GI
GUINEA PIGS

GI
GUINEA PIGS

How the Pentagon Exposed Our Troops
to Dangers More Deadly Than War:
Agent Orange and Atomic Radiation

Michael Uhl
and Tod Ensign

॥₽

A Playboy Press Book

Manufactured in the United States of America.

FIRST EDITION

Designed by Tere LoPrete

Library of Congress Cataloging in Publication Data
Uhl, Michael.
    GI guinea pigs.

      Bibliography: p.
      1. Veterans—United States—Diseases.
2. Atomic bomb—Physiological effects.
3. Radiation—Toxicology. 4. Herbicides—War
use. 5. Herbicides—Toxicology. I. Ensign, Tod,
joint author. II. Title.
UB369.U35   355.1'2   79-89164
ISBN 0-87223-569-6

For John David Herndon, Vietnam military resister
For all the victims of America's longest war
and
For Simon, who will be twenty-one in the year 2000

Contents

Acknowledgments

We want to gratefully acknowledge the contribution and support of the following friends and associates:

Carol Brightman made both an editorial and creative contribution. Joan Warch provided research, and Debbie Vanderhorst, secretarial and moral, support. Dolores Day transcribed dozens of interviews.

We discussed these topics at length with numerous friends, including Richard Schmiechen, Lee Meyrowitz, Pamela Booth, Jane Teller, Francine Smilen, Jeremy Rifkin, Dan Rosen, Kathryn Grody, Noreen Banks, and Len Rubin.

Diane Keaton, Martin Sheen, and our friends at Chiasma Films worked generously to help Citizen Soldier continue its campaign on behalf of all veterans.

Martha Millard sold the book to Sharon Jarvis, our editor, who also worked vigorously on the preparation of the final manuscript. Randy Matusow did the graphics.

Without the materials and enthusiasm supplied by Robert Stoldal, KLAS-TV, Las Vegas and James O'Connor, this book might never have been written. Maude DeVictor and Bethann O'Connor also helped a good deal.

Our adversaries at the Pentagon, Lieutenant Colonel William McGee and Lieutenant Colonel Darwin Way helped us more than they realized or perhaps even wanted to.

Technical assistance came from Dr. Susan Daum, Drs. Jeanne and Steven Stellman, Dr. Barry Commoner, David Kriebel, Professor Leonard Storm, John Stauber, Eric Jansson, and Paul Merrill.

The Vietnam Ranch Hand Association and the Nevada

Sagebrush Alliance are as different as any two voluntary associations can be. Both welcomed us warmly into their lives for several days.

Literally thousands of veterans were exposed to radioactivity or defoliants during the course of their military service. We wish them well and have to the best of our ability tried to tell their story in this book.

Introduction

In the last decade, the public's attitude about the development and use of science has undergone profound transformation. Gone are the days when a euphoric citizenry would sit transfixed before televised images of the astronauts taking mankind's first steps on the moon. In the years before that dazzling event, each scientific discovery was acclaimed as a boost to national pride and potency—and, of course, private industry was quick to exploit each scientific "breakthrough" by marketing new products and services. Rare indeed was the scientist or public official who dared to raise questions about the environmental or social hazards presented by many of these scientific and commercial triumphs.

At first, only a handful of "health faddists" and "eco-freaks" bothered to learn about the havoc being wreaked upon the environment by many of these new products and technologies. When they warned that the earth's delicate eco-system was being irreversibly damaged by the uncontrolled use of pollutants, they were dismissed as "effete snobs" who wanted to turn back the clock by crippling economic growth.

The average American, weaned on the irresistible logic of economic growth, tended to regard ecological concerns as an exotic pastime, purchased only by those with the leisure and money to indulge such lofty ideals. The slow seepage of radioactive waste into a town's water supply was at first perceived as a threat by those who lived only miles away. The death of western poet Billie Shoecraft, after she was accidentally sprayed with a herbicide commonly used for forest and crop control, was regarded as an aberration unique to a particular community. To many workers, particularly in the construction and energy industries, the environmentalists' protests seemed like callous invitations to join the ranks of the unemployed.

Rachel Carson's book *The Silent Spring* (1962) was the first exposé about the toxic effect of chemicals (DDT) to reach a mass audience. And as evidence of other environmental disasters accumulated throughout the Sixties, the number of concerned citizens grew proportionately. Ultimately came the dawning realization that each of us is being zapped by a growing barrage of gamma rays, microwaves, and X rays; pesticides; preservatives; and ten thousand other chemicals. Even the basic staples of life are no longer safe—neither the air we breathe, the water we drink, nor the food we eat. Indeed, the morning dew, age-old symbol of freshness and purity, is slowly turning to acid as a thousand pollutants infect the atmosphere. While the more industrialized societies are experiencing the effects of this massive poisoning first, eventually it will affect the entire human family.

Today, there is growing evidence that issues like radiation exposure and herbicide poisoning, to name just two apocalyptic vectors crisscrossing the nation, are beginning to get the hearing they deserve in that mythic realm of the pollsters, Middle America.

Opinion polls document the public's belief that the quality of life has badly deteriorated in recent years. The powerful myth that economic growth and scientific breakthroughs per se equals "progress" has begun to erode as an article of national faith, and coupled with this is a growing distrust of corporate and governmental decision making.

Of all those institutions, public or private, which have played a role in the development of science over the past forty years, none has been more active than the Pentagon. More than half of all scientific research in the United States today is financed wholly or in part by the Department of Defense, and the scope of funded research extends far beyond activities one would normally associate with the military mission. It is well known, for example, that many of the most significant scientific developments of the twentieth century—television, radar, microwave, satellite communication, penicillin, to name just a few—were results of military research.

In these pages, we will examine two products of Pentagon "research"—each claiming its generation of guinea pigs. First, its program of atmospheric testing of nuclear devices (A- and H-bombs primarily) from 1945 to 1961; and second, the massive defoliation program in Indochina, during which five million acres were repeatedly doused from 1962 to 1971 with over twenty million gallons of highly toxic herbicides.

Before Vietnam deflated a robust tradition of Yankee patriotism, military service was an honorable calling. Young men routinely volunteered to fight to preserve our sacred way of life, no questions asked. Now it appears that a few questions might have been in order, given the generals' willingness to expose millions of GIs to highly dangerous substances and then justify such risks on the basis of "military necessity" and "national security."

The use of troops at the nuclear test blasts in Nevada provides a microcosm of this mentality. When the radiation-exposure standards imposed by the Atomic Energy Commission interfered with the commanders' desire for realistic nuclear-battlefield training, they invoked these doctrines to justify taking control of safety standards. By arbitrarily raising the limits of allowable radiation, the Pentagon recklessly exposed the soldiers to even higher doses of radiation.

The toll for this lack of concern for the welfare of both GIs and civilians has only begun to be tallied in recent years. Today, countless World War II and Korean War vets may be suffering from disproportionately high rates of radiation-induced cancers and leukemias. The hell-bent-for-leather, zap-the-Japs decision to drop the Big One in 1945 is finally bringing Hiroshima home to the American heartland.

Unlike their counterparts from earlier wars, it has taken only a few years for the deteriorating bodies of Vietnam veterans to begin to tell the story of Vietnam in the only language that seems able to penetrate the consciousness of most Americans—the language of death. Thousands of young vets who should be at the peak of physical health are instead coming apart at the seams. Some say there was just too much trauma to the collective psyche of all those zip-gun and deer-rifle warriors caught flatfooted in the Asian jungles, and, proceeding on this assumption, the Veterans Administration has become the postservice quartermaster, equipped with its indispensable survival kit—Valium, Thorazine, and a host of other space-out medications, drugging veterans whose faraway eyes say they've never quite returned from Vietnam. But the undiagnosable traumas may not be entirely psychogenic in origin, the product of a million dreams which have mutated. A new culprit has been found, another piece of the puzzle, leading, as these things always do, back to the bigwigs who just couldn't say no to another war, no matter what the cost. This is the exposure of countless GIs to poisonous defoliants used in Vietnam.

In communicating their plight, the veteran/victims of radiation illness and herbicide poisoning whose stories are summarized herein will, we hope, win for themselves and others the consideration and relief they deserve. Although much of this book focuses necessarily on the military's abuse of science, the human dimension of the problem emerges in the experiences of America's warriors, who have been treated like so many no-deposit, no-return soda bottles; once the contents are consumed, the empties are thrown on the junk heap. If they're lucky, they might get recycled.

The consequences of this massive negligence have been too long denied. Every dog soldier will have his day, and the day of the veteran–guinea pig is approaching. A critical mass of aggrieved victims of both nuclear testing and the defoliation program is rapidly being reached, and the inevitable explosion may have unforeseen results. In the short run, the victims must educate themselves, learn to articulate their experiences, and fight against the forces of anonymity, political impotence, and bureaucratic indifference. In the last analysis, their experience teaches another lesson more difficult to absorb perhaps than the lesson brought home by the abuse of their welfare. Once a nation's military command throws its own soldiers into the path of its weapons of destruction, has it not already forfeited the support of its own people as well as its capacity for defense?

MICHAEL UHL
TOD ENSIGN
New York City, 1979

PART I

THE ATOMIC MYTHS: VICTIMS OF THE NUCLEAR BATTLEFIELD

CHAPTER

1

James O'Connor—Poet of the Nevada Test Site

It is 1957. The sun is setting over the harsh, awesome Nevada desert. A restless group of GIs are waiting for maneuvers to begin after the detonation of an atomic bomb. They are apprehensive, and a concerned chaplain waits with them. . . .
This is a scene from "The Big Picture," an army-sponsored television program that has brought viewers directly to the Atomic Energy Commission's proving grounds to watch live GIs maneuver on a nuclear battlefield. The visuals are accompanied by a voice that narrates quietly and with authority.

NARRATOR: Chow in the growing dust settling over the flats brings an end to the day. Dusk on the desert is always a reflective time . . . this one, perhaps, a bit more than most. . . . Everything is ready, but in the minds of men who are about to become part of an awesome experience, fundamental questions remain.

CHAPLAIN: What seems to be the trouble, soldier? You look a little bit worried.

GI # 1: Well, I am, Chaplain—just a little bit.

CHAPLAIN: Actually, there's no need to be worried, as the army has taken all necessary precautions to see that we're perfectly safe here.

GI # 2:   Sir, have you ever been out at one of these shots before?

CHAPLAIN: Yes, I've had the opportunity to see a number of atomic tests. I feel that as a chaplain it is my responsibility to be with my men.

GI # 1:   What's it like, Chaplain?

CHAPLAIN: First of all, one sees a very, very bright light, followed by a shock wave. And then you hear the sound of the blasts. And then it seems as though there's a minor earthquake. And then you look up and see the fireball as it ascends up into the heavens. It contains all of the rich colors in the rainbow. And then as it rises up into the atmosphere, it turns a beautiful, pale yellow . . . and then assembles into the mushroom. It's a wonderful sight to behold.

An ex-GI with less faith, but undoubtedly more gray matter, described an atomic spectacle he witnessed from a somewhat different perspective:

"I was petrified, with my hands clasped tightly to my eyes and head between my knees; perspiration ran down my cheeks. The sizzling flash stung my body. The bones in my hands glowed through my closed eyelids. Suddenly the rumbling noises turned to a roar. The desert seemed to be rolling. The trench crumbled in its wake, throwing me to the ground. My God! The world is ending!"

Jim O'Connor, who wrote this less-rosy description, was nineteen years old when he soldiered in the Nevada desert, laying miles of telephone wire beneath the flats of the A-bomb test site. O'Connor began his journal twenty-five years later, when he discovered that the radioactivity to which he was involuntarily exposed might be killing him.

"I am dying of polymyositus," he says today, and when he explains the medical jargon, the whine of the condemned is noticeably absent from his voice. "It's eating away at my muscles, and it's a slow, painful, and expensive way to die."

His doctor thinks that this and his other ailment, skin cancer, may be caused by radiation exposure. For the past six years, Jim O'Connor hasn't been able to work. He last used the muscles on his bulky frame to drive stock cars and to pull wrenches on high-performance engines.

"I started falling apart in 1973. It began with blood clots. I had three that year. Then two fingers on each hand started going to sleep. I couldn't hold the wheel anymore." There's a snapshot of a cherry-red stock car on a sideboard in O'Connor's Burbank, California, bungalow. "I built it from scratch and never got to drive it. In 1972, I was doing real good on the circuit. I was rookie of the year."

He has turned to writing to pass the time and to satisfy some deep literary urge he didn't have the leisure to pursue earlier. But mostly he writes to find some meaning for himself and others in that strange experience of many years ago when his country sent him to the desert to catch a sneak preview of the end of the world.

Bethann, Jim's wife, also writes. She has laid siege to the political establishment and the Veterans Administration with a torrent of letters on her husband's behalf. She berates senators and bureaucrats alike, demanding that they do right by Jim and the untallied legions of other vets who were irradiated as they watched with prophetic apprehension the "beautiful, pale yellow" fireballs of nuclear bursts in the Nevada desert or on some remote Pacific atoll.

The government has responded to the allegations of atomic-test vets in characteristic fashion: After twenty-odd years of doing absolutely nothing for these men, it has suddenly unleashed a rush of federal activity. President Carter has ordered the creation of an interagency task force, led by the Department of Health, Education, and Welfare, to take another look at the increasingly sensitive issue of biological effects of low-level ionizing radiation. There appears to be a growing recognition in Washington that official policy concerning the risks and benefits of man-made radiological technologies is lagging behind public awareness of potential health hazards.

In March 1979, the task force released its first reports, which satisfied neither critic nor advocate of nuclear technology.

After first finding that it's not possible to "provide an un-equivocal answer" to the hazards of low-level radiation, they then acknowledged that many unanswered questions exist. Predictably, they urged further study while proposing a citizen "self-help" campaign in which people would be encouraged to reduce voluntarily their exposure to radiation.

The government's task force is heavily weighted with pro-nuclear advocates who must attempt to assuage mounting public fear of any policy or product that increases the amount of radiation in the natural environment. Thus critics labeled this effort a clever campaign to defend long-standing pronuclear policies in the face of growing opposition. Public pressure may ultimately force the government to budge from its position that nuclear pollutants are a bitter, yet necessary, pill which we all must swallow if our country's energy and defense needs are to be fulfilled.

On the specific issue of the irradiated veterans, the Pentagon, a member of the Health, Education, and Welfare task force, has initiated a monumental investigation to identify all 300,000 ex-GIs who received nuclear-weapons indoctrination over a fifteen-year period beginning in 1946. The Defense Department's effort involves the historical reconstruction of the entire test period, including the examination of all available radiation-exposure records measuring the dose received by individual participants.

Conventional scientific wisdom concerning radiation's effects on human health holds that while all unnecessary exposure should be avoided, biological damage occurs only when exposure rates are much higher than those allowed for both the atomic workers and the GIs who witnessed the numerous atmospheric tests. But the leukemia rate among the veterans of shot "Smoky," a highly publicized 1957 test, may indicate that levels of radiation exposure allowed at that time were far in excess of what is now believed to be reasonably safe. The massive and immediate response of government to these findings is at least a partial recognition that the atomic-test veterans may have received more radiation than previously believed, which may prove extreme negligence on the part of the military, or that doses at lower levels than once thought, can cause serious illness.

Since it is virtually impossible to pinpoint the exact cause of disorders like cancer, leukemia, and genetic damage, the outcome of the current debate on low-level radiation's biological effects is unlikely to be resolved by science in the near future. Scientists on both sides of the issue can present credible, statistically supported arguments. Ultimately, the issue becomes one of energy versus epidemic, benefit versus risk. Government will talk of minimizing the risk while promoting the benefits, understandably motivated by its desire to protect billions of investment dollars already consumed by the nuclear industry, both military and civilian. Critics will point to numerous accidents like the near disaster at the Three Mile Island reactor, along with the irradiated veterans whose plight may foreshadow the fates of millions should the development of nuclear technology proceed unchecked.

Proving or disproving in the public mind that even the lowest levels of radiation are dangerous to human survival will be the principal axis around which the entire debate will revolve for years to come. Each skirmish pitting pro- and anti-nuclear forces against each other can be viewed as an evolving microcosm of the controversy, rippling outward and gradually involving larger and larger sectors of the public in the final decision, which may only be made years from now.

In late March 1979, one such skirmish took place in a Philadelphia courtroom when five alumni from an AEC atomic test series code-named Teapot were reunited. Jim O'Connor, Howard Hinkie, Jerry Dobbs, Ned Giles, and Nick Mazzuco hadn't seen each other since they'd trooped together at Camp Desert Rock twenty-four years earlier. The occasion for their reunion was a novel class-action lawsuit brought by lawyers for Howard Hinkie on behalf of all veterans who may have suffered genetic damage due to radiation exposure during the A-tests. After Hinkie returned from Nevada, he fathered two normal children. Then, ten years later, his wife delivered a massively deformed baby who died eighteen months later. Three years after that, another child was born, this one severely retarded. It may be that, during the ten-year interval, radiation ran its damaging course, permanently impairing Howard Hinkie's reproductive capacity. At any rate, his four buddies came to Philadelphia from around the country to bear witness to the test experience they'd all shared at the Nevada proving ground.

Did the army really take all the necessary precautions to protect the safety of the 300,000 American soldiers present during the atmospheric testing of the nation's nuclear arsenal? Or were the GIs merely pawns of political and military leaders who were quite willing to sacrifice them for grand strategic purposes?

Perhaps both these questions can be answered in the affirmative. Once certain assumptions were made about the "benefits" of nuclear weapons and the harmlessness of "small" doses of radiation, all known and "necessary" precautions were taken to protect GIs. At least on paper. In practice, the radiation-safety procedures governing permissible exposure often bore very minimal relationship to the true hazards of contamination. While every GI's experience was unique and personal, the broad pattern of participation in nuclear exercises remained the same throughout the years. Jim O'Connor's story is both his own and that of every GI who ever pulled a tour of duty at Camp Desert Rock, birthplace of the pentomic unit and the nuclear battlefield. We tell his story in the pages that follow.

It began in the late fall of 1954. Fort Huachuca, Arizona, was the home of the 232d Signal Company, United States Army. Many of the outfit's "communications specialists"—a fancy name for linemen and switchboard operators—were recent graduates of the Korean "conflict"—also a military euphemism, in this case for humankind's most ancient occupation, war.

The 232d didn't have a real mission at Huachuca, so the troops paraded like some raw basic-training unit. Something was in the air, however. Suddenly, without explanation, the entire company was given a battery of psychological tests. Eventually 120 men were culled from the unit and told they would soon be going on a highly classified operation for four or five months. They were issued special ID cards with their fingerprints and pictures, and then they left Huachuca by truck convoy en route to mysterious parts unknown.

It was in Tombstone, Arizona, that they first learned of their secret destination. "We'd never even heard of the atomic proving grounds in them days, much less radiation," O'Connor recalled.

It was still snowing in the high Nevada desert when late one night the caravan rolled into a compound of weather-beaten Quonset huts. These huts had been used in the previous year's atomic tests, but were abandoned afterward. The desert wind had all but reclaimed the godforsaken spot, but Camp Desert Rock would once again be resurrected as a Class I army base.

There was a camp dining hall, beer parlor, barber shop, outdoor movie theater, and, providentially, two chapels for religious service. An adjacent bivouac area could accommodate an additional 3600 servicemen if necessary. Meanwhile, the men from the 232d slept in the open for a couple of nights, then cleaned up the huts and moved in. For heat, they had potbellied stoves. Wells dug to 1200 feet produced no water, and it had to be trucked in, with considerable effort, from surrounding towns. So although Desert Rock was a complete facility, living conditions were, even by army standards, rustic.

Just up the road was Mercury, Nevada, the Atomic Energy Commission's headquarters for the nuclear testing program. But the GIs remained segregated and in the dark. Since full operations had not started, there was little work. O'Connor's squad, Wire Team B, was to lay cables for the Teletype operators and GI typists, who would then transmit the news stories.

"The old theory, 'Keep 'em out of trouble by working their asses off' went to hell. Here we were, eighty-five miles north of the playground of the world, Las Vegas, and only thirty-eight miles south of where the call girls were in Beatty, and what were we doing? Sitting there with our fingers up our butts, for security reasons. We had nothing much to do except drink, look for a hole in the fence, and bitch."

Few, if any, of the men knew what their assignment was. So they drank the weak beer the army sold them at the so-called PX, and they improvised for entertainment. Gambling was big; there was lots of poker, just as in the war movies. GIs will bet on anything, and occasionally there was some real excitement, a main event. Take the "great critter race" on the latrine floor, between the Greek's mouse, Speedybutt, and a big green lizard with the smashing handle Crockopotamus, owned by Joe Stack, a meek young fellow off the farm. Both men were pals of O'Connor over the months at Desert Rock. The big money was on the Greek's mouse, but Joe just applied a basic law of nature to defeat his slick West Coast rival. Joe didn't train his entry; he merely starved him for three days. The track favorite never got out of the gate. The big green lizard ate the rodent, leaving the spectators in hysterics, while the Greek fumed and pledged revenge.

Thus, mundane garrison life proceeded apace. Like most civilians of the period, GIs were ignorant of the grand events that were taking shape. But these early arrivals at Desert Rock, and the thousands of servicemen who were to join them during the course of the atomic exercises, were definitely part of the larger picture, whether they knew it or not.

The year 1955 was the height of the Cold War scare. Military analysts believed that world war could be deferred only for five years, because by that time the Russians would have closed the United States's lead in strategic bombers. For the army, the next war was synonymous with the Bomb: if not the shiny new hydrogen bomb (which further blew the national mind when it premiered in 1954), then at least a tactical or fission weapon of the Hiroshima class.

For military scenarists who dreamed of conventional battle-fields awashed with nuclear mushroom clouds, logic dictated that troops be trained to defend themselves against atomic attack—both offensively and defensively. So according to the official report, the Desert Rock VI exercises were to teach

American GIs "to respect, but not fear, the atomic device." But like the poison gases of World War I, radiation would not distinguish between partisan and foe; military commanders with the power to commit tactical nukes would be threading a fine needle—to inflict great damage on the enemy could expose their own troops to the same hazards. The American GI involuntarily took his place on the big board, between the proverbial rock and the hard place. It was Russian roulette—with or without the Russians.

Both the AEC and the army had big plans for the 1955 blasts, as did the Federal Civil Defense Administration (FCDA). Mercury itself began to bustle with activity in anticipation of the spectacular events soon to be unveiled.

One news story leaked from Washington announced the construction of a new "Doom Town," a name first coined by the press two years earlier when the FCDA built two suburban ranch-style homes and sacrificed them to the atomic fury. The entire hamlet, complete with "paved streets and utilities," was slated for demolition.

But it wasn't until a month after they'd arrived that the Desert Rock GIs were told anything substantial about their mission impossible. The news came early on a Friday morning as they bunched together in platoon formation.

"Gentlemen," began the first sergeant, "I have some good news and some bad news. First, the good news: You guys get your three-day liberty starting at 12:00 today and ending Sunday at 17:00. The captain has arranged for each of you to get a twenty-five-dollar flyer on your pay."

First Sergeant O'Reilly paused. For a moment O'Connor thought he saw the top sergeant's wide smile take a mean twist around the edges. When the din about the pass faded, O'Reilly filled his lungs and cocked his jaw to one side.

"There's been a lot of scuttlebutt concerning the reason we are here. We are in fact cordially invited by the Atomic Energy Commission to participate in maneuvers and as observers, in testing of A-bombs blasted from towers. In the near future, this camp will be invaded by thousands for the biggest war games maneuvers in history. On Monday, you will start working in restricted areas in Mercury, Nevada, under indirect orders from the AEC."

The AEC rules were then enumerated in a staccato military delivery: IDs would be displayed on the right breast pocket of fatigues at all times; film badges would be issued to measure radiation exposure; the penalties for security violations would be extremely severe; and so on.

By 10:00 A.M., a line of men had formed in front of the orderly room. O'Connor thought that most of them looked like winos waiting in line to eat at the mission on Thanksgiving. Many of the men had brought only the fatigues they'd been issued at Fort Huachuca. The guys who didn't have civilian clothes wore fantastic combinations that they had begged and borrowed. O'Connor's sidekick, the Greek, looked like a Ringling Brothers clown. He wore a bright green shirt with no buttons and khaki pants he'd rolled up four times but still dragged on the ground.

To get the three-day pass, each GI had to sign a statement that he had read and understood the AEC rules for the upcoming exercises. "Security" was again the watchword.

O'Connor read the printed bulletin over and over, as if it contained the answers to some very personal questions. As a teenager, just being in the army was a strange and overwhelming experience. Then there was the combat of Korea, an adventure so violently atypical that the experience seemed to exist outside of himself, as if it had happened to some other intelligent being in his body. Now this. Why was *he* in this desert, waiting for an intimate glimpse of the nation's potential fury?

O'Connor stared at the regulations. He never signed anything that he hadn't read thoroughly, and he had a vague but deep feeling of apprehension. There was something menacing in the AEC's demand that the GIs "remain silent, now and in the future, about activities and assignments while at Desert Rock, Nevada."

A confused O'Connor was holding up the line. The eager men behind him started griping. Hell, he thought finally, I've read enough. Just give me my twenty-five bucks and my pass.

I'll read it again Monday morning on the army's time, not mine. He signed, and along with the Greek and some other buddies, took the bus provided to Beatty, where they all hoped to visit the best little whorehouse in the state of Nevada.

The frustrated crew never did manage to find the infamous Red Rooster brothel. They settled for the local gin mill instead, where they drank real beer and listened to a fellow trooper play the guitar. There they also met a guy named Flippy who lived on a small ranch down near the junction heading off toward Death Valley. Flip offered to drive O'Connor and the Greek back to camp, and on the way they dropped by the ranch where Flip and his wife served as caretaker for a California doctor who had once planned to retire there—that was before A-bomb testing started at Mercury. In time, Flip's place would become the winter spa for O'Connor and his team. It was also the launching pad for a GI campaign to pilfer whatever test-site materials weren't bolted down. The main target would be the "Doom Town" construction site, where the building of the mock village was just getting under way.

Until the installation of the "all-volunteer" army in the early 1970s, GI pay envelopes were notoriously light. So the GIs took aid and comfort from Flip and his wife in exchange for items such as crates of cheese and gasoline. O'Connor, who dabbled a little in the GI black market, didn't know the full extent of the Greek's operation until one day when the wind blew his friend's fatigue hat across the desert floor. A piece of paper flew out from under the lining, and the Greek scrambled for it, leaving the hat to the fate of the elements. O'Connor snatched the paper and read it. It was a list of many items: refrigerators, suits, rifles, frozen foods, even a jeep. All these items were to be used for the various "effects tests"—they were supposed to be placed near the A-blasts and blown to bits.

The day after they returned from liberty, the troops of Camp Desert Rock began work in earnest. For the men of Wire Team B, this meant reporting to the Mercury gate at

6:00 A.M. each morning. The nights in the desert were always still, the sky always full of stars. Even the sunsets were enjoyable at that time of year since the chill at dusk wasn't uncomfortable. Daylight, however, brought gushes of icy wind that seemed to blow right through you as if you were a screen door. Then, as the day went on, the wind became constant and colder.

Despite the frozen desert floor, the wire team had to bury hundreds of miles of land lines for field-telephone networks. Normally the lines were rolled out along the surface of the ground, but since this communications system was being constructed on an atomic battlefield, often within yards of ground zero (the exact location of the bomb's detonation), the cable had to be buried in a trench eight inches deep.

The first day the team arrived in the work area, the wind's cruelty provoked a revolt among the men. "Come on, you guys," O'Connor pleaded. "Grab a shovel and start burying this cable. The Fat Man [the platoon sergeant] will be coming soon and I don't want him bitching about how far behind we are." The men picked up their tools and began to hack at the frozen ground. Each time a shovel hit, it made a sharp clang. After a few minutes of this, frustration set in and, one by one, the men crawled back into their truck, bunching up in their ponchos to get warm.

The army then decided to bring in a special truck, a weapons carrier with a newly designed plow attached to its tailgate. The plow truck would slowly follow another truck that fed cable from large reels. One man would follow, placing cable in the trench; two others were to come after him, shoveling the loose dirt back into the trench; and O'Connor would bring up the rear to make sure the cable was properly covered.

Day in and day out, the men of Wire Team B followed this routine. Pacing off hundreds of square miles of desert was boring and, despite the new equipment, the cold was unbearable. But they faced a far greater menace than the cold or boredom, although none of them was even dimly aware of the danger at the time. Much of the desert on which they worked had been contaminated by radioactive fallout from twenty-six previous bomb tests. While a great deal of the initial radio-activity generated by those blasts had decayed away, no one at the test site seemed to know just how much of the alpha-, beta-, and gamma-emitting elements remained to imperil these men.

A number of leading scientists, however, had become quite concerned about the long-term health effects of radioactive residue. By 1955, even as soldiers were facing exposure to such radiation, both in Nevada and the South Pacific, a national debate on the hazards of fallout began to rage. A number of eminent scientists, among them laureates Linus Pauling and Hermann Müller, found evidence that lingering fallout from past atomic detonations could precipitate a catastrophe: One of the by-products of radiation was the irreparable mutation of human genes.

From O'Connor's vantage point at the time, the potential radiation hazard was the equivalent of a great cosmic secret. He and the rest of his team continued, unawares, to carry out their assignment.

After several weeks of hard work setting up the switchboards and the telephone grids, it was announced that the AEC nuclear detonations would begin in mid-February, weather permitting. The first shot scheduled for Operation Teapot, the AEC's code name for the series, was a device expected to yield four times the energy released by the Hiroshima bomb.

As it turned out, the same treacherous winds that bedeviled the men of Wire Team B also frustrated the planners' desire to kick off the series with a large and dramatic first blast. The thousand GIs who had expected to witness the spectacle on February 15 were treated instead to a tiny blast that disappointed them by its puny dimensions.

Jim O'Connor actually saw his first A-bomb at a later date, either February 22 or March 1, both test-shot days for larger bombs. O'Connor is confused about the exact date of this experience—the memory fogs after twenty-five years—but, in any event, it was during his atomic baptism that he believes he was given a dusting with radioactive particles for the first time. Medical records show that he went on sick call on both dates, and he insists that on one of these occasions it was for radiation overdose.

O'Connor recalls that immediately after the detonation all the observers were evacuated. Only the men of Wire Team B remained behind, to repair any damaged equipment. Suddenly the wind shifted, blowing the mushroom cloud right back over them. One soldier turned to Jerry Dobbs and said, "Hey, my badge is black!" He was referring to the film badge each GI wore on his chest, which registered the total exposure to gamma radiation. All the men gathered around and compared badges. All of them were black.

Everyone panicked, O'Connor reports, "because of our ignorance in a situation like this." Nobody had the slightest idea what to do and there wasn't an AEC monitor in sight. They called the control center at Mercury and were told to return immediately to Camp Desert Rock.

"By the time we reached the infirmary, we were all expecting to fall over dead," O'Connor recalls. "The closest doctor was at Nellis Air Force Base twenty miles away. We had a pretty good medic, but he was studying for a degree in math. The poor guy was not ready for this."

Their film badges were collected, and the men heard nothing more about them. The medic wrote "seven-day bed rest" excuses for four of them, but a day later they were all ordered back to work.

Had O'Connor read the newspapers in those days, he would have learned that the AEC was quite emphatic on the question of human exposure to nuclear fallout. The very week O'Connor and his friends were showered with hot radioactive particles, a Commission report stated that only relatively small nuclear test explosions were conducted at the Nevada test site and that no individual in the vicinity would receive a radiation dose high enough to seriously affect the genetic constitution of human beings.

With fresh film badges and no wiser about the dangers of radiation, the men of Wire Team B headed back to the desert to prepare for another "relatively small" shot—this one with enough destructive power to wipe out four Hiroshimas. Again they dug holes in the frozen ground and laid cable in wind, rain, and snow. The preparations for this bomb, dubbed "Turk," were much more complicated than those for earlier shots had been.

Two hours before countdown, the main cable to Desert Rock went out. O'Connor, another man named Dobbs, and Lonie Turley, who had been sent over on temporary duty, jumped in a jeep and headed north toward the terminal box. They'd guessed right and were able to locate the damaged cable that had caused the short. While Dobbs and O'Connor struggled to repair the trunk line, Turley wandered in the vicinity of the tower, taking pictures.

At the 2500-yard line, the army had set up a display area where weapons and other equipment were to be tested for blast and radiation effects. O'Connor and the other wiremen were already familiar with these displays, having laid cable to a mock communication bunker earlier in the week. The use of cameras, however, was strictly forbidden, so when Turley sneaked up on them and snapped their picture, they were upset and frightened. Convincing him to hide the camera under the jeep seat, they asked Turley what he had photographed up by the tower. "A bunch of weirdos," he replied. He told them that some people, along with dogs and sheep, were being exposed to the bomb's potency at a significantly closer distance than other observers.

This confirmed a rumor that had been circulating along the GI grapevine, and it presented a mystery that nourished Jim O'Connor's fertile young imagination. This would have to be investigated after the shot, he decided right then. But, for the moment, their mission was complete; the cable had been repaired, and they were overdue back at the observation point.

They started off, but hadn't gone far when suddenly all hell broke loose right behind them. The jeep bounced from a tremendous explosion. "My first thought," O'Connor recalls, "was that the bomb had gone off. Looking behind us, I saw that the AEC had set off a thousand-pound 'test charge' of TNT just a hundred yards from where we'd just finished working. We never found our terminal box."

Such explosions were routinely conducted an hour before countdown, to check prevailing wind conditions. On this day the winds were wrong—the troop-observer trenches were adjudged to be directly in the expected path of fallout from the bomb—and the shot was again postponed. The AEC waited a week for a wind change; then, to be on the safe side, decided to move the trenches to another area. Wire Team B had labored long hours to meet the original deadline. It was frustrating to learn that much of their work had been in vain and would have to be done all over again.

O'Connor recalls an interesting thing he learned of during that period. It was on a Sunday morning, a few days before the rescheduled "Turk" shot. The Greek asked him if he wanted to take a ride; there was something on the test site he wanted to show him. O'Connor, curious, agreed. There was no road where they turned off the Mercury Highway, but about two miles from where they had entered the desert a newly graded, unused road appeared. The road turned slightly to the right, and they drove up a small rise.

"As we straightened out again, my mind flipped," says O'Connor. "There it was. Like something straight out of the Twilight Zone. A city right there in the middle of nowhere."

There were prefabricated houses which had been hauled to the site in sections. Brand-new refrigerators and stoves were neatly stacked in their crates on the ground. There were sofas still encased in their factory plastic. Huge steel beams and building materials were stacked everywhere. There was also a steel tower with its thick cement slab base, a ubiquitous sight throughout the test site. The metal structures held the various atomic devices aloft; in their height they reached up to 700 feet, for many of the shots.

This was Doom Town, the simulated American village that the Civil Effects testers planned to incinerate at the end of the Teapot series in late April. Construction had begun in early February. The plan was to simulate authentic American community life. The houses were full-scale and would eventually be fully furnished. As stand-ins for real people, the houses would have dime-store mannequins dressed in the latest fashions.

Doom Town was not yet complete—and might never be. According to O'Connor, the Greek was picking the place clean. It was the centerpiece of his black-market operation.

A Department of Energy official, Joseph Deal, confirms that Doom Town was constantly being sacked, apparently by the GIs. Deal, who was deputy chief of the AEC's Civil Effects Test Branch in 1955, says, "We called that 'midnight requisitioning.' We put something out, and if it wasn't nailed down, it would disappear. There were just too many people who had access to the general area, and particularly, with the troops, we had no real control."

The revelation of Doom Town added to the aura of "weirdness" that O'Connor and the others sensed when they returned to the desert after the weekend liberty.

"Turk" was eventually detonated, with O'Connor among the observers who watched from a trench 3500 yards from the blast's epicenter. The final checks for "Turk" were made, and at last all systems were go. Around dusk everyone in Wire Team B except O'Connor headed back to Desert Rock for chow. On Fat Man's orders, O'Connor remained behind to guard the switchboard and to tidy up any loose ends he might discover in the Signal Company display. He took his "hot" meal of cold meatloaf off the mobile chow truck, and then sat down to wait for the others to rejoin him around three o'clock in the morning. VIP officers and other troops slated to view this shot at 5:20 A.M. wouldn't arrive until H-hour minus one.

It was around 2:00 A.M. when O'Connor was stirred from his reverie by the whirring sound of a truck engine somewhere in the vicinity of the test bunkers, a thousand yards in front of him. A panel truck stood spotlighted by a beam from the 500-foot steel tower, where the atomic device sat waiting. The night was clear, and a full moon illuminated the desert. "You could see the outline of 'em putting people into this bunker," O'Connor said later. At the time, however, all he could think of were Turley's words: "a bunch of weirdos."

He mentally retraced the first visit he'd made to the special bunker. They had been on the blast site burying cable at the 2500-yard perimeter. They'd dug a foxhole and placed a mannequin inside with a field telephone. On the dummy's helmet the GIs printed the name "Private Slovik," in memory of the only enlisted man shot for desertion during World War II, on orders of General Dwight D. Eisenhower. In the switchboard back at the observation point was another mannequin whose helmet bore the appropriate legend "Ike."

O'Connor had walked a good portion of the perimeter that day out of curiosity. There were other trenches containing dummies, and weapons such as M1 rifles and machine guns. But most interesting to him was that special bunker and the way it was constructed. It was quite different from the six-foot-deep open trenches used by the other test participants. The whole structure was above ground like those he'd seen in Korea. A line of sandbags faced the small hole used for the entrance, and inside there was a straight bench going all the way across. At dead center he saw a terminal box of unconnected wires, covered with plastic for protection. He and the other wiremen had wondered if this meant they were supposed to connect some equipment to this terminal, but Fat Man had passed the word that they were to stay away. They'd noticed that to the left of the bunker, about sixty yards to the front, there was a remote-control camera mounted on a pole and trained on this bunker and nothing else.

What in hell was going on? he wondered now, alone in the darkness. But he had no time to ponder. His solitude was disrupted again by the arrival of more vehicles, this time his mates from Wire Team B. Howard Hinkie gave him a shot of his whiskey and took his place in the switchboard bunker. The Greek assumed his position in front of a mound of C-rations that he later would distribute to the GI and VIP observers.

Among the VIP officers this morning was Major General William Frisbie Dean, a Medal of Honor winner and prisoner of war during the Korean War. O'Connor had been on hand in September 1953 when the Americans and North Koreans exchanged prisoners and remembered having seen the general then from afar. On this occasion he went up to Dean to shake his hand.

The Greek was less cordial to the old soldier when the C-rations were being passed out. It was standard operating procedure to pass the food cans to the troops upside down so they couldn't read the labels and begin griping about the selection they'd received. General Dean flipped his can right side up and apparently didn't like what he saw, according to Hinkie who stood nearby. Dean requested spaghetti in exchange, but the Greek told him he'd have to take what he was given.

It was now 4:30 A.M. "Good morning, gentlemen," the loudspeaker crackled. "This is Mercury AEC control."

The desert and all life in it were suddenly still. The approach of daylight outlined everything that was visible. The men listened as the confident voice, so smooth and yet forceful, took command.

"You are invited to participate in, experience, and evaluate the blast of an atomic bomb that is four times greater than the one that fell on Hiroshima. That bomb stands ready for firing on the aerial tower in front of you. At the given order, you are to make an about-face, kneel on both knees, head down with both hands over your eyes."

Shot "Turk," delayed for almost a month, was all and more that O'Connor and the others had expected. O'Connor's eloquent and terrifying description of the blast is the one that begins this chapter. The dust was still swirling everywhere when the orders were given to evacuate the observers. O'Connor remembers shooting a final glance at General Dean as the general boarded a helicopter. The former POW's nose was bleeding, and he needed steadying by his aide-de-camp.

Once more, the men of Wire Team B remained behind for postshot cleanup. Fat Man had told them earlier that there was only one piece of equipment they'd have to salvage after the blast—the test cable leading up to the field telephone where "Private Slovik" kept his lonely vigil. This was the chance

O'Connor had been waiting for all night. Armed with Fat Man's order in case any AEC radiation monitor challenged him, he headed off toward ground zero. Now he would finally satisfy his enormous curiosity.

Walking through the postshot haze along a service road, O'Connor soon came upon the communications foxhole. The heat from the ground burned right through the soles of his boots. For a moment he froze; instinct signaled him to flee. Then, looking ahead in the direction of the bunker with the mysterious unconnected wires, he saw it. It was some fifty feet in front of him, along the same service road that ran the length of the 2500-yard line.

"There was a guy with a mannequin look who had apparently crawled behind the bunker. Something like wires were attached to his arms, and his face was full of blood from his nose and mouth. I smelled an odor like burning flesh. I knew this smell all too well. In Korea, we were right next to where the South Koreans disposed of their dead. They used to put them in double barrels and burn 'em. There's no smell like burning flesh.

"The camera I'd seen before was going, zoom, zoom, zoom, and the guy kept trying to get up. Instead of approaching him, I remember trying to run back the way I came. I fell on one knee and began to vomit. Then things started getting foggy. With that awful smell in my nostrils, I began to feel faint. The next thing I remember was some AEC monitors yelling at me, helping me into the rear of the jeep. They looked like spacemen with their rad-safe suits."

The monitors drove O'Connor directly to Mercury headquarters.

"My next recollection was lying on a cot. A guy dressed in civvies reached down and ripped off my film badge. He was cursing me for going near their hush-hush experiments."

Then the rad-safe men stripped off his clothes and put him in a portable shower. "The water had a greenish color and tasted of disinfectant. I can remember it burning my eyes."

He was still feeling sick and had the dry heaves. "I told the guy I had to heave and he told me to do it in the shower."

It wasn't long before the monitors dressed O'Connor in a wraparound hospital smock and put him in a white government sedan headed south toward Las Vegas. "I can remember little about the trip—I kept dozing off. But I do remember the gate at Nellis Air Force Base."

Medics helped him walk to an isolation wing in the camp infirmary. "Out of the window, I could see the PX and air force guys walking in and out." He was given some medication he remembers hearing them refer to as "thizine."

"I'll never forget that. It was a small cap, a red-colored liquid, and it tasted like iodine. The guy left, and about five minutes later the shit hit the fan. I felt so sleepy, I could have slept standing up."

Soon after, a smiling doctor appeared and told O'Connor he had been through a traumatic experience and that the medication was to help him settle down. "He asked me about the whole incident, and when I told him, he patted me on the back and said I had nothing to worry about."

Another doctor came in the evening. "He looked in my ears, mouth, nose, and eyes with a light." When the medic came in with more of the red medicine, he refused to take it. A few minutes later, the medic returned with a shot, promising it was something different. "This made me sleepy too. I felt like a damn robot." O'Connor slept the night through.

"The next morning, they gave me breakfast and I couldn't keep it down. The shrink they sent in ordered me some tea and soup. He asked me questions, but I don't remember what we talked about. I found myself in a struggle with my brain just trying to think."

Today, Jim O'Connor suspects that the mind-deadening drug he was given in 1955 was Thorazine, a potent tranquilizer now widely used to calm society's most shell-shocked casualties.

Jim is very hazy about what happened in the seven days between his first conversation with the psychiatrist and his return to Camp Desert Rock. His next memory is of being in a Quonset hut several hundred miles away at Camp Irwin, California. Maybe, he says, he was taken by helicopter med-evac. There were endless films and rap sessions about radiation and the bomb, all in very positive terms and images. The message was that the bomb would only hurt "them"—not "us." "But when I would ask someone about the poor guy I saw behind the bunker, they'd just ignore me."

O'Connor, looking back, has formed the strong impression that he was being deprogrammed. His wife, Bethann, remarks, "It seems very strange that Jim remembers so well everything before this time, but is very hazy after the 'Turk' shot. Things just didn't seem as important or outstanding in his mind as they did before."

Lieutenant Colonel Darwin "Dart" Way, a member of a Pentagon team currently investigating the long-term radiation effects on the Desert Rock troops, offers a personal explanation: "Couldn't he have seen a mannequin blown from a foxhole, and imagined it was a live person?"

It's a plausible theory. It's possible that O'Connor was so stunned by the disorienting shock of the huge blast and the barrage of radioactive waves and particles that the man behind the bunker was merely a figment of his imagination, an apparition.

The official response to Jim O'Connor's story was articulated by Lieutenant Colonel William McGee, chief spokesperson for the Defense Nuclear Agency: "We can neither confirm nor deny Mr. O'Connor's allegations." Reports state that there were no volunteer observers at that shot. Unofficially, McGee thinks O'Connor is just telling a tall tale. But Jim refuses to budge an inch: "I know what I saw."

Only one other man, Lonie Turley, supposedly saw the "volunteers" preparing for the "Turk" shot, but Turley disappeared after the incident with the camera. He was not a regular on O'Connor's team, and, in the army, replacements come and go without much fanfare or notice. For years O'Connor hoped that Turley would turn up to confirm or deny that the "weirdo" volunteers were actually present during the "Turk" exercise, but in February 1979 he received shocking news from the Pentagon. Using the Freedom of Information Act, O'Connor succeeded in obtaining unit rosters for the 232d Signal containing both his and Turley's names. The roster notes, however, that Turley was killed in a freak accident on the desert at precisely the time O'Connor says he disappeared.

Jerry Dobbs, who doesn't remember Turley or the camera incident, recalls that someone was killed at the test site in late February when a demolition crane's ball accidentally smashed through a truck's windshield. This was a fact that O'Connor either never knew or just completely forgot. It would not be the first mystery that the Nevada desert has swallowed over the past thirty years during the atomic testing program. But with the death of Lonie Turley, Jim O'Connor may remain the sole surviving witness to a test that measured the effects of radiation on human volunteers.

Jim O'Connor claims he may have been heavily irradiated on two occasions, in addition to his prolonged exposure to ambient ground radiation still present from earlier shots. A quarter of a century later, his account of these incidents is authenticated by the depth of detail he provides, particularly when he describes persistent nausea, a symptom long associated with exposure to 20 rads or more. Like his somewhat impressionistic account of the pathetic "volunteer," the story of his deprogramming seems farfetched until placed in the context suggested by recently declassified documents. Staff memorandums from the army's Training Methods Division, which worked with the "human-research units" of the various service branches, reveal a disturbing pattern of systematic manipulation of soldiers' attitudes toward the bomb and atomic testing. These reports fairly rejoice at the success with which the average GI was misled and misinformed about the dangers of radiation and its biological effects.

Other studies, like one conducted by the Operations Research Office (ORO) of Johns Hopkins University during the 1952 tests, suggested that too much brainwashing might backfire. ORO used lie detectors on GIs before and after each blast to measure their "fear reactions." Concerned that there wasn't much change in the emotional reactions of soldiers despite the varying types of preshot orientation, ORO offered two possible explanations: "Either the psychological effects of atomic weapons are overrated [or] the maneuvers with their emphasis on safety precautions and the virtual elimination of . . . danger were not realistic enough to evoke fear responses." ORO suggested that training might be more effective if the maneuvers were "more realistic, if some actual danger existed or if the troops were led to believe they might be in danger."

In Jim O'Connor's case, there was indeed concrete evidence of actual danger, but no way to interpret it, much less act on it. According to O'Connor, some weeks after his return from convalescent leave, the Fat Man told him he'd seen a field report stating that Jim had received a 10-roentgen exposure. Depending on how the dose was calculated, Jim could have exceeded the 6-rad limit set for an entire series with the one exposure. Moreover, in establishing the 6-rad limit, the military consciously exceeded the 3.9-rad ceiling that the AEC set for its own radiation workers over a thirteen-week period. The folly of this policy is seen when we consider that civilian site workers at Mercury could not be exposed to much more than 5 rads per year, total, while GIs were allowed higher exposure.

In any event, the radioactive battlefield was a given in training as well as in warfare. Anything short of a dose that would cause direct and incapacitating sickness didn't interest the military. The radiation O'Connor and the other linemen may have accumulated from the more slowly decaying by-products of fission deposited by the Teapot or earlier test shots was not considered dangerous in the short run. And the long run was not part of the planning.

The military planners reasoned that GI observers were statistically unlikely to receive much additional radiation after their Desert Rock tour, therefore this one-time overexposure, should it occur, was not particularly hazardous. In effect, the policy of allowing exposure levels that were higher than the already inflated standards set for radiation workers merely expressed the long-standing doctrine of "military necessity," which places the military mission above all other considerations.

Dr. Edward A. Martell wants to stay out of the argument about the military's responsibility at the Nevada test site. Martell, a West Point graduate, spent twelve years in the army, assigned to the Armed Forces Special Weapons Project. Some of those years were spent as a radio-chemist at Desert Rock. He now works with the National Center for Atmospheric Research in Boulder, Colorado. He offers the personal opinion that the military exercises there were pointless. He believes that the military was trying to associate itself with a new generation of weapons for future wars, but he feels it was futile to develop nuclear tactics and strategy for the battlefield because in a nuclear war there would be no battlefield. He is willing to offer a scientific opinion, however, on the potential hazards to which GIs were routinely exposed.

"The soldiers at the Nevada test site were exposed to relatively much more contamination of fission products in the surface dust of Nevada than the Japanese at Hiroshima and Nagasaki who received more prompt [immediate] radiation."

While he believes the biological effects of internally induced radiation to be much greater than previously estimated, it is virtually impossible to distinguish between the damage caused by external and internal dose. "They [GIs] are subject to multiple sources of insult. If they're going to crawl around and stir the stuff up and inhale it, they're going to get something from prompt, something from neutrons, something from residual, and so on."

While scientists know much about the immediate bioeffects of large doses of penetrating radiation such as X rays or gamma rays, Martell holds that "the whole health physics and radiobiology community is nothing but ignorant about the delayed effects and the chronic health effects of internal alpha emitters, for example."

And delayed effects of low levels of radiation are precisely what service veterans are saying has caused their premature decline in health. Martell confirms their fears without ambiguity: "Among the service vets, [these declines are] delayed effects of single or repeated exposures to various types of radiation. Ignorance is massive, overwhelming. But we learn by the unfortunate experience of the victims."

Martell offers one explanation for the military's failure to measure the full range of radiation exposure on test-site troops. "They were just measuring what they thought was the important component of the external, prompt radiation, and that's all. They didn't know the importance of the neutrons, and they had no feeling whatsoever for what they were inhaling."

While displaying little sympathy for the Pentagon's behavior during the tests, Martell doesn't point the finger of blame at the military planners. "Military leadership had no experience with the chronic health effects of radiation. They had no background in the radiation field. They wouldn't even accept the recommendations of people who had limited experience with radiation effects. The military simply assumed that the radiation health physicist was being ultraconservative, when, in fact, he was rather ignorant and wasn't being conservative even when he thought he was. The military wanted more realism. And they didn't know the effect, just like we're proceeding ignorantly now to build a lot of nuclear reactors when we don't know the ultimate consequences to mankind."

Who, then, is responsible for the victimization of irradiated GIs? Society? "Yes, I would say so," responds Martell. "It is the ignorance of our elected officials and leaders that is responsible. Our elected officials appointed these military leaders and let them conduct these questionable exercises. Naturally, it's a government responsibility."

One could argue that both the AEC and the military could have known much more about these delayed effects than they did.

Until not many years ago, some nuclear scientists believed that there was a "safe" threshold, below which exposure to radiation was harmless. Today, it is held almost universally that *any* exposure to radiation will have some consequence for human health. What is not understood, however, is that atomic scientists both inside and outside the federal government accepted this fact *before* American soldiers were brought to the atomic exercises. At a 1978 congressional seminar on low-level radiation, Dr. Victor Bond of Brookhaven National Laboratory allowed that ". . . it was in the late Forties and early Fifties that the ICRP and the NCRP [both nuclear-standards-setting agencies] made the very important change in philosophy—from a threshold . . . concept to a nonthreshold concept." He also noted this change was spelled out clearly in the NCRP Handbook #59, issued in 1954, but agreed to formally in 1951.

Had the AEC followed this principle religiously, it is unlikely that the atmospheric tests or even the nuclear industry would have proceeded very far. This "philosophy" was hidden from the public and, in its place, ALARA—As Low As Reasonably Achievable—was substituted. This became the rule of thumb applied to both the atomic workers and others for whom the AEC had decided that the risk of exposure was outweighed by the benefit of expedient government policy.

John Gofman is a health physicist who used to work for the Lawrence Livermore laboratory where much of the research and design work for atomic weapons is conducted. In 1969 he was ousted after he publicly dissented from the "official line" on radiation safety. He has a very blunt definition of what ALARA means to those whom the government "allows" exposure: "It permits human deaths. Because ALARA doesn't say the only way you could avoid deaths from the nuclear fuel cycle is to have zero releases. ALARA says keep releases as low as you can reasonably achieve with the [money] you want to spend on it. . . . So, it is a planned emission of radioactivity, and that, in effect, means planned deaths."

Even those scientists who still believe there are allowable levels of exposure feel that the present allowable dose of 170 millirems for the average citizen is ten times too high. (*Rem*, from *roentgen equivalent man*, refers to the dosage of any ionizing radiation that will cause the same amount of biological injury to human tissue as 1 roentgen of X ray or gamma ray dosage.) Contrast this to the 6000 millirems permitted for Jim O'Connor and the Desert Rock GIs in 1955.

CHAPTER

2

In the Beginning . . . When Bikini Was More Than a Bathing Suit

The tests in which Jim O'Connor participated had begun about ten years earlier when the United States dropped atomic bombs on Hiroshima and Nagasaki. In the Department of Energy's listing of the 600-odd explosions touched off by the U.S. since 1945, those two bombs are listed as the second and third "events" (their term).

The world's first fission bomb was built in absolute secrecy by the Manhattan Project in the midst of World War II, and strict secrecy continued to be the policy followed by the postwar nuclear test program until well into the 1950s. The fact that basic policy decisions about the development and use of nuclear power were made by a closely knit circle of scientists and public officials, insulated from public pressure and opinion, was to have enormous consequences.

Once nuclear weapons were added to the Pentagon's arsenal, military strategists came to regard them as legitimate weapons, to be refined, tested, and, where appropriate, used. Moreover, because the nation's political leadership had irrevocably crossed an invisible line, done the "unthinkable," when they'd dropped a nuclear bomb on Hiroshima, the cynical expectation that other nations might act exactly as we had became common among America's political and military leaders. Thus, the pressure to test and build ever-more-powerful atomic weapons grew irresistible.

Seventy of the nuclear scientists who'd worked on the top-secret Manhattan Project had foreseen the consequences of "first use" and tried desperately to convince President Truman not to take the fateful step without first warning Japan of our nuclear weapons and giving them an opportunity to surrender. Since his inner circle of nuclear advisers unanimously approved his decision to launch a secret atomic attack on both military and civilian targets in Japan, Truman felt he could brush the dissidents' objections aside. Sobered by their inability to exert any influence over the use of these hideously destructive weapons, large numbers of atomic scientists at the Oak Ridge, Chicago, and Los Alamos facilities later organized themselves into chapters of the Federation of American Scientists to work for disarmament and international controls on the use of nuclear weapons. Possessing few resources other than the persuasiveness of their expertise, these scientists banded together to dispel three principal myths on which the military use of nuclear weapons rested: one, that there can be a "limited" atomic war; second, that an effective "civil defense" against nuclear attack can be organized; and lastly, that there are "atomic secrets" which, if kept from our enemies, will insure America her nuclear monopoly.

When President Truman announced the bombing of Hiroshima on August 6, 1945, it was the first time the American people knew anything about the five-year, $2-billion program to build the atomic bomb. The proponents of nuclear technology understood that this widespread public ignorance, coupled with an enormous relief that a long and costly war was over, meant that they could pursue their nuclear experiments without significant opposition.

And indeed, no sooner had Japan surrendered than proposals for additional A-bomb tests began to be made. Senator Brien McMahon (D-Conn.), who later served as the first chairman of the Joint Congressional Atomic Energy Committee, urged that the United States conduct tests using captured warships. Within weeks, the navy announced plans to tow Japanese ships to sea and use them as atomic targets. The navy explained that the tests would measure the ability of ships to withstand nuclear attack. Clearly, the admirals wanted to demonstrate that their battleships were not obsolete in the Atomic Age.

In early October, President Truman proposed to a joint session of Congress that all means of producing atomic energy be nationalized and that all use of nuclear technology be strictly controlled by a civilian atomic energy commission. "The hope of civilization lies in . . . renunciation of the use and development of the atomic bomb," intoned the man who'd squeezed the nuclear trigger just two months earlier. He urged that other nations join the United States in restricting atomic energy solely to peaceful uses. At the same time, he reassured congressional skeptics that he planned to guard America's nuclear secrets strictly.

With this speech, Truman established what was to become an American political tradition: Denounce the proliferation of nuclear weapons, urge disarmament, and advocate peaceful uses of atomic energy, while continuing to produce and test nuclear weapons under the guise of national security. Truman enlisted Great Britain and Canada to join the United States in proposing that the United Nations oversee the exchange of scientific information on nuclear fission and begin work to eliminate all atomic weapons. He also announced that America wanted to share its atomic technology with its allies as soon as safeguards against unauthorized use could be developed.

But even these carefully hedged proposals began to draw political fire from many hardliners in Congress and the daily press. Senator Ed Johnson (Democrat-Colo.) spoke for many in Congress when he asserted that the best way to preserve the peace was with "vision, guts, plenty of A-bombs, modern planes, and strategically located airbases. . . ."

President Truman named a blue-ribbon panel—chaired by David Lilienthal, later to head the Atomic Energy Commission, and Dean Acheson, a future Secretary of State—whose responsibility it would be to draft a comprehensive proposal for international control of all uses of atomic energy. A different consensus, however, was emerging in American politics. Perhaps Winston Churchill defined it best in his famous "Iron Curtain" speech, which he gave in Fulton, Missouri, during this same period. After condemning the Soviets for lowering an "iron curtain" across Europe and the Balkans, Churchill argued it would be "criminal madness" for the United States to share any atomic secrets in this "agitated and ununited world." He also warned about the perils of "communist fifth columns" functioning throughout the West.

Nevertheless, two weeks after Churchill's call to arms, elder statesman Bernard Baruch presented the Acheson-Lilienthal plan for the gradual assumption of international control of atomic energy by the United Nations. In brief, it proposed that an international authority be established which could assume ownership of all nuclear processing plants and all stocks of uranium and thorium (principal bomb-making materials) in the world. It envisioned a carefully phased timetable for transition to U.N. control. In the first phase, a worldwide inventory of all uranium/thorium sources would be taken, while the actual production of nuclear weapons would cease until the final stage.

The Soviets made a counterproposal: All production of nuclear weapons would immediately cease and all stockpiles would be destroyed within three months.

These two proposals would generate endless debate within the United Nations for the next several years—all to no effect. In the meantime, both the U.S. and USSR relentlessly developed their nuclear capabilities.

Clay Milligan was a nineteen-year-old sailor serving aboard a destroyer in San Diego when the Joint Chiefs of Staff announced in January 1946, just after Truman's appointment of his blue-ribbon panel, that they would conduct the first atomic tests in the South Pacific later that year.

"Word came down that we were going to Bikini, but not to worry, that there was no danger," Milligan recalls. "You could get out of going if you wanted to, but most of us looked on it as an adventure. About a month later, our squadron of destroyers pushed off for Pearl Harbor where we rendezvoused with a lot of other ships that were also heading to Bikini."

Asked to produce the first nuclear show in history, the Joint Chiefs clearly planned an extravaganza, with hundreds of ships and a cast of thousands. Initially they'd planned to have 97 ships and 20,000 men participate, but by shot time this had ballooned to 42,000 men, 200 ships, 150 planes, and 4400 test animals.

The official histories, "Operation Crossroads: The Official Pictorial Records," and "Operation Crossroads: 4th Cruise of Mighty Mac," depict a veritable frenzy of scientific experimentation on the islands. Over 10,000 different instruments measured everything from the radioactivity in fish to the blast effects on swatches of army uniforms.

David Bradley, M.D., was another recent military recruit when Operation Crossroads was unveiled. He and twenty other physicians were given a crash course in radiological monitoring and then sent to Bikini. Bradley describes in his journal, later published as *No Place to Hide*, how the navy's experimentation snowballed.

"The target fleet [was] a sample of almost everything that floats, American ships, German ships, Japanese ships, flat-tops, submarines, battleships, cruisers, destroyers, landing craft, ships made of riveted plates, welded plates, floating drydocks made of concrete, even seaplanes. . . ."

The primary mission of Crossroads, according to the Joint Task Force One command, was to test nuclear blast effects upon naval vessels, although many tests of army weapons and equipment, as well as tests on thousands of farm animals, were also conducted. The first bomb ("Able"), scheduled for May 15, 1946, was to be dropped from a bomber and detonated in the air above the moored target fleet, while the second ("Baker") shot was to be detonated underwater near the fleet. A third ("Charlie") shot, a deepwater experiment, was scheduled for March 1947.

President Truman ordered a six-week postponement of the first test, however. The reason given was that Congress was preoccupied with legislation—particularly his own bill to create a civilian atomic energy commission—and the congressmen scheduled to observe the blast couldn't be spared from Washington. In retrospect, it's difficult to understand why 42,000 men and 200 ships would be kept waiting six weeks so that a dozen congressmen could personally witness a blast. It's more likely that the Crossroads test was a pawn in the enormous chess game Truman was playing with powerful forces both in Washington and abroad. The Pentagon had been opposed to Truman's plan for civilian control of nuclear technology, and legislation that would keep nuclear weapons under control of the military had passed the House. The Senate, however, favored civilian authority. An effective lobbying effort by the Federation of American Scientists on behalf of the AEC concept, coupled with a number of concessions made to promilitary congressmen, finally resulted in approval for the civilian agency.

Bikini atoll, consisting of thirty small islands which form a semicircle, is typical of many such chains in the Marshall Islands. Located about 2000 miles southwest of Hawaii, it was chosen after an intensive survey of the various atolls that had been captured from the Japanese. One small problem remained: The atoll had been the ancestral home to Bikinians for centuries. Nonetheless, military histories report that once the grand purpose of irradiating their islands was explained to them, the people agreed to relocate. They were moved—lock, stock, and outrigger—to Leo, Waltho, and Rongelop, other islands in the chain. These folks were presented as uncivilized primitives by news reporters. Journalists reported that when King Juda, the group's leader, was asked what he thought of the first atomic blast, he merely grinned and said, "Big boom." (The Bikinians made news again many years later when, in 1977, they were finally allowed to return home, only to be hastily reevacuated when it was found that the islands were still dangerously radioactive.)

As ships of the fleet arrived, Seabees and army engineers began dynamiting the extensive coral reefs to permit ship movements in the shallow lagoon. They constructed pontoon bridges and roads, erected huge instrument towers, and built airstrips and baseball diamonds. Within weeks, nine of the islands were transformed.

To heighten the drama, the Joint Task Force summoned to Bikini famous battleships and carriers that had seen action in one or both world wars. Legendary battleships like the *Pennsylvania, New York, Arkansas,* and *Nevada,* along with such well-known aircraft carriers as the *Independence, Saratoga,* and *Shangri-la,* were sailed thousands of miles to participate in the big event. Some of these historic ships were made part of the target fleet, as if to underscore that their military utility was at an end. The venerable *Nevada,* which had survived countless Japanese attacks, was painted a bright orange-red so that it would present a better target for the bombardier. Ships of the defeated enemy—the Japanese *Nagato* and *Sakawa* and Germany's *Prinz Eugen*—were also brought to Bikini and made part of the target fleet.

The U.S.S. *Appalachian* sailed from San Francisco with 170 reporters from every major American and European news service, newspaper, and magazine. The "dean" of atomic-blast journalists, William Laurence of the *New York Times,* was among the passengers. He had been the only reporter allowed to be present when the first atomic device in history was detonated at the Alamogordo, New Mexico, test site in July 1945. He also went along as the only civilian passenger when the A-bomb was dropped on Nagasaki. The Joint Chiefs and the boosters of nuclear power obviously appreciated the importance of favorable public relations to their fledgling enterprise. The U.S.S. *Appalachian* was stocked with the latest in communications technology. It could transmit 258,000 words a day, offering simultaneous translations in five languages: English, Spanish, French, Russian, and Polish. Its film labs processed over 50,000 still photos and a million and a half feet of movie film during the brief stint at Bikini. American newspapers received, via radio transmission, photos of each blast within three hours after it had taken place. Wherever there was a newspaper, a movie theater, or just a radio station, the story of Operation Crossroads would be told.

Meanwhile, the Federation of American Scientists issued a statement which flatly denied that there was any need for the Bikini tests. "Nothing of scientific value and little of technical value" would be gained from such explosions, they argued. The Federation was critical of the hasty test preparations and inadequate safety measures for participants, and concerned about the negative effect that the tests might have on the international talks on atomic control, which were just getting underway. In May 1946, Albert Einstein expressed his alarm about the failure to inform the general public as to the implications of nuclear energy. As chairman of the newly formed Emergency Committee of Atomic Scientists, he wrote: "Our world faces a crisis as yet unperceived by those possessing power to make great decisions for good or evil. The unleashed power of the atom has changed everything [except] our mode of thinking and thus we drift toward unparalled catastrophe."

On Bikini, however, no one in authority paid any attention, as one of the most elaborate military exercises in history wound to its emotional climax. In the spirit of the times, B-29 bomber crews strenuously competed for the honor of being allowed to drop the first A-test bomb.

On July 1, the big moment finally arrived as the prizewinning crew of "Dave's Dream" approached the lagoon carrying a 23-kiloton bomb dubbed "Gilda" after one of Rita Hayworth's recent movies. Forty-two thousand servicemen and observers were deployed on ships anchored between ten and twenty miles from ground zero. The seventy-three ships of the target fleet had been arranged for maximal blast effect; twenty were moored within a radius of a thousand yards. Just before countdown, the audience, except those equipped with special goggles, was ordered to turn their backs on what was to be a four-star performance.

When the bomb went off about a thousand feet above the prophetically named target ship, the *Nevada*, five ships were sunk immediately and nine others were heavily damaged. Manned and pilotless "drone" aircraft immediately began to fly sorties through the mushroom cloud taking radiation readings and samples. Drone boats circled the target ships, taking similar measurements. The official histories report that radio-activity soon diminished to "safe" levels and that ships carrying VIPs and members of the press were allowed into the target area just a few hours after the blast.

Bill Scott of Camarillo, California, was a member of the huge corps of photographers and journalists that arrived aboard the *Appalachian*. Bill had served in the army air force as a photographer during World War II. Discharged at the war's end, he returned to the South Pacific to work as a civilian filming the nuclear tests. According to his widow, Helena, he rode in a photo plane that flew in and around the radioactive cloud immediately after the first blast. As Mrs. Scott tells it: "Starting in 1955, Bill had nosebleeds, backaches, and coughing attacks, followed by vomiting, nausea, and upset stomach. His nosebleeds would last for days at a time. His teeth rapidly decayed and his feet became very dry and scaly. In 1971, he was hospitalized for tests which found that bone cancer had spread to his spine, ribs, and the exterior of one lung. He rapidly lost weight, and six months later he was gone."

Two other California widows believe that their husbands' lives were shortened by working on or around target ships. Mrs. Annette Tjeerdema says that her late husband, George, was a member of a 250-man navy work crew sent aboard one of the target ships, the U.S.S. *Bladen*, in an effort to decontaminate it. For at least two weeks they lived aboard the *Bladen*, scrubbing its radioactive surfaces with a solution of Tide soap and water. George told his wife that none of the cleanup crew wore protective gear and that they consumed food and water that had been aboard the ship during the blast. In 1963, Mr. Tjeerdema was diagnosed as having Hodgkin's disease, a proliferation of tumorous growths throughout the body. Their son also suffers from a blood condition, possibly leukemia. After extensive blood and bone marrow tests, it was decided that he had a congenital spherocytosis instead, a disease of the red blood cells; he must be regularly monitored for this condition.

Mrs. Mary Demuth coincidentally lives only miles from

Mrs. Tjeerdema. In 1969, her husband Albert died from a rare type of adenocarcinoma. He had been a deep-sea diver at Crossroads and for six months after the blasts he had been sent down to examine sunken target ships and to remove specimens for testing.

Both widows have applied, without success, for VA survivors' benefits.

In his book, Crossroads participant Dr. Bradley expressed concern about false confidence in the face of radiation's dangers. "The fact that radioactivity is apparently decaying away makes caution more imperative. [There are] dangerous materials which are not detectable on Geiger counters, notably plutonium remnants." Bradley noted that his safety team had only one instrument that could measure deadly alpha emitters and that it was fragile and extremely difficult to operate. The question arises: When someone with as little radiological training as Dr. Bradley could recognize the gross deficiencies in Crossroads' rad-safety program, why wasn't it equally apparent to planners of the exercise? Apparently they had other fish to fry.

The second Bikini bomb, named "Baker," was designed to test the effects of an underwater nuclear blast on the hulls of eighty-seven battleships and submerged submarines. Since the radioactive materials relased during such a blast would heavily pollute the surrounding waters and would pass more slowly into the upper atmosphere, the scientists knew that "Baker" would be dirtier than the previous blast—but how *much* dirtier, no one knew for sure.

The sailors shared the scientists' uncertainty. Texan Clay Milligan recalls: "We passed around a newspaper which had printed an artist's sketch of what might happen with an underwater blast. It showed a hundred-foot tidal wave that was flipping a destroyer on its back like a toy. When the bomb went off, I thought the initial blast *was* the wave. Man, I was scared to death!"

While the monster tidal wave didn't materialize, the underwater bomb drove a half-mile-wide column of contaminated water over a mile into the air.

James McCauley of Fairborn, Ohio, had been en route to China aboard the *LST 871* when his ship was rerouted to assist in the evacuation of the Bikini islanders. Like Milligan, he remembers being told to prepare for a possible tidal wave during the second shot.

"Just before the detonation, our commander came on the loudspeaker and told us to look away from the blast area. He also said we wouldn't be allowed back into the lagoon for at least seven days due to radioactivity. However, a few hours after the blast we left the main flotilla and cruised toward the lagoon in preparation for entering it the next morning. I believe our orders were changed because the scientists aboard our ship were curious and wanted to view the damage as soon as possible," McCauley recalls.

"When we entered the lagoon, I saw that destroyers, submarines, and the Japanese battlewagon were sunk. The hulls of two American cruisers were melted to a crisp, but they were still afloat. We sailed among the target fleet for at least five hours and on one side we were so close we could have touched them with a long pole. No one on *LST 871* wore any sort of protective clothing."

On the long voyage home, McCauley remembers experiencing severe dizziness and headaches as well as weakness and loss of appetite. He was admitted, along with several other crew members, to a naval hospital where he spent nearly six months before he was dropped from the navy with a medical discharge. He reports that since 1971 he has suffered from an unexplained blood disorder.

Jerome Martek, who now lives in Gaylord, Michigan, was exposed to the highly radioactive waters of Bikini after the first Crossroads blast. "One of my jobs in the engine room was to replace the zinc plates which were exposed to water drawn from the lagoon. Cold seawater was drawn in as a coolant for the engines. A technician with a Geiger counter walked by just as I had finished replacing the plates. The counter showed I was highly contaminated; he asked me how I got so 'hot.' He told me to get out of my clothes and to shower immediately. The same technician ran the counter over me again and told me to shower again and to scrub thoroughly."

Martek went to sick bay when he began to experience numerous nosebleeds but he received no treatment, nor was any medical follow-up ever conducted. Nosebleeds and nausea can be early-stage symptoms of radiation poisoning.

After discharge from the Navy, Martek married and, for many years, he and his wife tried to have children. His local physician, Dr. Gerald Drake, recently ordered a sperm count which found Jerome to be sterile. Dr. Drake has told the VA that he believes the sterility to be a result of radiation exposure.

Nor is sterility the extent of Martek's problems: "In 1959, I had a third of my lung removed because of internal bleeding and bronchiectasis. I had a brain abscess in 1965, which the doctors believe was due to my bad lungs. The brain damage left me with no feeling in my arm, hand, or face. I take daily medications to prevent Jacksonian attacks, an uncontrolled jerking and trembling of the affected side."

Today, at fifty-two, Jerome finds it hard not to give in to bitterness: "I have been denied the chance of fatherhood and my poor health has made it impossible to qualify for adoption. My disabilities *are* service-connected and the VA's denial of my claim is an injustice."

We have located three other sailors who worked on various decontamination efforts after the blasts. One of them, James Zepede, was ordered to board the U.S.S. *Salt Lake City*, one of the target ships, just hours after the first blast. Zepede and twenty-five other sailors lived aboard the "hot" ship for several weeks while they unloaded contaminated ammunition from the ship's hold. They ate K rations they'd brought with them, but they drank from the ship's water system. As he remembers it today: "It took a while for our group to get organized and begin following basic safety precautions, such as wearing breathing equipment and using Geiger counters and film badges. After the second bomb, we were moved on to other target ships for similar cleanup work. Even at the time, everyone in our group thought we were guinea pigs. We were never tested for radiation poisoning."

When the rest of the fleet sailed for home, Zepede's unit stayed behind to finish its work. They worked on the contaminated fleet for another six months. Today, Zepede suffers from an unexplained skin discoloration on his back and a chronic eye infection. However, compared with what he's heard about some of the other test observers, he considers himself lucky.

A thirty-year career employee of South Dakota Bell Telephone is not someone you'd normally think of as an angry man, but Ken Marshall defies the stereotype. He worked with decontamination teams during Crossroads.

"I never saw a Geiger counter or a film badge the whole time I was there. They talk about 'em now, but it's a lie." He was serving aboard the captain's ship when a group of men who evidently had been heavily contaminated were brought aboard. "It was pretty secretive—they examined and bathed them; a day or two later they were flown out," he recalls.

Marshall remembers experiencing health problems shortly after the tests. On the cruise home, "Everyone was nauseous and our hair fell out in patches. The hair under my arms turned a bright red. When we arrived at the pier in San Francisco, I remember that the civilian dock workers refused to unload the guns we'd salvaged from the *Nevada*, so sailors had to do it. It was Navy Day when we tied up at Mare Island. Although we were left aboard, the ship carried warning signs to would-be visitors: 'ship radioactive.' Huge containers of acid were loaded aboard and then we sailed out past the twenty-mile limit where we flushed the acid through the ship's fire mains." Marshall doubts that it did any good, though, since the ship was immediately placed in dry dock and decommissioned upon its return to port.

In 1954, when he was 29 years old, doctors removed a tumor from Marshall's thyroid. The surgeon told him that he'd never seen one like it before. At thirty-nine, Marshall suffered a heart attack, and since then he's suffered from a long series of unexplained ailments. Three sons born after Crossroads suffer from the same congenital defect in their knee joints, although they're healthy in all other respects.

A third witness is Ivan Kirk. He served aboard the U.S.S. *Creon,* whose mission was to take periodic radiation samples of the lagoon water. He relates that after radiation monitors came aboard to take readings at Honolulu, the ship was ordered to put out to sea. After cruising up and down the California coast for two weeks, they were finally allowed to dock at Long Beach. Every crew member was bathed with special soaps. The U.S.S. *Creon* was placed in dry dock and every inch of her paint was painstakingly chipped off.

Kirk developed severe migraine headaches about two years later. He is now 100 percent disabled.

Writing in his journal a month after the second blast, Dr. David Bradley appraises the decontamination effort: "Having proven at last that salt water, lye, Foamite, and soap applied with liberal amounts of navy profanity have no value in cleaning these ships of their coat of radioactivity, the navy has decided to try sandblasting." Bradley warns that this technique will create yet another danger: inhalation of radioactive dust. He also concludes that given the shortages in lab equipment and personnel, the ongoing monitoring of sailors by rad-safe teams is extremely speculative, at best.

The government indirectly confirmed the paucity of film badges in the South Pacific when Dr. Donald Kerr, today the Department of Energy's Assistant Secretary for Defense Programs, conceded that badge information could be found for only 11,500 (out of 42,000) present during the '46 test and 1500 (out of an estimated 20,000) during the '48 test.

Some of the photos in the official pictorial history of Operation Crossroads display an almost touching naïveté. One is captioned: "To prove island was undamaged, five officers pose in front of healthy palm trees." In another, crew members of the submarine *Skate,* one of the target ships, are standing on her wrecked bridge under a sign that says, "Keep Clear—Danger! Very Radioactive." A third shows sailors and reporters clambering around a badly damaged ship be-

neath chalked graffiti warning "No souvenirs." As the weeks
passed, however, no amount of press agentry or atomic boosterism could conceal the fact that the test blasts had badly
contaminated the ships, water, and possibly the men of
Bikini Lagoon. When President Truman canceled the third
test without explanation, the press didn't ask *what* had happened to make the long-planned third shot no longer necessary. With all aspects of the A-bomb's development shrouded
in mystery, news accounts of the period tended to be both uncritical and prone to error. Not atypically, the *New York
Times* passed along a report that the canceled blast was to
have been set off at a depth of two *miles*, even though Bikini
Lagoon is only 200 feet deep. In the hands of skillful press
agents, the complex technology of nuclear power was made
to seem awesome indeed.

In any event, Operation Crossroads, which had cost an
estimated $90 million, was brought to an end, and most of
the fleet sailed for home. Nearly a hundred ships had to be
left behind in what was called temporary quarantine. Scientists would find them still highly radioactive two years later.
These ghost ships were to spark fresh controversy in 1948
when two of them, the *Independence* and the *Salt Lake City*,
were towed to San Francisco despite the lingering radioactivity.

At least two servicemen who boarded these ships off the
California coast have died in recent years of what may have
been radiation-induced cancers. Marine Colonel Charles
Broudy was a young student at the Naval Radiological Defense School when he was ordered to board the ships. He
probably received additional doses of radiation when he
participated at several A-tests at the Nevada site in 1957.
According to his widow, Pat, when they tried to pursue a claim
for service-connected disability, the marines claimed to have
lost his medical records for the years 1948–60. One of the
Broudys' children was born with hypothyroidism, which some
scientists believe can be linked to radiation-induced genetic
damage.

Colonel Nicholas Kane also paid a visit to the Bikini ships

off the California coast, and, like many career officers, he was later sent to Nevada to observe several A-blasts in 1955. During one shot in March 1955 he was in a trench only a mile or so from the blast. He succumbed to leukemia in December 1978.

Finally, the *Independence* and the *Salt Lake City*, which had bested Japanese warships in thirty different battles, were sent ignominiously to Davy Jones's Locker by torpedoes of the U.S. Navy.

Both the armed forces and the civilian scientists conducted literally hundreds of detailed experiments and studies at Bikini. Reports often running several hundred pages were published within a few months after Crossroads. (Until recently, nearly all were classified.) In retrospect, it seems like nearly anything was considered a fit subject for study *except* a survey of radiation's possible effects upon the 42,000 men who served at Bikini. Not a single test participant we interviewed was ever contacted by any government agency concerning radiation exposure until after public reports of A-bomb-test victims began to appear in 1977. In response to a growing controversy over the allegations of GIs that they were harmed by radiation either in Nevada or the South Pacific, the Pentagon commissioned DASIAC, a division of General Electric, to review the entire body of scientific studies conducted during the nuclear tests from 1946 to mid-1963. Even though DASIAC looked only at studies that seemed likely to assist the identification of military participants, its researchers came up with nearly 2000 separate reports and studies. In its 200-page index of these reports published in March 1978, not a *single* study of possible radiation exposure of Crossroads personnel appears.

The military did, however, make extensive use of these scientific findings to modify and improve military equipment and hardware. The Joint Chiefs' evaluation panel made bold recommendations for changes in military armaments, strategy, and tactics based on effects tests at Bikini. For example, two battleships, the *Kentucky* and the *Hawaii*, were halted in the midst of construction. Their superstructures were redesigned to take into account pressure from a nuclear blast.

CHAPTER
3
Eniwetok: Out of Sight, Out of Mind

No sooner had things begun to cool down on Bikini than a new controversy over atomic weapons brought political temperatures to a boil in Washington. It began when Secretary of Commerce Henry Wallace (dumped by Roosevelt as a running mate in 1944 in favor of Truman who was not identified with New Deal liberalism) sent a private letter to President Truman during the Crossroads tests. The letter began: "Americans [feel] that war is coming and that the only way to head it off is to arm ourselves to the teeth." He suggested that this mood was encouraged by Truman's foreign policy and wondered whether the administration's public appeals for nuclear disarmament and international control of atomic energy were sincere. He closed by warning that other nations would soon have their own A-bombs and that international agreements, not bigger and better bombs, were the only way to head off a nuclear holocaust.

The truth was that while the United States still enjoyed its nuclear monopoly, no knowledgeable scientist believed that it would take the Soviets more than a few years to develop equivalent nuclear weapons. Nonetheless, when Wallace delivered a public speech that was mildly critical of the "get tough with Russia" approach a few weeks after the letter, all hell broke loose. Secretary of State James Byrnes threatened to resign if Wallace wasn't disciplined, Navy Secretary James Forrestal (later Secretary of Defense) publicly attacked Wallace, and excerpts from his July letter turned up in the nationally syndicated column of muckraker Drew Pearson. Truman let Wallace twist in the wind for a few days and then fired him.

The message was unmistakable: A "bi-partisan" foreign policy had been worked out by America's political leadership, and one of its tenets was that no limits on America's nuclear strength would be tolerated. Woe unto any official who dared to question publicly the new hard line against the Soviet bloc. This monolithic policy had the effect of enshrining the development of nuclear weapons as national gospel.

Meanwhile, the armed forces concerned themselves with adjusting to the new civilian Atomic Energy Commission, which was to assume complete authority on January 1, 1947. On his return from Crossroads, Secretary of War–designee Robert Patterson conducted a series of briefings on atomic warfare for top army officers. He reportedly told them that the military must proceed on the assumption that there would be no adequate international controls.

Looking back thirty years later, it seems that those who fought for a civilian-controlled atomic energy commission seriously underestimated the pressures for conformity that the Cold War would exert on nuclear planners—civilian and military. One of the AEC's first official acts was to announce that tests of "new atomic weapons" were needed, and from then on the AEC consistently supported the principle of maintaining American "nuclear preeminence" through the development and testing of nuclear weapons.

Evidently the civilian commissioners found it difficult to reconcile the constant pressure for new weapons development with other concerns about safety. One commissioner, Eugene Zuckert, who served on the AEC from 1952 to 1954, told a Senate committee probing offsite fallout in June 1979 about tensions within the Commission. "The AEC was set up really as a check on the military [however] it attempted to safeguard the needs of the military. So you had a basically adversary situation . . . we were doing something that the military felt it should do."

When Zuckert was asked whether he thought the AEC favored the development of new nuclear weapons over concern for public safety, he answered, "When the two came into conflict, the balance was apt to tip toward the military programs." Zuckert also described the effects of operating in secret: "So much of what we did was [based] on restricted data; it limited the field of people who had expertise. I think we got a group that tended to become too introverted about the problem and [to] become too unanimous."

In the fall of 1947, a joint AEC-Pentagon project, Task Force Seven, was formed to build and operate a new atomic proving ground on Eniwetok in the South Pacific. Hence the natives of Eniwetok received an unwelcome surprise for Christmas—they were told that their islands were needed for nuclear tests. The series was dubbed Sandstone, and the Foreword to its official yearbook, *Operation Sandstone*, constitutes a bit of nuclear-testing history. For the first time, the test program was justified not just on military or "national security" grounds but on the basis that it would yield "valuable information pertaining to the civilian employment of atomic energy." This rationale would become very common in the years ahead.

While the nature of the bombs tested was similar, Operation Sandstone differed from the earlier Crossroads as night from day. The polarization of the Cold War had settled over Bikini; thus the Sandstone series was conducted in virtual news blackout. Gone were the press ship and the instant replay of each blast. "Secrecy" was the new watchword. The ships were festooned with posters depicting a fish with an open mouth. "Don't be a sucker," the posters warned, "keep your mouth shut." The only outsiders allowed were members of the Joint Congressional Committee on Atomic Energy.

Jeremiah Murphy of Portland, Oregon, was a young naval officer just out of Yale when he was given a .45 pistol and sent to the science labs at Berkeley. He was to pick up the top-secret operational plans from the previous tests. The documents were handcuffed to his wrist in a special pouch. He immediately rushed to Washington, D.C., by plane, only to find that no one was there to meet him . . . Perhaps even his arrival time had been declared top secret. . . . A few months later he was serving aboard the U.S.S. *Perkins* in San Diego when security personnel came aboard to check the ship's crew. Evidently no spies were uncovered, for a few days later his ship was en route to Eniwetok to participate in Operation Sandstone.

"We were probably twelve miles from Touchstone (ground zero) when the first shot went off. Nobody aboard our ship had a film badge or a dosimeter; I don't recall seeing anyone wearing one the whole time I was there. We were given no briefings, no films, nor booklets; we were in the navy—you did what you were told."

Murphy doesn't remember much fear or concern among the men. "After Crossroads, it was pretty well known that if you were far enough away, there wouldn't be any damage." He recalls that each of the three shots went off precisely on time. "First, we'd feel the heat, like someone had turned a sun lamp on. This was quickly followed by the blast's impact.

"We had some 'activity' at one of the tests when a rain squall passed over our ship after having passed through the mushroom cloud. I don't remember exactly what I did, but I can assure you I wasn't standing out in a rainstorm." He recalls that the command was quite concerned and ordered all the decks washed down as soon as the squall passed.

Confirming an atmosphere of strict security, Murphy reports: "Sandstone was a hush-hush operation. They thought the Russians might try and monitor our tests; we didn't want to be paying the bill while they got the benefits. If a Russian sub had been found, we would have bombed it."

Operation Sandstone resembled Crossroads in the plethora of exotic experiments that were conducted. John E. Knights of Tampa, Florida, conducted one such experiment which may have permanently damaged his health. Trained as an electronics engineer, he was placed in charge of a remote-controlled tank unit that was to retrieve radioactive soil as soon after the blast as possible. Aboard a helicopter near ground zero, Knights was guiding a tank into the bomb crater when it became stuck. Later, Knights was sent in to extract the stuck tank. Wearing only canvas booties, ordinary fatigues, and no film badge, he entered the highly radioactive crater which had been gouged by a 37-kiloton bomb only days before. When tow lines attached to the upper part of the tank failed to do the job, Knights crawled under the tank, pushing away the "hot" soil with his hands as he attached the cables. A rad-safe monitor who was present testified later at a VA disability hearing that Knights had received 800 rads of exposure. Records produced by the government at the same hearing indicated that he'd received only half a rad of exposure.

When Knights returned to the rad-safety ship, he was ordered into the showers for a thorough scrubbing. He thinks he was also given some sort of emetic to flush him out internally. Before he returned to the States, his hair began falling out in patches. It never grew back.

"No one ever again asked me about my health; they only seem interested in secrecy. 'You didn't see anything, you don't know anything,' they told us."

In 1969, doctors found bladder cancer. Knights has undergone eight different operations since then. This, coupled with an unexplained disorder in his hands, made it impossible for him to work as an engineer, or indeed to work at all, at age fifty. For nine years he has waged a fight, unsuccessful to date, to win a service-connected disability.

At the end of the tests, one wag had an elaborate scroll printed which admitted its bearer into the "Sacred Order of Guinea Pigs." While it was taken as a joke by John Knights and the other men, perhaps the prankster knew more than he realized.

A careful reading of the official yearbook, *Operation Sandstone*, reveals that a subtle shift of atomic policy had occurred. While the first tests were justified solely on the basis of national defense, the Sandstone yearbook marked the first time that they also were extolled for producing "valuable information pertaining to the civilian employment of atomic energy." This rationale was employed with increasing frequency in the years that followed.

Two brothers-in-law, Frank Turner and Jim Grandy, served together as airmen on Kwajalien during Operation Sandstone. They were assigned to electronics supply, and all the instruments and test equipment for the B-17 "drone" aircraft came through them. The mother ships would fly the drones through the atomic cloud and then land them, by remote control, on Eniwetok.

According to Frank, these drones were left on Eniwetok to "cool off" for a few days after a test blast, then were flown back to Kwajalien, where he and other crew members would remove the scientific instruments from them. He remembers a couple of incidents that caused him to wonder about the decontamination program.

"I was taking something off one of these drones when an officer told me, 'Put it down, I think it's still hot.' Of course, I went and washed off with gasoline, but obviously some of the stuff hadn't been checked out too closely."

Frank remembers worrying even then about radioactivity. "I'd seen a lot of those people in Japan who had radiation—big sores all over. I had a good idea what that stuff could do, but, to be honest, I don't think most people at Sandstone knew the power of the bomb."

He doesn't recall seeing any ground or air crew members wearing film badges, and there was no radiological monitoring equipment in his hangar. "We handled things that were brought back from Eniwetok. They were supposed to be already cooled off."

At fifty-four, Frank Turner has fortunately not manifested any of the health problems normally associated with radiation damage. However, his brother-in-law, Jim, may not have been so lucky. One son is dying of incurable cancer and another child was born with a congenital head defect that required corrective surgery. Scientists have long known that radiation can severely damage genes so that children produced after exposure may suffer from gross birth defects.

The photos in the Task Force's official yearbook suggest that radiation-safety practices were casual at best. In one, ground crew members, wearing ordinary fatigues, are shown standing a few feet from a "hot" drone airplane while they spray it with garden hoses. Another shows men (perhaps Bob or Jack) gathered around a drone plane with the caption: "Planes returned with their load of samples, were unloaded and readied for future missions." One sailor, wearing a regular uniform and gloves, carries a box of radioactive samples.

Some press accounts at the time speculated that the long-postponed "deepwater" test had been conducted, but they were wrong; perhaps the scientists had soured on underwater testing after the "Baker" shot in 1946. Each of the three bombs (which ranged from 18 to 49 kilotons in blast force) was detonated from a steel tower several hundred feet high, and the Task Force Seven command evidently made quite an effort to "stabilize" the sandy beaches of the atoll prior to the tests. This could have been out of concern for the danger of alpha particles attaching themselves to granules of sand as they were swept up high into the mushroom cloud. General Hull, task force commander, is shown in one photo watching as his troops shower some substance from heavy bags onto the beach. Another photo depicting men working states cryptically, "Ground conditioning continues." Colonel William McGee, the Defense Nuclear Agency spokesperson, was at a loss for an explanation; he stated that he could find no information about any such effort to stabilize the contaminated sand.

When the test series ended, Bob Harris reports, virtually every instrument and piece of equipment used during the tests was carefully logged, packed, and shipped back to the States. Whether radioactive particles were brought home with the salvage will never be known.

Three years would pass before the United States conducted another atomic bomb test. During this hiatus, though, America's military and political leaders continued to sound alarms about Soviet threats and aggression, insinuating that nuclear warfare was all but inevitable. World War II hero Lieutenant General Jimmy Doolittle urged Americans to be "prepared physically, mentally, and morally to drop atom bombs on Russia at the first sign of aggression. Our people must be conditioned to accept this type of retaliation."

America's brief whirl as belle of the nuclear ball ended abruptly, however, on September 23, 1949, when President Truman announced that the Soviets had successfuly detonated an atomic bomb. Soon, powerful voices in Congress and the military would begin urging that the U.S. regain the "lead" by resuming the testing of nuclear weapons.

CHAPTER

4

Environs Las Vegas: New Gambler in Town

In late June 1950, the long-simmering conflict between the northern and southern portions of Korea broke out into open warfare. The country had been temporarily partitioned by the Soviet and American troops who liberated it from Japanese occupation at the end of World War II. Now President Harry Truman immediately sent American troops to fight on the South Korean side, and a massive mobilization of the U.S. military was begun. After several months of bitter fighting, the Americans and other allied forces succeeded in pushing the northern forces back across the provisional border that divided the two parts of Korea. Heady with victory, General Douglas MacArthur relentlessly drove his troops toward the Chinese border despite the continued warnings from both Peking and Washington. As they neared the Chinese mainland, 60,000 Chinese troops attacked, and soon the U.S. forces were in full retreat. Truman warned that he might authorize MacArthur to use atomic weapons at his discretion.

It was against this backdrop of international crisis that Truman issued orders that a nuclear-testing site within the continental United States be established and that the pace of testing be accelerated. The National Security Council (NSC) asked the Atomic Energy Commission to recommend a domestic site "at which a few relatively low-order detonations may be done safely." Three years earlier, the NSC had debated the wisdom of such a domestic site, and the Pentagon's nuclear arm, the Armed Forces Special Weapons Project (AFSWP) had conducted a top-secret feasibility study under the code name "Nutmeg." Its recommendation that such a site be located in the "arid Southwestern U.S." was shelved for "possible later consideration in the event of an emergency."

We interviewed a nuclear scientist who participated in nearly all phases of the nuclear weapons testing program from 1949 to 1962. While he can't be identified publicly, the Defense Nuclear Agency, which arranged the deep background interview, confirmed his service during those years. He remembers: "During 1947, first thought was given to a continental site. Military and AEC personnel surveyed sites on the North American continent. . . . If the weapons labs had a backyard site, [test] results could be reflected in weapons development months sooner than with tests in the South Pacific."

Minutes of an AEC meeting on December 12, 1950 (recently declassified) refer to staff memos which admit that data as to potential safety risks at the test site were incomplete. "These questions may be answered satisfactorily as test knowledge increases . . . but they're not satisfactorily answered at present," reads one memo. The site was chosen over other possible locales because it was close to the main scientific labs at Los Alamos, New Mexico, the land was already part of an air base, and, according to the AEC, the favorable climate meant that "some of the most urgent weapons tests can be conducted . . . within acceptable limits of radiological safety."

With the new trump card of domestic testing up their sleeve, leaders continued to stir the cauldron of international tensions, which were heading toward flash point. On Christmas Day, 1950, President Truman broadcast one of his patented Cold War tantrums in which he endorsed a worldwide mobilization against the Soviets, whom he called "the heirs of Mongol killers . . . the greatest killers in the history of the world." Several high-ranking military commanders advocated a first strike using atomic weapons against the Soviet bloc. "The Communists will understand the lash," said General Emmett "Rosie" O'Donnell, "when it's put to them."

A week before the AEC announced the Nevada test program, Congress approved the creation of the Federal Civil Defense Administration. Most of the agency's funding was earmarked for the construction of "community-type" bomb shelters in cities and towns across the country.

Just six weeks after Truman signed the authorization, the Nevada desert shook from its first atomic blast. Over the next years, until the Limited Test Ban Treaty between the U.S. and the Soviet Union ended atmospheric testing in 1962, eighty-three other atomic bombs, ranging up to five or six times larger than those dropped on Japan, were detonated in Nevada. Nearly 100,000 servicemen, mostly soldiers and marines, were brought to the test site to witness one or more atomic blasts.

No military troops, however, were present to observe or skirmish during the first test series in Nevada, since the AEC was anxious to begin blasting as soon as possible. Also, the entente between the AEC and the Pentagon, which would open the way for the nuclear orientation of tens of thousands of GIs, was still being negotiated. The AEC brahmins, privy as they were to the truth about radiation's punishing effects, most likely foresaw the nightmarish problems of control and radiation safety dissolving into full-blown chaos as thousands of GIs hiked over the contaminated desert.

When the five shots of the initial series were completed, the scientific staff shuttled back to the South Pacific for the Greenhouse series. One of the four bombs tested during Greenhouse was particularly significant: It was the first successful test of tritium and deuterium, two essential components of the hydrogen bomb. A powerful bloc within the nuclear community had been lobbying for a crash program to build a thermonuclear (hydrogen) bomb ever since the Soviets had developed an atomic bomb.

Bernard Durkin of Scituate, Massachusetts, witnessed these four tests while serving aboard the U.S.S. *Curtis* as a young sailor. Now suffering from lymph cancer, Bernie sought VA disability, contending that his malignancy is due to the radiation he encountered at Eniwetok. He recalls that he and other sailors were made to scrub the ship's decks with a special rock (called a "holy stone" in Navy jargon) even though the decks had been drenched with radioactive water during the test blasts.

Durkin also accompanied teams of scientists when they went to and from the radioactive atoll before and after each test. "We wore shorts, no shirts, and rarely shoes," he recalls. "As a result, we frequently had cuts and scratches from the coral reefs. It's interesting to note, in retrospect, that the scientists wore clothes, shoes, and at times, heavy protective garments."

He also remembers making many trips to Enjebi, a nearby island in the Eniwetok chain. He recently saw a news photo taken in 1978 when scientists returned to Enjebi—wearing protective gear against the continuing hazard from plutonium traces. "Twenty-five years ago, such things were considered a luxury," he notes with a bitter laugh.

The VA denied his claim, relying in part on a radiation exposure record which indicated he'd received only 1.4 rads during the entire series. The use of such "data" upsets Bernie since he never wore a film badge during his time at Eniwetok.

Rather than admit that their dream of nuclear supremacy was a Faustian pact with the devil, these scientists and their allies in the military urged that America reclaim its dominant position by building vastly more powerful thermonuclear weapons. They won Truman's support, and, eighteen months later, on Halloween, 1952, the dirtiest, nastiest bomb ever—a 10.4-megaton H-bomb (equivalent to ten million tons of TNT)—was detonated at Eniwetok.

By that time, however, the Soviets, driven by a fear that was not entirely paranoid, already had poured enormous resources into their own atomic-weapons development; they had detonated their own H-bomb a few months earlier. As Albert Einstein prophetically observed in 1950, "The idea of achieving security through national armament is, at the present stage of military technique, a disastrous illusion."

By the time the nuclear road show had returned from the South Pacific in early summer, the armed forces had developed extensive plans for the use of ground troops during future tests at the Nevada site. Sixth Army Commander Major General W. B. Kean approved the use of troops "to provide training in the employment of atomic weapons and [protective] measures." He expressed the hope that GIs could be marched through the detonation area "as soon after the blast as possible." The Military Liaison Committee had urged in a July memo to the AEC that such exposures were needed since "the psychological implications of atomic weapons close to our own front lines in support of ground operations are unknown."

To coordinate and direct troop operations during the Buster-Jangle series, which was to commence on October 22, 1951, Lieutenant General Joseph Swing's staff wrote a detailed battle plan. Similar plans were written for each of the subsequent tests at which troops were present. The battle scenario for this series assumed that an "aggressor enemy" had already conquered all of the western United States to the north and west of the test site. Leaving no doubt as to whom they thought the "aggressor enemy" would likely be, the plan's authors designed the battle based on the "typical formations and current tactical doctrines of Communist armies." One of the principal test objectives was to experiment with the tactical use of atomic weapons against conventional ground forces. Exhaustive surveying of every hill and ravine preceded the writing of the mock battle plan.

Just before the series began, the AEC's chairman, Gordon Dean, presented his views on the future of atomic strategy in the future. "We're entering an era where our power to wage [nuclear] warfare is so great that our concept of atomic warfare must undergo revolutionary change. We can begin to meet the military's retaliation. There is now a new kind of atomic warfare much more promising as a means of halting aggressors without the risk of destroying large parts of the world in the process," he concluded optimistically.

A number of magazines and newspapers published articles

on nuclear warfare and the possibilities of global war with the Soviet bloc, around the time of this series. *Collier's,* then one of the large weeklies in the United States, devoted its entire October 27 issue to the subject, under the heading "Preview of the War We Don't Want: Russia's Defeat and Occupation, 1952-60." Various contributors, ranging from Walter Reuther to Senator Margaret Chase Smith, tried their hands at forecasting the nature of the "next" war.

Adding its voice to the chorus, the Joint Congressional Committee on Atomic Energy released a statement urging the nuclear planners to "greater boldness and more scientific daring." The AEC should "risk failure," they argued, to speed development of new atomic weapons.

Construction began, and in just a few weeks Camp Desert Rock rose from the mesquite brush of the Nevada desert. From the beginning, the test site functioned under a strict security system. A fifteen-page booklet, *Camp Desert Rock Information and Guide,* was printed and distributed to all arriving units. The guide's section on security began with the warning: "Everyone will want to know what you've seen, officials, friends, as well as the enemy." It went on for two pages listing what GIs could and could not (mostly the latter) talk about.

This near-obsession with security resulted in numerous delays and occasional absurdities. For example, the toilets at Camp Mercury happened to be in an area to which only persons with a "Q" clearance could be admitted, so one had to have the highest security classification before one could go to the bathroom. A scientist, taking matters into his own hands, commandeered a bulldozer and knocked down the fence around the toilets.

Everyone, down to the lowliest private on KP, was screened for evidence of possible disloyalty. A small number of GIs were sent home, mostly for not having U.S. citizenship. All civilians at the site, including members of the press, were similarly screened. In its "after-action" report, written after the series, the army criticized the AEC for making public much test data that the military believed should have been kept secret. They urged that a "firm and inflexible press and public relations policy" be strictly enforced at future tests. However, the same report candidly acknowledged that "the Soviet Union and its satellites possess other and more fruitful means of collecting U.S. atomic energy information; therefore they found overt or clandestine intelligence activities at Desert Rock unnecessary." One wonders whether the primary purpose of the security system wasn't to instill fear among test observers, the better to secure their unquestioning obedience under conditions of nuclear combat.

The Buster-Jangle series was inaugurated on schedule with a small 1.2-kiloton shot on October 22, 1951. It was, in many ways, a blueprint for the tests that followed over the next six years. Vehicles, weapons, and military equipment of all kinds were positioned both on the ground and in trenches at varying distances from ground zero at 1000, 1500, and 2500 yards, and so on—so that the effects of blast, heat, and radiation could be measured. Sheep also were tethered at similar distances from the bomb's epicenter.

During the fourth shot, "Dog," the troops only observed from trenches, but on the next shot, "Easy," touched off on November 5, large numbers of ground troops maneuvered for the first time on the "atomic battlefield." Immediately after the 31-kiloton bomb went off 1400 feet in the air, an 833-member battalion combat team moved into trenches just 3500 yards from ground zero. Another 4300 GIs occupied trenches farther back. Ninety minutes later, the battalion combat team marched to within 500 yards of ground zero, following in columns behind rad-safe monitors. The troops then executed a complex set of maneuvers set out in the battle plan.

Don Smith and William Bires, who both now live near Portland, were among the first GIs ever to maneuver at the Nevada site. Smith was assigned to the 374th Convalescent Center while Bires served with the 231st Combat Engineers. Smith remembers being trained in atomic warfare before arriving at Desert Rock. He summarized this indoctrination as follows: "Radiation will not hurt you, even if it passes over your trench by a fraction of an inch, you'll be safe."

Both men had been in the army about eight months when they were sent to Nevada to watch five different atomic tests. Smith remembers sitting on the desert floor before the first blast, facing away from the bomb. He guesses that his unit wasn't more than two miles from ground zero, although the official reports state that no one was closer than seven miles when it was detonated. When the bomb went off Smith felt a sharp stab in his neck; then his whole body felt warm. After a few moments they were told to turn and look at the rising fireball. Smith remembers that "it was an awesome sight, sort of beautiful in a way."

Bires's experience is similar: "I observed a total of five blasts. I and my fellow soldiers frequently went into the test area to repair and construct the gun emplacements, animal pens, et cetera, between tests. No consideration was ever given to radiation exposure except once when I observed a busload of officers being swept with a Geiger counter after they returned from a visit to ground zero." Don Smith is emphatic that he was never given a film badge to measure radiation exposure.

Both men suffer from crippling ailments today. Smith has severe joint pain throughout his body, rendering him unable to work; Bires reports a long history of gastrointestinal problems in addition to his joint problems. Both are worried men today: two army buddies of Smith who served at Nevada have died of cancer in the last six months.

During the early tests, the firing of a red cluster bomb meant that "Condition Black"—a radiation emergency—was in effect and that all troops were to assemble at the nearest trucks for evacuation from the test site.

During the Buster-Jangle series, each GI was issued a film badge, which he wore pinned to his chest. The photo film in this badge registered the amount of gamma radiation received by the badge. Unlike a dosimeter, which indicates the dose *currently* being received, the badge merely recorded the total exposure; it would not warn the wearer that he or she was encountering levels of radioactivity beyond predetermined limits. So troops maneuvering in "hot" areas were totally dependent upon rad-safe monitors operating survey meters for warnings as to current dose. As we'll discuss later, there are serious questions about whether even this equipment was capable of taking accurate measurements under field conditions. Moreover, one of the official Desert Rock I–III reports concedes that, while the tactical dosimeters are "satisfactory for measuring gamma radiation," beta and neutron radiation can have "important biological effects" as well. This concession is significant because it establishes that the military was aware at the very first test series that its equipment could not accurately measure certain types of radiation.

During the first series, when a GI was given a film badge his name and badge number were entered on an alphabetical roster. After the test, the badges were collected, analyzed, and exposure data was to be entered next to his name. However, when a House subcommittee probed the issue in January 1978, the army admitted it could find exposure data for only 2770 of the 7224 GIs present during this series. And apparently this was the case with later tests as well; exposure readings could be found for only a small percentage of GIs who were present.

Other questions involve the adequacy of the decontamination procedures employed at the test site. According to Desert Rock reports, three methods of decontamination were used in the field: "dry," which consisted of brushing soldiers off with a broom; "semiwet," which entailed wiping off "hot" items or persons with wet rags; and "wet," wherein exposed parts were bathed or washed. While brushing or washing would remove certain hot particles from the clothing or skin, obviously it would have no effect on particles that had been inhaled into the lungs or swallowed. Nowhere is there any mention of the problem of internal dose.

According to a Defense Nuclear Agency source, there was only one medical officer with radiological decontamination experience present when the Buster-Jangle series began. Since the army lacked sufficient numbers of trained personnel, a number of rad-safe monitors who had worked at the Greenhouse tests in Eniwetok were brought in. Fifteen soldiers from Fort Mc-

Clellan who'd received some radiation-safety training gave on-the-job training to sixty other GIs in the use of radiation-monitoring equipment.

Probably because this was the first test series in which it was given an active role, the army produced an enormous number of reports and studies on every nuance of the operation. Every branch of the army, from Artillery to Signal Corps, prepared detailed reports, complete with criticisms and recommendations for changes at future tests. The career officers were undoubtedly concerned about the degree to which atomic weapons might render the conventional army obsolete. As a result, the authors of the reports, mostly ambitious young colonels, frequently outdid each other in maximizing the "can do" spirit of overcoming all obstacles, while minimizing the potential hazards from radiation, blast, and heat.

For example, a Lieutenant Colonel Brewer, writing for Ordnance and Armor said: "There should be as much troop participation as possible in order that unjustified awe in the minds of soldiers about the A-bomb be dispelled. While there's no desire to belittle this weapon, the troops who will fight a war should judge it in its proper perspective."

Colonel Boyd Bartlett, of the Transport and Military Police, wrote: "A gradual lowering of security classification and accumulation of data will enable us to tell the 'consumer' more facts. Training must avoid 'scare' information and stress nuclear weapons solely as a new and very powerful means of fighting battles. [Endorse] the concept that a nuclear blast will not kill them any deader than a direct hit or a near-miss by conventional explosives."

A Lieutenant Colonel Holmstrom of the Engineers offered a particularly bold proposal: "Drop an atomic bomb in Korea on a suitable tactical target sufficiently close behind the lines for a quick link-up . . . drop parachutists into the area to capture maximum numbers of prisoners . . . [then] interrogate them closely to determine the bomb's effect on the enemy."

A somewhat morbid note of reality was injected by Colonel Joseph James of the Quartermaster Corps: "Specialized training in procedures for recovery of remains, decontamination of bodies, mass burials [is needed] based on projections from Hiroshima."

Beginning with the very first tests in 1951, independent defense contractors were given grants to produce studies on all manner of human response to the blasts. For example, the Human Resources Research Office (HumRRO) of George Washington University was given a military contract to perform elaborate psychological studies of troop attitudes and reactions during nuclear bomb tests. HumRRO divided the GI observers into various categories and "control groups" and subjected them to a barrage of questionnaires, polls, surveys, and even lie-detector tests, before, during, and after each blast. To a typical survey question, "When do you think we'll have war with the Soviet Union?" 64 percent of the troops responded, "Within ten years."

Desert Rock Reports I, II, and III set the stage for the use of tens of thousands of troops at subsequent tests. At one point the reports conclude that the tests proved "that combat troops can safely cross the area of a nuclear explosion within minutes of the [blast]." According to the reports, "Residual radiological contamination from explosions of this size (21–31 kilotons) is of no *military* significance at distances greater than 1000 yards from ground zero." After studying the bomb's effect on the tethered sheep, it was concluded that "it's *possible* that humans would have been free from serious harm if they were in trenches at least 1000 yards from ground zero [italics ours]." The report noted, however, that because sheep's wool provided unusual protection against some of the effects of radiation, further study was needed. These reports were written within a few weeks after the tests, so long-term effects, such as various types of cancers and genetic birth defects associated with some types of radiation exposure, are not dealt with at all—nor is the possibility of such future effects even taken into account. Because only immediate health effects were deemed to be of "military significance," it was perhaps inevitable that no medical follow-up or monitoring ever was conducted.

The social scientists from HumRRO were equally sanguine about the value of further troop maneuvers at nuclear blasts: "Widespread and thorough indoctrination, careful planning, strong leadership, together with [test site] experience will result in a reasonable attitude toward the weapon." Summarizing its interviews with individual soldiers, HumRRO enthused: "It was a memorable experience for the men and much of the superstition and mystery surrounding radiation was removed. They are [now] convinced that the [blast] area can be safely entered after the explosion; that effects decrease rapidly with distance; and, most important, of the life-saving protection of a hole in the ground at any distance [from ground zero]." HumRRO did report that some GIs felt they'd been used as "guinea pigs" and questioned why they had to participate in these maneuvers if the army already knew (as it claimed) what the effects would be. But HumRRO concluded: "Remove the mystery and deemphasize the radiological hazard and the thing is accepted in its proper proportion."

Apparently the social scientists believed that radiation hazards were merely an "attitudinal" problem, which could be overcome if enough indoctrination and training were applied. And evidently the army was pleased with HumRRO's work; they received contracts for similar studies at subsequent tests.

Turning to the assessment of the impact of nuclear weapons upon strategy and tactics in the future, the field commanders happily reported that an A-bomb of the size used in the tests would not knock out an infantry division (10,000–15,000 men) if the division was well dug in and dispersed. Nevertheless, they argued against using larger bombs against conventional enemy forces, since these bombs "are more difficult to deliver and a portion of the destructive area is wasted due to a lack of profitable targets." Instead, they urged the use of multiple small nuclear weapons which could "saturate critical areas, without creating major dead space." This doctrine would later contribute to the concept of "limited warfare" as a cornerstone of national defense policy.

The joint command made a number of recommendations for

future tests. First, they urged that atomic-weapons data be much more widely disseminated within the military. Further, all military personnel should be indoctrinated on the effects of A-bombs so that "widespread misconceptions can be overcome." They also proposed that definite radiation-exposure standards be established.

In a separate report, the Armed Forces Special Weapons Project (AFSWP) attempted to forecast radiation effects on humans by studying test animals and instruments placed at varying distances from ground zero and in various types of fortifications. Perhaps to remove any ambiguity, AFSWP recommended that human volunteers be used at future tests to allow more precise measurement of effects. This recommendation was implemented once the military gained full control over the use of its troops at the site.

The commanders were quite unhappy with what they considered "excessive safety restrictions" imposed by the AEC. Their report implored the Pentagon to exert pressure at the "highest levels of government" to remedy this annoying problem. They included the report of one of their university contractors who wrote: "Under AEC restrictions . . . it was difficult to make the maneuver realistic. The usual performance requirements . . . were absent. The troops moved across the terrain in single file [behind monitors], a formation . . . vulnerable to enemy fire."

Apparently the Pentagon took these complaints seriously, for the minutes of the December 23, 1951 AEC meeting report that General A. Fields told the commission that the military wanted to make changes at future tests; this would mean the existing standards for radiation exposure would probably be exceeded.

AEC chairman Gordon Dean played Pontius Pilate: "Since the Department of Defense considered it necessary to conduct the exercises in this manner, the AEC was not in a position to recommend that normal limits be observed."

But the commission saw to it that a public statement was issued by the Department of Defense prior to the tests "clarifying Department of Defense responsibility for the safety of the troops." By the time the Joint Chiefs of Staff had issued a standing order to AFSWP on January 18, 1952, authorizing the use of GIs at future tests, troop maneuvers on the "atomic battlefield" had become an integral part of military life.

The military defined its primary mission for the Desert Rock exercise as "troop indoctrination under nuclear conditions." Effects tests on weapons and equipment were assigned a lower priority than at the previous series.

Troops from the Eighty-second Airborne, the First Armored Division, and other elements were initiated into nuclear combat on April 22, 1952, during the third shot of the series, called "Upshot-Knothole" by the AEC. They watched from trenches four miles away as a 31-kiloton bomb was dropped from a B-29 and detonated over the desert. An hour later, rad-safe monitors reported that it was safe to advance and an Airborne company and some other units moved to within a half-mile of ground zero.

Never comfortable being too far from the action, marines arrived, many directly from duty in Korea, and two battalions participated in their first test on May Day. According to Los Alamos sources, several high-ranking Marine officers were so pleased with this exercise that they asked for a 1-kiloton bomb which they wanted to detonate for training purposes at their El Toro base, adjacent to San Diego. Fortunately for San Diegans, their request was denied.

On May 25, history was made when an atomic bomb was detonated for the first time from a steel tower in Nevada. Previous bombs had been detonated in the air after being dropped from a B-29, with the exception of two that were touched off at ground level. A 30-kiloton bomb was powerful enough to obliterate the tower totally, except for a small stump at the base.

In a section entitled "Clothing and Equipment for D-Day," the *Camp Desert Rock Information and Guide* stated that "gas masks and film badges will be worn and carried in the forward area." But the standard army gas masks would offer no protection against the inhalation of microscopic "hot" particles, and we have found only one participant who recalls his unit ever using gas masks. Dr. Edward A. Martell, of the National Center for Atmospheric Research, whom we referred to in Chapter 1, says on the subject of gas masks: "People have to breathe, and fine particles can get through anything that allows air to enter. The fine particles that can be inhaled and deposited deeply in the lungs get through these gas masks. That's one of the misleading things about these protective devices: you'll be inhaling the extremely small particles that can do the most harm."

From the standpoint of safety, these tower shots were the most hazardous form of detonation. Nevertheless, after-action reports contain virtually no discussion of the danger of radioactive particles becoming attached to tiny steel fragments and then being inhaled by maneuvering troops. In a response to a question by the Rogers Subcommittee about this danger, the Pentagon commented: "In a tower shot, much, if not all, of the iron in the tower is vaporized and made radioactive in the same process." Asked if troops entering the fallout area would risk inhalation of these particles, the Pentagon gave a one-word answer: "yes."

Although the towers were several hundred feet high, these blasts were considered "ground shots" since tons of sand from the desert floor were sucked high into the mushroom cloud as it ascended. These "hot" sand particles constituted an added hazard, for, when they fell back to earth, the whirlpoollike winds that buffeted the desert floor dispersed them in every direction. Still, detonating bombs from several hundred feet in the air seemed an improvement over the last two blasts of the previous series. These had been detonated on, or just below, the earth's surface and had so contaminated a large area of the test site that the AEC had had to declare it "off limits" for several days. At least now, it was felt, most of the "prompt" (immediately released) radiation would be propelled skyward into the atmosphere.

By the time the "How" shot brought this series to an end, the army had taken complete control over radiation safety from the AEC. The after-action report for Desert Rock provides a good insight into what the military deemed important. Achievements of the series: "Troops were in trenches at 7000 yards [from ground zero], nearer than any personnel have ever been, excluding Hiroshima and Nagasaki [!]" Other "advances" were: army personnel assuming more responsibility for rad-safety, and troops moving to within 175 yards of ground zero only minutes after a blast. During the last shot, troops advanced immediately after detonation without waiting for AEC clearance.

The 1979 Senate testimony of Eugene Zuckert, the AEC Commissioner we quoted earlier, is a good illustration of the pervasive attitude that soldiers are not deserving of the same consideration extended to other citizens. He opined that even today he would vote to permit the military to assume total authority for the safety of troops at the test site. His reasoning: "The responsibility of the AEC was to tell the military what we thought the implications were. We should not have had control over their final decision. They [had] responsibility for training and having been fully informed, I don't think it was our responsibility to try and override them."

Once the military succeeded in gaining complete control over the use of troops at the start of the 1953 series, they made several significant changes. First, they doubled the amount of radiation to which soldiers could be exposed from 3 to 6 roentgens, half of which could be from immediate radiation and half from fallout. (AEC site workers, by comparison, were limited to 3.9 rads for an entire test series.) Second, combat units began to be placed routinely in trenches as close as two miles from ground zero. These GIs then conducted maneuvers in and around the blast area just a short time after detonations. Also instituted was an experimental program wherein "volunteer officers" crouched in trenches a mile or so from ground zero during three of the tests. The exposure limits for these volunteers was raised to 10 roentgens per test, as long as only half was "immediate" radiation. This proved to be a wise decision because their exposure at the very first test exceeded the old 6-rad limit. They were allowed

25 rads for three shots. Army reports claim that the men chose the precise location of their trench, based on their own calculations of weather and other factors. Perhaps in this way the military hoped to absolve itself of responsibility for any future effects of radiation on these men.

During the 1952 series, the army's rad-safe monitors had gradually replaced those provided by the AEC. Beginning with the 1953 series, the military also assumed full responsibility for film badging and lab analysis. Unfortunately, the army's photodosimetry unit was hot adequately equipped or staffed so that each GI could have a film badge, so the reports state that one or two men in a unit would have a badge.

We interviewed four soldiers who participated in different shots during this first "all-army" series. They confirmed the military's success at finally providing a "realistic" experience on the nuclear battlefield. Two of the four are seriously ill today, suffering from health problems that may be related to radiation exposure.

Stanley Jaffee, age forty-seven, is a pharmacist from River Edge, New Jersey, married, with three teen-age daughters. In November 1977 he underwent emergency surgery for breast cancer. Unfortunately, the cancer had already spread throughout his lymphatic system. He undergoes chemotherapy, living a day at a time. He has sued the federal government, charging it with responsibility for his cancer. For his lawsuit, he has testified that he was given no radiation-safety training prior to participating in the test and that at no time did he see anyone wearing a film badge during the exercise. "We were given no special clothing, nor were the trenches lead-lined or designed to keep out radiation," he recalls.

"The explosion itself defied description. After the initial blast, I opened my eyes and saw a fireball which looked like a red sun setting on the desert floor. While I can't be precise about the distance between me and the point of explosion, I don't believe that it was more than two or three thousand yards.

"We felt an incredibly powerful shock wave, followed by

another shock wave moving back toward the bomb site. It was this reverse wave that [created] an enormous mushroom cloud. While this was happening we were ordered . . . to march in the direction of the fireball. I don't know how far we were able to [go], but I do recall that the heat was incredibly fierce and that later a number of men were ill on the trucks which removed us from the site."

Ken Watson, fifty, of Tacoma, Washington, was sent to Nevada for the first shot of the 1953 series. Like Jaffee, he states that he received no training or indoctrination prior to the test and he doesn't remember seeing anyone with a film badge at the site.

"They kept stressing that everything was top-secret. They told us that two GIs who'd been at the last test had talked with strangers about Desert Rock and now they were doing long prison terms at Leavenworth. We were warned that FBI agents might buy us drinks in Las Vegas and then try and get us to talk about what we'd seen at the test site."

Watson says he was so frightened by these warnings that when he later underwent surgery for cancer he didn't dare tell his doctors how he might have been exposed to unusual amounts of radiation.

After witnessing a blast from trenches that he estimates were about 2500 yards from ground zero, Watson was shipped back to Fort Carson, from whence he was sent to Korea. It was after he returned from Korea that army doctors removed a football-size tumor from his abdomen. He has been plagued since that time with arterial and vascular problems that have rendered him unable to work.

Chuck Willmoth and Richard Larzelere, two young draftees from Detroit, became pals while serving in an army unit that was guarding the Soo Locks in northern Michigan.

They and four other GIs were suddenly sent to Chicago where they boarded a special troop train. Willmoth remembers that the train had many cars and was pulled by several engines. In the dining car they were served what tasted like army food. "They wouldn't tell us where we were going, other

than that we should take summer clothes. As I'd just spent
a winter on the Canadian Border, that was okay with me,"
Willmoth reminisces. "Only when the train pulled into Las
Vegas did some of the guys begin to guess we were going
to the atomic bomb site."

Unlike Jaffee and Watson, both Willmoth and Larzelere
remember being given rad-safe briefings and lectures at Desert
Rock. They also remember a pleasant afternoon when the
GIs were entertained by a variety show from Las Vegas which
featured comedian Jan Murray. They confirm, however, that
they saw no one wearing a film badge during their time at
Desert Rock. The two Detroiters participated in the last shot
of the test series—the only time the army got to fire an atomic
shell from its 280-millimeter field cannon. The shot was
called the "Grable" test, named for the movie star with famed
legs.

Now a draftsman with Fisher Body in Detroit, Larzelere
recalls: "They placed us in shallow trenches I would guess
were about 3000 yards from ground zero. They told us that as
soon as we saw the flash we could get up. I did, and got
knocked on my butt when the shock wave passed. A few
minutes later, we followed rad-safe monitors toward ground
zero. For protection, we wore our gas masks during the entire exercise."

Chuck Willmoth, now forty-six and chief of police in
Garden City, Michigan, remembers watching, fascinated, as
a pickup truck drove right down to where the bomb had just
gone off. "A guy jumped out, picked up some sort of instrument, and drove off again."

As the men moved forward, Larzelere remembers seeing
sheep on fire. "The closer we got to ground zero, the worse
shape they were in." Both men recall being ordered out of
the area after they'd gone over half the distance to ground
zero. They were taken to a rear area, told to wash and shower,
and given new uniforms to wear.

Willmoth shared a bit of Desert Rock scuttlebutt: "We
heard that they took alarm clocks and tied them around

the necks of rabbits. Supposedly, they were timed to ring so that the rabbits' eyes would be wide open just when the bomb went off."

The postmortems for the 1953 series again display the brand of atomic boosterism peculiar to the military. Among "advances" claimed for the series was the placing of troops 3500 yards from ground zero, "the nearest any known large body of troops has been deliberately exposed to date." The "volunteers" qualified for an even more impressive entry in the *Guinness Book of World Records*—2000 yards, "the closest any known personnel had been since the atomic bombs were dropped on Japan." The official report argues that by studying the volunteer officers "who accepted larger doses" one could deduce proper radiation-exposure limitation. Finding that the volunteers suffered no apparent ill-effects, the report concluded that the placement of their trenches was "sound and should be used in the future."

Jim O'Connor and the men of the upcoming Teapot series couldn't have known it at the time, but the report writers urged that future tests emphasize "tactical operations rather than weapons effects," thus "recommending" even greater radiation exposure for the unfortunate GI participants. Nevertheless, effects tests, as we shall see, were anything but devalued. In fact, effects tests were promoted and became the subject of a national spectacle when the armed forces returned to Desert Rock in 1955.

CHAPTER

5

Doom Town: Dress Rehearsal for Armageddon

After his overdose, Jim O'Connor continued to be stationed at Camp Desert Rock until the completion of the army's exercises. After "Turk," however, he saw very few of the Teapot detonations. He didn't return from his convalescent leave until around March 21, 1955; after three more weeks on the job laying land lines he persuaded Fat Man to grant him another ten days' leave to again return to Burbank, this time to marry his high school sweetheart. (The marriage ended in 1964, but Jim and his first wife did succeed, after many years, in producing a healthy son despite a period of sterility after his tour of duty in Nevada.)

The march of the Cold War continued in O'Connor's absence. On his wedding day, April 15, 1955, the AEC exploded shot "Met," a 22-kiloton device intended to measure, among other things, the effects of radiation and blast on the winter and summer uniforms of Chinese Communist and Russian soldiers.

On April 22, 1955, when O'Connor again returned to Desert Rock, only four days remained before the scheduled "Apple II" spectacular. "Apple II" was to be a media event that served up the vision of nuclear attack for the edification of the American public.

Many federal agencies and private-sector industries shared

the action at "Apple II" with the AEC and the Defense Department. Their activities were planned and coordinated by the fledgling Federal Civil Defense Administration (FCDA). This civil defense portion of the test was code-named Operation Cue. All told, there were sixty-five associated experiments conducted during "Apple II," including forty-eight by the civil defense consortium.

Hardly in the mood to surrender the spotlight entirely to these civilian irregulars, the army offered a major innovation in a grab for public relations points of its own. On April 18, the largest tank convoy ever assembled left Camp Irwin in California and made an unprecedented drive across the Mojave Desert en route to the atomic test site. The 160-mile journey took four days, and on April 21 the 238 vehicles of Task Force Razor—including tanks, armored personnel carriers, mobile artillery, and a host of jeeps, trucks, and tank-recovery vehicles—bivouacked in a staging area 16,000 yards from the designated ground zero.

Armor, "the combat arm of decision," had arrived at Desert Rock with their engines all revved up. Army tank mavens were jealous of the infantry ("Queen of the Battlefield") domination of the nuclear maneuvers. They argued that ground troops couldn't instantly assault an objective that had been softened up by a battlefield-size A-bomb, whereas "present-day armored vehicles might have a high degree of suitability for employment with atomic weapons." One Las Vegas newspaper reporter, who would ride in the lead tank during the assault, wrote with macho approval before the shot how Task Force Razor would "hurl a punch" at the mighty atomic device. The implication was that armor was immune to the effects of radiation.

The ability of tank exteriors to repel radiation was an open question, however. In fact, Task Force Razor was at the Desert Rock exercises precisely to determine whether or not the "shielding effect of armor against gamma" was adequate to make tanks a viable postblast assault weapon. And apparently, the "instruments" on which the "shielding effect" would be measured were the 800 tank-crew members and support troops ordered to rumble through the deadly radio-active dust bowl just minutes after the blast.

But the bold armored foray into the contaminated cloud was only a sidebar compared to the main item on the agenda of the "Apple II" designers. With some of our military leaders issuing almost daily warnings about the possibility of an enemy attack, the population could hardly help feeling in great peril. What would happen, in fact, if an American community actually did become the target of an enemy atomic weapon? This was the question being posed in the most dramatic possible terms by the superpatriotic civil defense advocates. And so "Survival City" was built to provide the answer.

Against the background of the Cold War, "Apple II" was a dress rehearsal for Armageddon, and Civil Defense was being offered as the five-star recipe for survival. What form survival would take following the atomic holocaust and whether it was even desirable was a more subtle question that remained largely unformulated and unimagined at the time.

Old AEC hand Joseph Deal is still a true believer when it comes to defending the need for massive doses of public information on civil defense during the Fifties. "The difference between surviving and not surviving could have been knowing what to do," he said recently. But destruction, not survival, was the message conveyed by this and previous atomic-related civil defense exercises. It was no accident that the model town introduced as Survival City by the government's PR flacks was prophetically renamed Doom Town by the troops.

Over 500 newspaper, TV, and radio reporters were on hand to transmit the civil defense melodrama into every home along with the morning soap operas, telling Americans what to do in the event of nuclear attack. "The world's most expensive premiere will be unfolded out on the Nevada desert, and nothing that Hollywood has ever produced will be able to equal it," wrote one reporter.

Two days before the scheduled detonation, the public, via

network television, was given a tour of Doom Town, the village brought to life for a single day, only to be instantly destroyed. Television crews would film the interior of a yellow frame house, symbolic of a dwelling occupied by a "typical American family." On D-day itself, featured network personalities like Dave Garroway, John Cameron Swayze, Walter Cronkite, and John Charles Daly would be on hand for live coverage of what another journalist described as "the greatest horror program ever produced."

For some people, the prospect of viewing Operation Cue at home on TV was just too vicarious. Las Vegas was a much smaller town in 1955 than it is today, but the "nation's playground" was growth-oriented and the local Chamber of Commerce had been quick to grasp a golden opportunity to inject a few more fast bucks into its coffers. Atomic tourism was promoted shamelessly. One hotel called itself the Atomic View Motel because its guests could view the flash and mushroom spectacle without ever leaving their lounge chairs. It had become a Las Vegas tradition to pack breakfasts and drive up to nearby Angel's Peak in the early morning hours on shot days to catch the show. But Operation Cue brought an unprecedented crush of curious outsiders, the vanguard of whom began arriving on April 21. "No Vacancy" signs went up all over town, and the Chamber of Commerce had to divert the overflow to surrounding towns.

The FCDA, in the course of conducting its forty-eight civil-effects tests planned to expose everything from food to fallout shelters to the shock, heat, and radioactivity of the 30-kiloton explosion. The key ingredient giving Doom Town an almost eerie quality of authentic American community life were its ten full-scale homes. (The reinforced structures of the houses were designed by an architect who had studied the damage to Japanese houses after the A-bomb raids.) Many of the houses were fully furnished and had late-model autos parked outside in carports or garages. Gas stoves were connected in the kitchen, as were all the fancy new appliances that mass production could make available to the American consumer of the Fifties. Dime-store mannequins, wearing the latest in ready-made fashions, were liberally distributed throughout the town to represent civilian inhabitants.

The mannequins, which included dummy infants and children, lent a particularly macabre aura. Indeed, the author of this unusual display of bureaucratic imagination remains anonymous today. No one seems eager to take credit for this bizarre touch. What was once apparently a somewhat controversial inner-agency policy—that is, blowing up fully clothed dummy people with atom bombs—now seems a downright embarrassment to some former test-site personnel. To DOE official Joseph Deal, a solid sort of man for all middle-American seasons, the idea was, and is, offensive. "It was just a stunt," he says. The mere discussion of this topic seemed to make him uncomfortable.

Not so Harold Goodwin, however. Goodwin was the FCDA's civil-effects-tests director during the Operation Cue exercises. Goodwin says that using the mannequins was a "deliberate attempt to get attention." According to Deal, Goodwin was a "very imaginative public-information type, concerned with the public impact." And Goodwin in turn, offering further explanation for the policy, said, "We wanted to really dress up the set, so we used mannequins. It was for the TV cameras and the movies. The newsmen wanted drama—not reality."

And drama was what they were given. Official photographs from the test show mannequin families in a mundane series of "stop-action" poses: at the breakfast table, nestled in the fall-out-shelter bathroom, entertaining guests in the living room, and so on. Baby mannequins sit on the laps of their simulated mommies. One dummy is posed looking through a window at the bomb tower, awaiting the final solution. The planners of this humanesque drama clearly had their existential sides.

This calculated use of mannequins as surrogate humans almost certainly secured the involvement of the public, albeit through a field of TV microwaves in the semireligious atomic spectacle linking most Americans in the logic of Cold War ideology.

The Civil Defense Agency also brought live folk to Las Vegas for its desert classic—about 2000 all told. Some were civil-defense volunteers, mobilized from practically all the forty-eight states. Others were "technical project personnel," some representing the government and others the more than 200 corporations which had eagerly stocked the site with their wares. Now these industrial researchers, otherwise excluded from the elite ranks of the atomic scientific community, were given their day. Like a grade-school field trip, they assembled to monitor their own "effects tests" on the sacred objects of mass consumption. Perhaps Bendix believed a better washing machine was needed to withstand a nuclear explosion. In any event, industry participants who played sorcerer's apprentice in the forbidden nuclear laboratory later became boosters for the civil defense program in communities across the country.

In addition to the highly technical civil-effects tests which sought information on the ability of residential and commercial structures, foodstuffs, and a host of other items of common use to withstand atomic blasts, the civil-defense volunteers came to participate in field exercises. They were organized into teams, with each team conducting an array of exercises in simulated situations—such as mass feeding, sanitation, health, police, fire, rescue, and communications services.

The scope of the planned exercises was somewhat restricted, however, by what should have been by that time a thoroughly predictable circumstance. As with "Turk" and other earlier shots of the series, the still uncontrollable "variable" called weather intervened to cause ten days of false starts and postponements. By the time the weather cleared on May 5, the 2000 volunteers had dwindled to 500. The entire California delegation, responsible for the off-site fallout-monitoring program, had pulled up stakes and departed, taking with them a small convoy of emergency vehicles and communications equipment scheduled for use during the test.

One exercise, the mass feeding program, is a piece of Americana worth describing in some detail. In a sense, it represents the best in the spirit of Yankee volunteerism. Top execs and hotel chefs came to Nevada, like good scouts on an annual jamboree, prepared to rough it, but, at the same time, they wished to "contribute to the physical comfort and well-being of the official observers, media representatives, and field-force participants by providing hot coffee during the early morning hours before the shot, a tasty breakfast immediately thereafter, and a nourishing lunch on the day following." Like American backpackers, they would combine the best of available technology with the pioneer spirit of expediency—plus a dash of grandstanding—to accomplish their mission. In their own words, they set out to prove "how professional feeders could adapt to unfamiliar forces, equipment, and surroundings, and work as a team."

Undaunted by the numerous delays in the firing of "Apple II," not to mention the progressive erosion of their team roster, the feeding team bravely prepared snacks on seven occasions when the shot was expected, serving 55,000 cups of coffee in the process. But the mass feeders' real tour de force came on the day following the actual shot. Paper-cup-company vice-presidents joined such professional feeders as hotel operators and Red Cross canteen personnel in spooning out baked beans that had arrived piping hot from San Francisco by freight train. To drive home the point, whatever it was, more hot coffee was flown in from Chicago and it likewise was still steaming when it reached the final meal. A real garden-club touch was the souvenir menus for all the mass fed.

Looking back, even the mass feeders might experience some lessening of the joy of post-nuclear-disaster cooking when they note that their field grills were set upon the radioactive rubble of one test house decimated and contaminated by the 22-kiloton "Apple" II blast.

At "Apple II," the AEC allowed ordinary civilian volunteers a closeup look at an atomic detonation for the first time. At Position Baker, a trench like those used by the GI observers, twenty-nine "just folks" got a chance to experience the might of nuclear power from a distance of 3500 yards. "The reason for stationing people at Baker," according to the official Operation Cue history, "was to find out what the actual reactions from citizens who were not schooled in the atomic field would be to get some idea of what ordinary citizens might be able to endure under similar conditions."

Arthur Landstreet, a mass feeder from Memphis who volunteered to go into the trench, recalled his experience for the official history of Operation Cue: "The flash was so terrific that even with closed eyes it seemed as bright as looking into a flash bulb from a camera only a few feet away. Seismic shock followed immediately. The trench seemed to rock back and forth for several seconds, then the noise and blast, ten times the thunderclap of lightning within a hundred yards. The blast was sudden and sharp. It felt like someone had taken a sandbag weighing twenty pounds and struck me in the middle of the back."

In the event of heavy fallout from the blast, these volunteers had exactly five minutes to cover a distance of five miles—the distance from their trench to the road which connected the test area to Camp Mercury. No attempt was made by the AEC or any other agency to follow up on the civilian volunteers to determine if the radiation dose they almost certainly received on May 5, 1955, affected their health.

Hal Goodwin, the former Civil Defense official, was present at the Baker trench on that day. He schooled the volunteers in the drill for witnessing atom bombs at close range. Today, Goodwin believes that the volunteers were more likely to have suffered injury from stepping on a rusty nail than from the effects of ionizing radiation. "We would not have exposed a lot of old men and old ladies to hazards and we didn't," he insists.

As with the GIs, however, the "hazards" were not limited to the immediate danger of induced external radiation. Contamination from previous shots was by now ubiquitous in the desert environment—not to mention particles that the volunteers may have swallowed or breathed, never to be measured by the film badges worn on their outer garments. Landstreet reports that, after the blast, the Baker volunteers could see very little of the bomb's impact due to the fact that "tons of dirt were whirling and there was dust everywhere. We had nothing but a brown, drab sight as our only reward."

We may never know if the civilian volunteers suffered ill effects from radiation they received that day in the Nevada desert, but Goodwin concedes that the GIs may have a good case. "The government," he says, "didn't have the guts to follow through. We were wrong, we underestimated the danger. We did our best, but our best wasn't good enough." Goodwin blames the Cold War and the fear of imminent hostilities for the lack of official attention to radiation safety during the tests.

To be sure, Cold War paranoia and knee-jerk patriotism were widespread. The former governor of Colorado's response to university professors who warned of potential health dangers from test fallout was typical. When two Colorado professors, Doctors Ray R. Lanier and Theodore Puck, charged that dust from the tests might endanger public health, the governor retorted, "They should be arrested."

Keeping the vigil with the GIs and the civilian defense volunteers and sharing their disappointment with the miserable weather and repeated shot postponements were the superstars of American newscasting. Taking up his position in Baker trench was "Today Show" host Dave Garroway, the droll commentator on the daily American comedy. The other stalwarts—Cronkite, Daly, and Swayze—pitched camp at News Nob, the media perch eight miles from ground zero.

"To build up the suspense," *Newsweek* reported at the time, "on-the-air coverage began on D-day-2." From April 24 on, there were special editions of well-known TV shows like "Youth Wants to Know" and "Today." The coverage continued for the entire week during the delays, with the networks committing thousands of dollars to ensure that the shot would be the public spectacle the government planners had envisioned.

Endless streams of newscasters invaded the doomed village, going so far as to conduct one-sided interviews with a mannequin family called the Darlings. The food editor of the TV show "Home" inspected the Darlings' cupboard and refrigerator and speculated on the effects of the blast on such items as baby food, dishwashers, and children's pajamas.

Where there's the press, can "society" be far behind? Dame Sarah Churchill, Winston's daughter, dropped in at News Nob in blue ballet slippers—a move that would have brought a blush of shame to the cheeks of Isadora Duncan. Many great entrances were made at Operation Cue, and, after a while, a few premature exits. To paraphrase the irascible H. L. Mencken, nobody ever went broke underestimating the attention span of the American media.

Buildup for the main event had ridden the crest of headlines, feature stories, and on-the-spot coverage for over a week. News Nob was beginning to take on the tense atmosphere of a maternity-ward waiting room. But for those reporters from the large outlets, the news value of Operation Cue was perishing rapidly. When the national media, especially the TV personalities, pulled out before the actual firing on May 5, it was a major blow to the PR expectations of the military-regulatory complex. The federal information boys had lost their chance to score a first on prime time.

Still, the rumpled-suit crowd of working reporters from the wire services and the picket-fence dailies vowed to tough it out. These were the reporters who wrote for papers and magazines in those parts of the country where it was still believed that people lived in towns and villages—not major and minor "markets." Naturally, this assignment was hardly considered rough duty, if you didn't count the fallout and radiation hazards—and judging from the dispatches of the time, nobody counted them.

At dusk, veteran correspondent Bob Considine, president of the Ancient and Honorable Society of Bomb Watchers—whose membership was limited exclusively to reporters—would call a meeting to order around the pool of the Flamingo Hotel. Stories continued to be filed during the lull, and were no doubt discussed good-naturedly over cocktails: articles, for example, that reminded residents and visitors to reset their clocks since daylight saving time would occur in the course of the delays.

One reporter caught the mood of the city fathers with Polaroid simplicity, writing that "the test might run smack dab into the Tournament of Champions golf meet, sending hotel reservations out the window in a terrific mess." Atomic tourism would have its run, but it would not be extended.

Sticking it out paid off for some reporters; their postshot stories have the passion and liveliness of observations from the real front lines.

Dateline: Doom Town, Nevada
Real Folk Find Test Tribe Dead, by Archie Teague, *Las Vegas Review Journal*, May 6, 1955. [Excerpts]

Postshot inspection tours were held to learn the odds of survival in the atomic age. People played by dummies lay dead and dying in basements, living rooms, kitchens, bedrooms.

Civil Defense rescue teams worked briskly to free trapped families. Along Doomsday Drive, a dirt road 4,700 feet from the blast, everything and everybody suffered heavy damage or death and injury as expected. A handsome two-story brick house that could have been a bank president's caved in, bricks sent hurtling in every direction. Occupants of a reinforced bathroom were fatally injured.

A mannequin mother died horribly in her one-story house of precast concrete slabs. Portions of her plaster and paint body were found in three different areas. A mannequin tot, perhaps the size of your three-year-old, was blown out of bed and showered with needle-sharp glass fragments. The house withstood the blast, but not its occupants.

Anyone living in the one-story masonry brick house would have had no food problem. Civil Defense monitors said that kitchen cabinets stocked high with groceries withstood the blast. But a simulated mother was blown to bits in the act of feeding her infant baby food.

The fury and heat of the original blast killed many. Those surviving were so irradiated, they died before aid could reach them. The town was completely without contact with the outside world. The Power Station was knocked out, the radio tower was down, there was no way for people to receive instructions. Most cars can't be used to evacuate them. Survivors must sit and wait, hoping rescue is forthcoming.

With reporters' attention focused on such total and immediate devastation from the bomb's visible effects, the question of long-range damage from low levels of radiation must have seemed remote, even abstract, especially in a culture always rushing to catch up to the visible implications of its rapidly changing technological landscape. The good working press caught the action but failed to decipher the real message. Sometimes the reporters even are told how to think and what to write by "officials." Deficiencies in the "depth" of coverage during the period of atmospheric tests sadly reflect the rule, not the exception of American journalism.

In any event, the working press got its bite at the apple. All the networks got was sour grapes. One news magazine reported: "Last week, TV's biggest bomb finally went off with a bang and a whimper. The bang came from the 500-foot tower on Yucca Flat, Nevada, where a 35-kiloton nuclear device was detonated. The whimper came from the networks. After spending an estimated $200,000, they were left with only skeleton crews on hand when the bomb was finally triggered."

The "Home" show, whose reporter had interviewed the mannequin family, offered five minutes of film "between a lesson in meringue whipping and a promo for Mother's Day."

"An elephant has just given birth to a mouse," said a disgusted veteran of the preshot trenches, Dave Garroway.

On the other hand, Task Force Razor, the army's elaborate tank exercise, was considered an unqualified success. One change the tank experts recommended for subsequent atomic armor exercises was to allow the tanks to remain in motion at their assault line, like racing sailboats, and to use the blast itself as the starting gun. The tank troops complained that their assault was delayed during five minutes of radio silence following the detonation, during which they awaited their orders to hurl their knockout punch at the atomic cloud.

A military document reporting the results of Task Force Razor mentions that the leading columns of tanks executed a flanking movement away from ground zero when the interior radiation count reached 12 roentgens. Outside, the atmosphere was sizzling at 130–160 radiation units. A Defense Nuclear Agency spokesperson, without offering further documentation or comment, called the figures cited in the after-action report a "misprint."

There was, of course, no medical follow-up on the tank personnel of Task Force Razor, who may have deserved some special attention for another reason besides the radiation shower they received. When the tank convoy finally returned to Camp Irwin, California, on May 9, the troops had to complete one more exercise. On their way to the barracks, the men crossed a minefield contaminated with mustard gas. Five soldiers were reported ill. Their gas masks and rubber hoods were defective. Among war-game planners, it apparently is a short step from the atomic to the chemical battlefield.

After "Apple II," the AEC wrapped up the Teapot series with two more tests, including the unheralded gigantic "Zucchini" shot which weighed in at 35 kilotons. But "Apple II" was the real finale; it was a tough act to follow.

In June, the FCDA organized "Operation Alert" during which President Eisenhower, members of his cabinet, and 15,000 federal workers engaged in a mass evacuation from their Washington offices. Ike signed a mock declaration of national emergency and then spoke to the nation via TV and radio from his bomb shelter hidden in the Virginia countryside. Civil-defense workers and volunteers across the nation joined in the activities, but most of the work force ignored it. FCDA administrator Val Peterson estimated that the evacuation would have saved 4.25 million Americans from death or serious injury had the attack been real. He predicted that the "attackers" would have hit fifty-three United States cities and that without evacuation 8.2 million would have been killed and another 6.5 million injured.

The atomic season would soon draw to a close. Still remaining was a one-night stand somewhere off the coast of California, where the underwater "Wigwam" shot probably set back the clock on marine evolution for a few generations, but had little impact on the viewing public, accustomed as it was to far more spectacular displays. In December 1979 some ripples from Wigwam were felt when the Defense Nuclear Agency admitted that hundreds of sailors may have been exposed. Lawsuits on behalf of sailors who died from cancers have recently been filed.

But in Nevada, the Great White Way of atomic testing, it was time to strike the tents and clean out the cages. The nuclear circus would retire to winter quarters in the South Pacific and prepare for the events of the next season. Camp Desert Rock would mark time and remain empty for two years before more American GIs were oriented to the continental nuclear battle-field, where Cold War casualties never won purple hearts or decorations for valor above and beyond the call of duty.

For the boys in the weapons labs, 1955 had been a vintage year, full of firsts, not the least of which was the heady sense of American superiority in the development of nuclear weapons. Hadn't that venerable warlord Winston Churchill stated during Teapot that the United States was the only nation able to launch a full-scale nuclear attack with hydrogen bombs? And the AEC had in Dwight David Eisenhower a patron saint who would protect that semiautonomous federal agency from a chain reaction of public criticism aimed at the atomic juggernaut. To the rest of the nation, Eisenhower would appear as Moses leading the troubled and fearful masses from the captivity of an unlimited arms race to the distant promised land of the Peaceful Atom.

But in 1955 the AEC and military nuclear strategists were more concerned with being first in atomic war than first in atomic peace. Toward that objective, they had chalked up an impressive record during Teapot. There had been the development of the minibomb, an atomic satchel charge small enough to be carried by a single man. There'd been the flash from "Turk," the biggest domestic shot up to that time, seen a record 760 miles away. President Eisenhower had given his imprimatur to the concept of America's "first use" of tactical atomic weapons in war. Nuclear-loaded antiaircraft technology had taken a giant leap forward when a test showed that an entire fleet of bombers could be wiped from the sky with an A-bomb-packed guided missile.

On the peaceful side, the AEC announced that electric power produced by atomic generators would be available for commercial use by the fall of that year. Radiation? No problem, according to the AEC: "There were no known health hazards or hereditary damage caused by fallout." What about that Japanese fisherman caught in the wake of the first U.S. hydrogen-bomb explosion in 1954 and who, it was believed, later died of radiation sickness? Not so, said Dr. Burgher of the AEC. "He died of hepatitis, not radiation." Even a man of scientific stature like Nobel laureate Hermann Müller—who received the celebrated prize in 1946 for proving that ionizing radiation destroys genetic material—could not dent the armor of the party line when he charged that people in high places were falsely denying that atomic testing caused hereditary damage.

It came as no surprise, therefore, when in 1955 the AEC's medical experts denied the claims of three persons who were suing the government for $275,000 on the grounds that they were injured by Nevada test fallout. The three lived downwind of the so-called test-site window—the atmospheric pathway the AEC had selected for the release of its radioactive by-product. Today the AEC's successor, the Department of Energy, is besieged with hundreds of damage claims by folks in Nevada, Arizona, and Utah who lived along the path of the "window."

The AEC did admit a few of its mistakes in 1955, of course, such as the fallout cloud unexpectedly released over populous Las Vegas (albeit "posing no danger"), or the report that several GIs had suffered permanent eye injury through "failure to cover the eyes properly during the tests." Well, that's the price of progress. You can't split atoms without breaking a few DNA molecules.

CHAPTER

6

Preaching Radiation Blues in the Land of the Friendly Atom

The movie *The Green Berets* could have been based on the life of Paul Cooper—except for the last year of it, that is. With his muscled torso, close-cropped hair, and ramrod military bearing, Paul projected the classic image of the tough and resourceful Green Beret, so admired by many Americans, at least during the early years of the Vietnam War. Atop the color TV in his suburban living room sits a framed photo of Paul in his camouflage jungle suit, his green beret set at a jaunty angle. A large ashtray constructed of artillery shells stands next to the gold frame. A small plaque commemorates Paul's three combat tours as a member of the Fifth Special Forces in Vietnam.

When he returned from Vietnam, Paul's twenty years were up, and he retired from the army. In keeping with his law-and-order sentiments, he took a job as a deputy sheriff in a northern Idaho town. The only problem was that Elk City had never quite abandoned the wild and woolly ways of its Gold Rush heyday. Paul told his family that the job was worse than Vietnam. After countless fights and hassles with unruly locals, he threw in the towel, settling into the safer precinct of the state highway department.

It was in 1976 while he was working at his new job as weighmaster that Paul was first stricken; intense pain spread over the left side of his body. Six days of examinations in a local hospital produced no diagnosis. Not much later, it hit again, this time while he was alone on a highway. He drove at top speed toward the Veterans Administration hospital in Boise, hoping the police would stop him, as puddles of blood collected at his feet. After lab tests, the VA doctors gave Paul the bad news: acute myelogenous leukemia. He was transferred to the VA hospital in Salt Lake City, which has better facilities for cancer treatment.

One day a VA doctor there surprised Paul by asking him if he'd ever worked around radiation. Paul told him that he had participated at the "Smoky" test on August 31, 1957, as a member of the Eighty-second Airborne. After two weeks of training at the test site, Cooper's unit had been taken by truck to trenches about 4000 yards from the base of a 700-foot bomb tower on the morning of the test. Cooper recalled: "We were looking forward to it. It was a new experience, and we were sure that the government would protect us from any harm." While it was still dark, however, the troops were suddenly moved to a hillside just 3000 yards from ground zero. They were told that the wind had shifted; it was feared that their trenches would have been in the path of radioactive fallout.

"Just before they detonated the bomb, they told us to turn around and put our hands over our eyes. When it went off, we felt almost unbearable heat . . . we could see the bones in our hands through our closed eyelids as if we were taking a giant X ray. Then they told us to turn around and watch the bomb. We saw the fireball go off and shock waves knocked several of us off our feet," Cooper related.

By coincidence, one of Cooper's doctors at Salt Lake City had previously worked for the Center for Disease Control (CDC), which is part of the U.S. Public Health Service. He called his former colleagues and told them about Cooper. When the CDC asked the Pentagon for records on the test and its participants, it was discovered that such records as existed were fragmentary and incomplete.

Unable to work, with perhaps a year to live, Paul applied for

VA disability to support his wife and three young children. A few weeks later, he got his answer: His claim that the leukemia was service-connected was denied. Paul was stunned by the news. According to Nancy Cooper, his widow, Paul had always accepted the risks he took as a professional soldier; however, he had relied on the government's caring for him and his family should he be seriously injured or killed. He recalled that officials in Nevada had told the GIs that they'd be periodically checked for medical problems after the tests. "We never had a debriefing; I'm still waiting for one," he bitterly told a reporter.

As the government's refusal to assume any responsibility for his injuries sank in, Paul's shock and frustration slowly turned to anger. Faced with the prospect of his family's being forced onto welfare once he could no longer suport them, he decided, after some hesitation, to tell his story to the press. He hoped that this would draw attention to an injustice and also might help locate old army buddies who could corroborate his allegations about "Smoky." He started with interviews with local newspapers and TV stations in Salt Lake City, but before long he attracted national attention as *Parade*, the wire services, and "Good Morning, America" all did stories on his case.

As the effects of this bad press began to be felt in Washington, the Pentagon roused itself into action. In May, an ad hoc committee was convened, consisting of representatives from the Armed Forces Radiobiology Research Institute, the deputy chief of staff for operations and plans, the army's Public Affairs office, and the Office of the Surgeon General. The committee gathered in June at Yucca Flat to sort out what historical data and records on troop participation existed.

As the Center for Disease Control had been first out of the gate with a postmortem on shot "Smoky," the nuclear-weapons community had little choice but to go along with the CDC, although it's certain they would have much preferred to conduct the study "in house" or through a trusted private research contractor. In December 1977, however, after several months of bureaucratic infighting, it was finally agreed by all the concerned federal agencies that the Pentagon's nuclear arm, the

Defense Nuclear Agency, would serve as the "executive" agency to coordinate all administrative tasks of the follow-up effort. The National Research Council of the National Academy of Science, a private association composed of 1300 of the nation's most eminent scientists from all disciplines, agreed to design scientific protocols on which studies of other tests would be based. The CDC was left to continue its study of shot "Smoky."

Cooper's one-man publicity campaign had one other immediate effect: The VA reversed itself and decided that he was entitled to disability payments after all. The Appeals Board stressed, however, that it was granting relief for health problems detected while Cooper was on active duty—not for any connection between radiation exposure and his leukemia.

In July 1977, Paul Cooper tried to visit the Nevada test site, accompanied by officials of the Disabled American Veterans, but was refused entry. David Jackson, the test site's public relations man told us later that site officials regarded his visit as a "publicity stunt" and they didn't want to be responsible for what such stress might do to a man in Cooper's condition. Apparently it was fine for Cooper to have walked, without protective clothing, to within a few hundred feet of where a highly radioactive A-bomb had just been set off, but they didn't want to upset a dying man with these painful memories twenty years later. Still, as word about the health risks of atomic tests spread, large numbers of veterans began to check in with Congress, the Pentagon, and other federal agencies. The *Parade* story alone brought in nearly 4000 calls and letters to the Center for Disease Control. Clearly, something had to be done.

During this same period, another "Smoky" veteran, Donald Coe, forty-five, of Tompkinsville, Kentucky, also was told that he had leukemia. Coe was fortunate in having as his congressman Tim Lee Carter, a country doctor and well-known congressional maverick (he later hosted Richard Nixon's first public appearance as ex-president) who serves as the ranking minority member of the House Subcommittee on Health and the Environment. Carter had lost a son to leukemia, and when he learned that possibly thousands of military veterans might be suffering in silence, he became furious at the government's inaction. He worked effectively behind the scenes, and in late January 1978 the subcommittee, chaired by Paul Rogers (Democrat-Florida) commenced three days of hearings on the Health Effects of Ionizing Radiation.

Shot "Smoky" was easily the most ballyhooed A-test after the "Apple II" shot in 1955. The army used it as the subject of an installment of its nationally syndicated TV program "The Big Picture," a scene from which began this book. The show's theme was that the army had created a new military concept, the pentomic unit, which would allow it successfully to wage war on the nuclear battlefield. To demonstrate maximum mobility of its land forces, combat troops were ferried by helicopter into the blast area after detonation. Donald Coe rode in one of these helicopters with the Twelfth Battle Group. As "Smoky" also was designed to test aerial resupply techniques, these helicopters flew numerous sorties that landed all around the troops. Colonel Thomas Stedman, who piloted a helicopter that day, told the subcommittee that "The entire exercise area was covered with a heavy dust cloud . . . [which] extended up to a height of several thousand feet. Visibility was so poor that we feared collisions in midair."

Dr. Martin Sperling, a scientist with Science Applications, a military research firm based in La Jolla, California, testified before the subcommittee about the dangers of highly radioactive dust which could be propelled by the prop wash of these helicopters. Assuming a dust cloud ten feet high, Sperling calculated that Coe could have inhaled an additional bone-marrow dose of roughly 13.2 rads. He observed that while Coe's filmbadge reading was 2 rads, "that seems to agree with his external whole-body dose; film badges were never meant to measure inhalation."

Donald Coe reported that immediately after "Smoky" he was hospitalized with severe headaches, nosebleeds, nausea, and dizziness. However, when he tried to examine his army medical records for his VA claim, he was told they had been destroyed in the Saint Louis records fire in 1973.

Dr. Sperling also calculated that the men of the Eighty-second Airborne, including Paul Cooper, could have inhaled what he termed an "extremely high" dose of about 100 rads by walking from 3000 to 100 yards of ground zero within an hour after detonation and remaining there for thirty minutes.

Dr. Karl Morgan, who headed the AEC's health physics program at the Oak Ridge labs for thirty years, was the subcommittee's next witness. He told them that he'd been very disturbed by the military's conduct during "Smoky." He'd received reports at the time from an AEC team which was on-site studying the bomb's effects on specially constructed Japanese houses during the shot. "Even in 1957, I was frightened and appalled by the fact that troops were in trenches and would go to ground zero shortly after the blast." He disclosed that AEC workers sent in to retrieve test instruments at "Smoky" turned back three miles from ground zero when they encountered high gamma levels on their survey meters. (The instruments were never recovered.) Morgan also quoted Dr. J. A. Auxine, the AEC official in charge at Desert Rock, as saying that "Smoky" was the "dirtiest" test he'd ever worked on, either in Nevada or in the South Pacific. It is a comment on the closed nature of the nuclear community that Dr. Morgan didn't publicly express his concerns about the safety of military personnel until many years later.

As both Cooper and Coe were too sick to testify, a third veteran of "Smoky," Russell Jack Dann, age forty-two, of Albert Lea, Minnesota, gave the GIs' version, albeit from a wheelchair. He was in Cooper's unit, the Eighty-second Airborne, although they were not friends at the time. He described two weeks of indoctrination run by the "white suits" (as the GIs called them) from HumRRO. Every morning and afternoon his unit was drilled in a series of test procedures which they would perform immediately after the shot: crawling under barbed wire, throwing hand grenades, and reassembling rifles. The plan was for the GIs to repeat the exercise on shot day so the researchers could measure their performance under nuclear conditions against their pretest results. Dann's unit was in fact participating in yet another HumRRO experiment. According to HumRRO, this one tested troop reactions to initial effects of atomic detonation and to "the contamination of the terrain by nuclear radiation."

His description of shot day is chilling. "We were trucked into position to await the shot. It was still dark and the tower was lit up like a Christmas tree. I could see an elevator going up to the top; it was evident that the shot had the green light."

After they were moved to a hillside about 4000 yards east of the bomb, Dann recalled widespread fear among the men. "It was as if observation was more important than safety. No one found any humor in what was about to happen. There was a devastating blast which words cannot explain. I could see the bones in my arm and within a few seconds the shock from the blast hit us. It knocked me ten or fifteen feet. It blew off my steel pot [helmet] and I never found it. After the shot, our company loaded in trucks and moved down to within three hundred yards of ground zero. This was to monitor the tower, to see what shape it was in. It was nothing but a pile of rubble.

"Before loading on the trucks to leave, we were checked for radiation. My count was very high. I was required to remove my fatigue jacket and shake it out. A whisk broom was used on my jump boots."

The next day, the men in Dann's unit were given passes to go into Las Vegas. He recalls that no sooner had they arrived in town than special TV and radio broadcasts announced that all men of the Eighty-second Airborne were to return to Desert Rock immediately. Apparently a last-minute decision had been made to hold the field tests that had been canceled during "Smoky" due to excessive radiation. During the "Galileo" shot, Dann and his mates were forced to crawl all over the radioactive desert so the behavioral scientists could collect their data at last.

Dann described for the subcommittee the physical deterioration that set in after he was discharged the following year. "I lost my hair in blotches . . . my teeth began falling out, and I lost my hearing in my left ear. For several years I experienced severe dizziness. In 1961, I found out that my wife and I were having no children due to my very low sperm count. In 1963, I began having trouble with my knee joints and both shoulders. I spent nearly a year in a VA hospital, during which time they told my wife that I had a weird blood-cell count. For years I've said that these symptoms were the result of shot 'Smoky,' but who'd ever have believed such a Buck Rogers story?"

After he returned home from testifying in Washington, Russell Dann received a telephone call from Lewis Ginn, his old first sergeant, who now lives in Norfolk, Virginia. Ginn did quite well by the army, finally retiring as a brigadier general. Dann says that Ginn agreed with his account of Desert Rock in all essential respects and offered to serve as a witness on Dann's behalf.

Dr. William Foege, director of the Center for Disease Control, appeared before the subcommittee after Dann. He read HEW Secretary Joseph Califano's letter which fully committed the parent agency to support for the "Smoky" study and urged that additional studies of other tests be conducted. Pointedly, he underscored the importance of complete independence for researchers doing this work. Foege reported that eight cases of leukemia had been found in the first 500 "Smoky" veterans they'd located. Based on National Cancer Institute tables, if the average age of the soldiers was twenty-two at test time, only two cases would be expected in a general-population group of this size. By September 1979, the CDC had succeeded in getting some health data from 2029 of the 3225 "Smoky" veterans. Dr. Glyn Caldwell, who's directing this study, told the authors that 111 cases of cancer had been reported from this group while 101 would have been the norm for men in this age group. He doesn't, however, consider this excess "statistically significant," although he notes that the cause of death for thirty-six of the 278 veterans who've died since "Smoky" still has not been determined. They've found no new leukemias, but the eight cases still represent four times the number that would be expected in a "normal" population.

Witnesses for the Department of Energy (successor to the AEC) and the Veterans Administration proved well practiced in the time-honored bureaucratic art of ducking and dodging any responsibility for the ailing veterans. The head of defense programs for the Department of Energy, Dr. Donald Kerr, testified that AEC and military functions were kept as separate as possible at the test site. When a congressman challenged his assertion that the AEC never authorized the military to exceed safe exposure levels, he responded lamely, "The AEC had no control over the army." This is also the same Donald Kerr who testified earlier that badge information was missing for most of the men exposed during the 1946 and 1948 Bikini tests. Like the proverbial Tar Baby, no federal agency wants to get any closer than necessary to the lowly GIs who maneuvered on the nuclear battlefield.

One interesting fact brought out in the Department of Energy's testimony was that only $18 million is being spent annually for research on radiological health effects. Of that, a third goes for follow-up studies among the Hiroshima and Nagasaki survivors; nearly $3 million is used for a continuing study of 1500 workers who hand-painted radium on watch dials before 1920; and a paltry $1 million is spent to study the health of 150,000 workers at two uranium-processing plants. Needless to say, not one dime has been spent conducting research or medical follow-up on any of the 458,290 Americans that the Department of Energy lists as having been present at one or more of the atmospheric bomb tests.

The doctor in charge of the VA's Nuclear Medicine Service, James J. Smith, outlined a nearly perfect Catch-22 for the would-be radiation claimant. He cited the "prevailing medical opinion" that an exposure of 75 to 100 rads would be necessary to cause leukemia. Therefore, unless a veteran can prove such a massive exposure to radiation or unless his symptoms appeared during or shortly after service (remember, leukemia and other radiation-induced cancers have a latency period of between eight to thirty years), his prospects for receiving any compensation for health problems are very dim. In fact, of the 231 claims lodged for radiation-induced disability as of February 1979, only 19 have been allowed. Three hundred other such claims are pending.

Pentagon spokesperson Major Alan Skerker had perhaps the

most difficult job of any witness. Since the military had assumed complete responsibility for the safety of their troops from the last tests in 1952 onwards, they had to acknowledge some culpability if their testimony was to enjoy any credibility. It fell to Major Skerker, a nuclear scientist with the army's Strategy, Plans, and Policy Directorate (nuclear division), to weave a cautious path between total candor and defiant stonewalling. The result was a mixture of trivial detail and important admissions concerning some of the tests.

Skerker stated that, out of the eighty-odd Nevada tests from 1951 to 1957, "there are around fifteen tests that we ought to be looking at." His description of the difficulties with one of these "problem" shots, "Nancy," of March 24, 1953, was quite candid. "A wind shift blew the radioactive cloud over trenches [4000 yards from ground zero]. The troops launched their attack three minutes after the explosion and moved to between 500 to 700 yards of ground zero. There was heavy fallout in the maneuver area and an intensity of 14 rads per hour at some unknown point. Monitors proceeded into the area without giving . . . readings to their commanders."

Concerning another suspicious shot, "Badger," detonated on April 18, 1953, Skerker reported that "units were entrenched at 4000 yards . . . a wind shift blew fallout over the eastern portion of the trenches. The First Battalion was taken out of action since 6 rads was recorded on their pocket dosimeters. As with 'Nancy,' this shot has considerable potential for overexposures."

The "Hood" shot on July 5, 1957, earned a paragraph in the Desert Rock book of records for being the largest atmospheric bomb (72 kilotons) ever detonated in the United States. (It also is a good illustration of how "nuclear diplomacy" was practiced during the period. On July 2, the United States, with great fanfare, had made a new proposal to the U.N. disarmament conference that all nations agree to an immediate moratorium on atmospheric testing. Three days later, the giant bomb was touched off.) According to Skerker, it was a "problem" shot. Troops were helicoptered to within 400 yards of ground zero just fifteen minutes after the blast. Although the subcommittee had made an advance request for more details on "Hood," Skerker came unprepared and passed the buck to the marines, whose troops had maneuvered at "Hood."

Skerker's testimony was deficient in other respects, too. On a number of important issues, he cited the military's own Desert Rock reports as though they were established fact. Unfortunately, the members of the congressional panel, with two exceptions, were poorly prepared, and Skerker deftly parried their anemic queries. Even a cursory reading of his testimony raises far more questions than he answered.

Another shortcoming was that the hearings failed to examine any aspect of the South Pacific tests, in which over 70,000 American serviceman participated. When Paul Rogers, subcommittee chairman, tried to ask Peter Haas of the Defense Nuclear Agency about the Pacific tests, Haas responded: "No troop exercises; there were exposures . . . we're not prepared."

Haas later unintentionally made clear the distinction between the nuclear scientists and the lowly troops: "In dusty areas [of the site] I wore appropriate gear, Band-Aids and covers for my mouth. I don't know about the troops."

Tim Lee Carter finally lost his cool. "The scientists," he said, "went in completely equipped, dressed in protective clothing; at the same time GIs were sent in without protection. I think that constituted a heinous crime—such unfeeling men should be prosecuted to the full extent of the law." He later exploded again at the government's witnesses: "I don't trust you people with the national security. Nuclear war is not a practical instrument for our defense. Do you want to kill us all?"

In its written response to follow-up questions submitted by the subcommittee after the hearings, the Pentagon admitted that the film badges could not accurately measure: (1) ionizing (gamma) radiation having energies below the film's range; (2) alpha radiation, which would bounce off the badge's plastic cover; and (3) beta radiation. However, they still defended the badges' use, arguing that they "provide a fairly accurate and complete dosimetry record" of radiation received by the individual at the time of detonation. This is so, they explained, because "high-energy gammas provide the large majority of radiation present [during the tests]."

This is a clever, but disingenuous, explanation that carefully skirts the crucial issue of residual radiation and fallout particles. When a plutonium bomb is detonated, for example, most of the "prompt" (immediately emitted) radiation *is* gamma radiation. However, as pointed out by Dr. Martell, alpha- and beta-emitting radioisotopes are also produced in large numbers, and they often attach themselves to tiny specks of dust or to particles from the steel bomb towers that are vaporized upon detonation.

In response to a subcommittee question about troops possibly inhaling or ingesting such particles, the Pentagon answered: "Film badges will not measure this [but] maneuvers through contaminated soil pose some risk of internal intake through the nose or mouth or superficial wounds." They didn't bother to mention that at no time during the Nevada tests were respirators ever issued to ordinary troops who would be entering radioactive areas.

After the Desert Rock I–III series ended on November 29, 1951, the military dismissed any concern about radioactive dust, saying, "A hazard doesn't exist . . . the particles which fell out in the immediate area were [too large] to be breathed in. Smaller particles were carried off in the atomic cloud and dispersed to such a degree that no hazard resulted."

This was to become the nuclear testers' stock answer whenever outsiders raised questions about the dangers of inhaling or eating radioactive dust. However, even their own reports acknowledge that two ground-level blasts during the Buster-Jangle series in 1951 (unlike other blasts detonated high in the air) resulted in extensive radioactive contamination blanketing a large area and persisting at dangerous levels for several days.

Another problem ignored at the time is that alpha and beta rays travel through the air with less force than gamma rays. This means that a reading of gamma radiation on a film badge worn chest-high may lead one seriously to underestimate the amount of alpha and beta being received by the feet or legs. President and Mrs. Carter, astute observers of newspaper photos may recall, wore booties wrapped tightly around their ankles while inspecting the damaged reactor at Three Mile Island. This was presumably to guard against such radioactive contamination from these lower energy emitters.

Apparently stung by the subcommittee's criticism that it was not doing enough to identify and locate test veterans, the Defense Nuclear Agency set up toll-free "800" lines so that participants could check in from anyplace in the country. Even though the agency relied entirely on news releases to spread the word, over 13,000 phone calls and letters were received in the first two weeks the phones were on. One wonders what the response would have been had they placed a notice on the 1979 Internal Revenue forms or on the 1980 census questionnaire. In August, a news story reported that 2400 of the callers had stated that they suffered from leukemia or other cancers. By October 1978, over 26,000 veterans had been logged. Callers were asked for brief biographic details and were also asked a series of questions concerning the tests they'd participated in. Each caller was then sent a one-page questionnaire that basically repeated the phone interview.

On the same day the telephones were belatedly being turned on, Paul Cooper died in a Boise hospital. He was buried on February 13 in his Green Beret uniform with full military honors, including a twenty-one-gun salute. Two days later, coauthor Tod Ensign arrived at the Cooper home in Emmet, a small town that nestles in a snow-ringed mountain valley about fifty miles north of Boise.

The first evening in Emmet he enjoyed the warm hospitality of the Cooper clan as they treated him to a venison dinner and regaled him with hilarious stories about parts of northern Idaho where the Law of the Six-gun still has some meaning. When he returned in the morning, however, the mood clearly had changed. As he set up his tape recorder for an interview with Nancy Cooper, one of Paul's brothers paced nervously, shooting frequent glances out the living-room window. A few minutes later, the front door swung open and in walked the sheriff, packing the biggest pistol Tod had ever seen. Evidently the brothers had decided that Tod was a dangerous radical or subversive. When he objected to the sheriff's hostile interrogation, he was told, "Out here people don't mind answering questions, unless they've got something to hide." With the Bill of Rights disposed of, it only took a few more minutes of wrangling before the sheriff ordered Ensign out of the house. Driving him to the town's main street, the sheriff made it clear it would be best if Tod was on the next bus out.

On the way over to the Coopers' that morning, the local female cabdriver had told Tod the story of Sorrowing Widow Ridge, which overlooks the Coopers' house. Local legend has it that a group of Indian women and their children were slaughtered there one day by white settlers while their braves were away on a hunt. The legend, in a way, seemed to fit the Coopers, although for them it was the brave who'd gone away and been slaughtered, leaving his wife and children to cope alone.

As thousands of vets reported in, the White House decided in May 1978 to appoint a task force to conduct yet another study of the issue of low-level radiation. Once again, all federal agencies having any connection to radiation or its victims were ordered to sift through America's nuclear legacy.

During the summer, some of the estimated 25,000 residents who lived near the test site in the tristate area of Nevada, Arizona, and Utah organized themselves into the Committee of Survivors. Aided by former Interior Secretary Stewart Udall and local attorneys, they began filing damage claims for cancers and other health problems they believed were caused by the radioactive winds that blew regularly off the test site. In the course of their research they uncovered a 1965 report done by Edward Weiss of the U.S. Public Health Service, who studied the health of area residents. He examined the death records for two Utah counties near the test site for the period from 1950 to 1965 and found what he termed "excessive" rates of leukemia. His study had so upset his superiors at the Public Health

Service, a branch of the Department of Health, Education and Welfare, that they barred its publication. It was not released to the public until May 1979.

As local residents came forward in growing numbers to report sickness and premature deaths in their families, the attitude of local officials toward atmospheric testing underwent a marked change. Utah's Governor Scott Matheson, a devout Mormon and a conservative on most social issues, became so concerned that he journeyed to Washington in November 1978, to demand that the federal government do more about the problem. A few days later, President Carter visited Salt Lake City, where he announced that the government would re-examine previous fallout studies for evidence of increased rates of leukemia or thyroid disease.

By April 1979, over 700 claims for injury or death had been filed by area residents with the Department of Energy. Under the Federal Tort Claims Act, the agency has six months in which to accept or reject a claim. If it takes no action in that period, the claimants can then file suit in federal district court. Another Utah official, Dr. Joseph Lyon of the state's Cancer Registry, released a study which found that children raised in the area proximate to the test site were two and a half times as likely to develop leukemia as children raised in other parts of the state.

The continuing furor prompted a joint House-Senate panel to travel to Salt Lake City and Las Vegas in April 1979 to conduct a probe of the federal government's activities with respect to this issue. Co-chaired by Senator Edward Kennedy (Democrat-Massachusetts) and Representative Bob Eckhardt (Democrat-Texas) the hearings were among the first ever conducted by legislators who didn't have concurrent responsibility for the development or promotion of nuclear weapons or nuclear power.

Dr. Lyon first summarized his findings for the joint committee; he then was asked if he thought the high leukemia rates were caused by the fallout. "It's a leading contender and whatever's in second place is a long ways behind," he responded.

Lyon also commented that the AEC kept its worries about safety to itself: "There was concern, yet they didn't seem to want to pursue it to its logical conclusion."

Governor Matheson pulled no punches in his testimony: "An all-out public relations campaign was mounted by the AEC. Although on occasion residents were advised to remain indoors [during tests] the AEC announcements were quick to remind listeners 'there is no danger.' Evidence shows a willful refusal to investigate threats to human health. It also shows a conscious suppression of important information on health dangers."

The panel also heard from Dr. Harold Knapp who had worked in the AEC's Fallout Study Branch during 1962-63. He described his discovery that AEC had been grossly underestimating the hazards of fallout since 1953. "The standard which the AEC had for determining an internal [body] hazard at the time . . . seems to me to have been too large by a factor of one thousand. At that time there were no statistics around the Nevada test site of the levels of various internal [radioactive] emitters, such as strontium 89, barium 140, or iodine 131 in milk."

He recalled for the panel his superiors' reactions to his discovery that fallout may have been grossly underestimated: "People had been saying for years that there couldn't be any hazard [by] pointing out that the external gamma dose . . . might have been only five or three rads and that never caused any trouble. So when I came on and said we may have missed it [by hundreds of times] people at first were skeptical and then very concerned."

Dr. Knapp recalled how his division head reacted when he told him about his research: "Harold, you're playing with dynamite." Knapp's study was criticized by other AEC scientists as amateurish and incompetent, but due to his persistence, it was eventually published and, just as quickly, forgotten. Not long after that, Knapp quit the AEC.

His conclusions about the underestimation of hazards from radioactive emitters within the body are significant not only for off-site residents but for GIs who maneuvered on the test site as well. "I have no reason to [suspect] gross error in external gamma measurements as reported. I was [concerned] about magnification factors for internal emitters," he summed up.

Sensing he was in a hostile forum, HEW representative Peter Libassi, who also chairs the Inter-Agency Task Force on Health Effects of Ionizing Radiation, opted for a conciliatory posture. He admitted that "recent studies of populations exposed to low level radiation suggest that risks may be higher than earlier predicted." He noted that his Task Force had already recommended that a "substantial portion" of the health research on radiation be transferred away from the Department of Energy.

Meanwhile, the Senate Veterans Committee conducted its own hearings on the VA's handling of disability claims from ailing veterans. It asked the VA to reconsider radiation claims it had denied. The VA referred 231 such cases to the Defense Nuclear Agency for reevaluation. The agency reported that it could find exposure records on only some sixty of these men, but that it would conduct a further search. A few weeks later, the agency sent back half of the cases, stating that only a few of the men had been exposed to significant radiation. So it goes.

Despite the numerous congressional hearings, not much sentiment for compensating radiation victims has yet emerged in Washington. One group, however, the families who lived downwind from the test site, received a boost in October 1979 when a bill was introduced by Senators Edward Kennedy and Orrin Hatch (Republican-Utah) which would impose strict liability on the government for either leukemia, bone cancer, or thyroid cancer. This would relieve the plaintiffs from the difficult, often impossible, task of proving in court that fallout from the tests was the cause of their cancerous condition. The legislation would draw a precise map, consisting of seventeen Utah counties, as well as several from both Nevada and Arizona. Anyone who resided within that area for at least a year during the period from 1951 to 1962 could hold the government strictly liable for their radiation-induced cancer. It would be up to a local federal jury to determine appropriate damages in each case. Congressman K. Gunn McKay (Democrat-Utah) introduced a similar bill in the House in August.

The bill doesn't provide compensation for other radiation-related ailments such as birth defects and sterility, nor does it cover either GIs or civilian workers who were present during the tests.

Although several influential senators have signed on as co-sponsors, most observers feel it has only a slim chance of passage. Many in government are frightened that it would create a costly precedent which would soon be offered to other categories of victims, perhaps eventually extending to citizens living near Three Mile Island or any of the dozens of nuclear reactors and other facilities throughout the U.S.

Efforts by ailing or dying veterans to gain compensation through the courts have not amounted to much. A few weeks before the April hearings, a U.S. District Court judge in Newark dismissed all four counts of Stanley Jaffee's suit for damages and injunctive relief. Judge Herbert Stern ruled that the first three counts which had sought compensatory and punitive damages for Jaffee and his wife for his breast cancer were barred by the time-encrusted doctrine of "sovereign immunity." While this doctrine had been softened by the Federal Tort Claims Act to permit some suits against the government, the Supreme Court held in the *Feres* case in 1950 that soldiers cannot use the Act to recover for injuries suffered while they were on active duty. When Stern expressed "the gravest reluctance" in throwing the Jaffee case out of court, noting that during oral arguments the government attorney had admitted that under the *Feres* doctrine a commander could consciously march his troops off a cliff and the government would still be immune from liability.

Jaffee's lawyers, Steven Phillips and Andrew Jacobs, took Stern's rulings to the U.S. Court of Appeals, but he was sustained on all but one point. The appellate court reversed his denial of the plaintiff's request for a public warning, holding that the government could be ordered to issue public notices to all veterans who may have been exposed during the atomic tests. In September 1979 counsel for Jaffee and the Defense Nuclear Agency agreed to the text of a public announcement which the agency is to release nationally. Unfortunately, it is couched in cautious language: "It is believed that radiation exposures were low . . . science has no proof that exposure to radiation levels as low as these is hazardous . . ." Worse, veterans are urged only to contact the agency via its toll-free phone system. This means that all names and addresses of veterans who respond will be bottled up in the agency's computers, safe from the prying eyes of independent veterans' organizations. When one such organization, Citizen Soldier, attempted to review the names and addresses of the 26,000 veterans who'd called in by December 1978, the Defense Nuclear Agency rejected its request, stating that such data were restricted by the Privacy Act and also covered by exemptions to the Freedom of Information Act. Thus, reform legislation which was passed recently to protect citizens *from* the prying eyes of government and to open up the governmental processes to scrutiny, is now used to keep the veterans' identities safe from outside groups who might criticize the government's conduct in their desire to help the veterans.

Despite these attempts by the government to defuse and discredit the just claims of many radiation victims, atomic veterans are beginning to seek each other out and are actually getting organized. The Committee for U.S. Veterans of Hiroshima and Nagasaki, based in Portland, Oregon, has called attention to the widespread evidence of blood and tissue cancers among American GIs who entered the radiation-soaked environs of the two unfortunate target cities. Committee founder Norman Solomon has been influential in the planning of a national conference for radiation victims, to take place in Washington D.C. in April 1980.

Another prime mover among irradiated soldiers is Orville Kelly, himself a cancer victim and a year-long participant in the South Pacific atomic tests on Eniwetok in 1957. Kelly has organized the National Association of Atomic Veterans from his home in Burlington, Iowa. The NAAV already has 1000 members and puts out an informative monthly newsletter. Kelly recently won on appeal a favorable ruling on his VA claim for service-connected disability compensation. He was fortunate to have the services and support of Dr. John Gofman and other nuclear scientists who helped reevaluate his case on appeal. In his testimony, Dr. Gofman concluded: "Mr. Kelly was put into a serious potential radiation environment. Given the fact that radiation does indeed induce lymphoma, this case should be adjudged in Mr. Kelly's favor on the basis of elemental fairness and justice to a veteran of the United States Service."

For Jim O'Connor and the men of Wire Team B, as well as countless irradiated vets, the results of their claims have been less felicitous. Howard Hinkie has suffered three serious heart attacks, and heart disease may be as radiation-connected as cancer, according to Dr. Edward Martell of Colorado—especially from the internal emitters that Hinkie, O'Connor, and the other wiremen were almost certain to have ingested in extremely dangerous quantities. The federal judge in Philadelphia dismissed Howard Hinkie's claim that his and every atomic vet's civil rights had been violated by the government's failure to warn them of possible genetic and health damage due to exposure to radiation.

Jim O'Connor has also been pursuing a separate claim with the VA for the past two and a half years, so far without success. In preparing his claim, he's amassed over 500 pages of medical records from the army and the VA, although, as stated earlier, all records relating to his service at Desert Rock are missing except for three fragmentary pages, one of which lists his dates on sick call. Like Donald Coe, Jim was told that these particular records were destroyed in the 1973 fire that swept the military's records repository in St. Louis. O'Connor finds it amazing that the fire would selectively burn only those portions of his records which could prove he was at Desert Rock and received medical treatment for radiation overexposure there.

PART II

DEFOLIATION MYTHS: VICTIMS OF AGENT ORANGE

CHAPTER
7

The Ranch Hands: "Only We Can Prevent Forests . . ."

It was a suffocatingly hot July day in 1962 when 900 soldiers from the Fourth Infantry Division became the first troops to conduct nuclear maneuvers at the Nevada test site since the Plumb Bob series with its ill-fated "Smoky" shot in 1957. As it turned out, they were also among the last GIs to participate in an atmospheric bomb test. Joining them on the sun-baked desert that day were two high-ranking members of the Kennedy administration—Attorney General Robert Kennedy and General Maxwell Taylor, special military adviser to the president. These men had taken time from their busy schedules to witness the testing of the new "Davy Crockett" atomic mortar shell. While the Kennedy administration was eager to show the nuclear flag in response to Soviet A-test initiatives, it's likely that the attention of the two men may have strayed to a real-life battlefield 10,000 miles away—Vietnam.

At the time, Kennedy and Taylor were serving as cochairmen of the Special Group Counter-Insurgency, an ultrasecret planning group created by President Kennedy to organize America's effort to fight revolutionary guerrilla movements in Vietnam and other parts of the world. As two architects of the grand American scheme to intervene in Vietnam squinted into the bright Nevada sun, the first sorties by air-force deoliation planes made lazy arcs over Vietnam's canals and roadways.

John Kennedy had won the presidency by a narrow margin, and he attributed his success in part to his campaign pledge to restore America's military supremacy over the Soviet Union. During the campaign, he had charged that the Eisenhower-Nixon administration had allowed U.S. military strength to erode. In his three years as president, Kennedy substantially boosted military spending in all sectors, including a tripling of spending on the development of weapons for chemical and biological warfare.

It had become an article of faith since World War II that the immense technological capacity and inventiveness of American industry allowed American policy makers to shape, and often control, events in even the remotest corners of the globe. In his inaugural address, John Kennedy asserted not only the ability but the *right* of America to do so. "Let every nation know . . . that we shall pay any price, bear any burden, meet any hardship, support any friend, oppose any foe to assure the survival and the success of liberty. This much we pledge—and more."

Over the next fifteen years, this presumptuous arrogance would bring death and destruction to Indochina. Only after a savage bloodletting, in which millions perished and much of Indochina was blasted to smithereens, would it be seriously challenged.

Defoliating agents had been developed originally for use in the South Pacific against the Japanese. These defoliants were to destroy vegetation in order to deny concealment to the enemy and to open up "fields of fire" around defensive positions and along transport routes. They also were to destroy food crops which might be of use to an enemy. But their military debut was delayed when atomic bombs brought World War II to a rapid conclusion.

After the war, army chemists continued to refine the technology by testing over 12,000 different compounds for their defoliating properties. (It wasn't publicized at the time, but Britain enjoys the distinction of being the first country to employ defoliants as a military weapon, using them in its campaign to suppress the communist insurgency in Malaya in the early 1950s.)

It must be stressed that when they decided to utilize chemical warfare in Vietnam, the Kennedys were only expanding upon an American tradition begun at Hiroshima and Nagasaki. After all, once you've poisoned whole cities and sown the heavens with deadly plutonium and other radioactive toxins, who's going to worry about the long-term effects of a few "weed killers"? The relentless development of nuclear weapons contributed to an attitude of moral agnosticism among most, but by no means all, American scientists. Given this moral climate, an entire subcontinent could be turned into a virtual laboratory for testing terrifying new weapons with scarcely a whimper of protest.

In October 1961, Kennedy's most trusted military adviser, General Maxwell Taylor, returned from an inspection tour of Vietnam with a deeply pessimistic report. The regime of Premier Ngo Dinh Diem was in serious danger from a determined insurgency led by the National Liberation Front. Anxious not to lose an ally to communism, Kennedy resolved to tilt the scales in favor of the Diem government.

Historian Arthur Schlesinger, a Kennedy intimate, reports in *A Thousand Days* that Kennedy made a priority of developing a counter-insurgency program for the U.S. military. He ordered Special Warfare Centers to be established at Fort Bragg (for Green Berets) and at U.S. bases in Panama, Okinawa, Vietnam, and West Germany. Among the new programs he personally approved was Operation Hades, code name for a program under which a squadron of cargo planes would defoliate guerrilla-controlled areas of Vietnam from the air. According to the military, Operation Hades would "clear jungle growth and reduce the hazards of ambush by Viet Cong forces. . . . Destruction of food [would be] undertaken only in remote and thinly populated areas under Viet Cong control and where significant denial of food supplies can be effected. . . ."

The defoliation scheme had been developed by the Pentagon's Advanced Research Projects Agency (ARPA). In May 1961, teams of scientists from Fort Detrick's plant-science labs were sent to Vietnam as part of Project Agile to conduct field experiments on the susceptibility of Vietnam's flora to various types of defoliants such as 2,4,5-T and 2,4-D. Experts from the Department of Agriculture and the U.S. Forest Service, as well as the air force's armament labs at Eglin Air Force Base, were also called in to lend expert advice. Evidently the project's name, Operation Hades, was too strong even for hardened military stomachs, for it was soon changed to Operation Ranch Hand. The satanic theme survived, however, at least on the shoulder patches worn by some Ranch Hands depicting a smiling devil with a pitchfork.

The Pentagon Papers tell us that Kennedy agreed to a substantial increase in U.S. commitment in Vietnam without having pinned Premier Diem down to a unified strategy for fighting the rebels. "By early 1962, however, there was apparent consensus . . . that the Strategic Hamlet program represented the unifying concept." By mid-1963, Premier Diem claimed that seven million Vietnamese (nearly half the population) now lived in 7000 such hamlets.

At the time the spray program began, two-thirds of South Vietnam's land surface was covered with forest, much of it extremely dense triple-canopied jungle. This dense foliage afforded the anti-government guerrillas excellent cover and relatively safe bases from which to operate. Furthermore, nearly four-fifths of Vietnam's population (the "hearts and minds" the U.S. so piously urged the Saigon government to win) lived in these rural areas. Over the next nine years, more than a third of this forestland would be sprayed at least once, while at least 15 percent of the croplands also was doused.

Once it was decided to organize a defoliation program, the air force naturally turned to its Special Aerial Spray Flight, a unit that had been flying insect-spray missions since the Korean War, using C-47 cargo planes. They flew missions throughout the United States and the Caribbean whenever aerial spray was needed on an emergency basis. When the air force adopted the two-engine C-123 "Provider" as its basic cargo and troop-transport plane in 1960, the "spray birds," as they were called, switched over to this plane also.

We met some of the original pilots at the twelfth annual reunion of the Vietnam Ranch Hand Association in Fort Walton Beach, Florida, on an October weekend in 1978. The Ranch Hand Association is sort of an alumni club for the men who flew missions with Operation Ranch Hand from 1962 to 1970. Unlike veterans of earlier wars, there've been few reports of Vietnam vets getting together to reminisce about the "good old days"; most of them threw away their uniforms and medals when they came home and tried to forget the whole thing. The men who flew the defoliation missions, however, are apparently an exception. Of the 1200-odd pilots and flight engineers eligible for membership in the Ranch Hand Association, nearly a quarter are on its active mailing list. Every fall, a number of these men travel hundreds, sometimes thousands, of miles to spend a weekend eating, drinking, and swapping stories about their exploits on what they affectionately call "the Ranch." At various times during the weekend, we noticed that nearly all of the thirty-odd men attending wore special shirts, scarves, and flight suits emblazoned with the Ranch Hand crest—a bright green patch bisected by a defoliated stripe of brown.

One of the pilots we met at the 1978 reunion was William "Robby" Robinson. Robby today is a deskbound warrior in the battle for insurance sales near Houston, Texas, but for twenty-one years he flew air-force planes, several of those years as a spray pilot. Despite his office pallor, he still retains the rugged bearing of an air-force career officer. Another pilot we met was Jack Spey, the association's president and its principal spark plug. Spey best fits the popular stereotype of the aviator hero—a reincarnation of Terry and the Pirates. Blond, tanned, and trim, with boyish good looks just starting to harden around the edges, he talked with enthusiasm about his record eleven years with the defoliation program. Robby and Jack are the two most senior Ranch Hands still alive and kicking. Together, they flew two of the original six C-123s on their maiden voyage to Vietnam near the end of 1961. Over nonstop screw-drivers, they sat down and reminisced about the birthing of Operation Ranch Hand.

In 1961, Robby told us, one of the men in his spray unit, Captain Mario Cadori, was sent to Vietnam to train the Viet-namese in the techniques of defoliation. According to Robby, Cadori decided, after taking the Vietnamese pilots up on a few test runs, that American pilots would be needed. "He told us that the Vietnamese would fly their planes at the proper alti-tude, just above the treetops, for a while, then they would start to inch higher, losing the effective spray application." Whether or not the decision to use American spray pilots was based on the alleged cowardice or simple ineptitude of the Vietnamese, the air force actively began to recruit American crew members for Vietnam in the fall of 1961.

Apparently the obsession with "national security" that per-vaded the atomic test program carried over to the defoliation project as well. Jack Spey remembers that when the air-force recruiters came to Pope Air Base looking for prospective crew members, they made the applicants sign statements that they wouldn't divulge anything that was said during the interview.

"After all that," Jack said, "they told us precious little about the mission. We didn't even know where we'd be sent if we were picked. Just a few days after we were chosen, we were told to be ready to ship out immediately."

The day after Thanksgiving, 1961, the six C-123s which had been specially refitted for defoliation missions, took off for Vietnam. Designed for troop hauling and cargo, the planes were stripped of all extraneous equipment, and a cylindrical 1000-gallon tank adapted from the B-50 was added. Spray booms with sixteen nozzles each were mounted under each wing and a small gasoline engine was installed to pump the defoliant through pressurized hoses from the tank to the wing racks. (Later, after field testing in Vietnam, a third spray rack was added across the rear, beneath the cargo door.) Each plane's crew consisted of a pilot, copilot, and flight engineer. The engineer rode in the cargo hold and operated the spray machinery. A fourth crew member, a navigator, was added to the lead plane on each mission, to direct the planes to the target.)

To accomplish the long trek across the Pacific, extra gas was stored in the defoliant tank. The planes island-hopped, first to Hawaii, then Johnson, Wake, and Guam, before finally landing at Clark Field in the Philippines. According to Robby, only two planes went on to Vietnam, and the rest remained at Clark because the defoliation program still was a "touchy" situation in diplomatic circles. James Camden of Greenville, South Carolina, was a flight engineer with the original party. He recalls that the Vietnamese would only allow three planes and their crews to be in Vietnam at any one time. This meant that crews had to shuttle back and forth to the Philippines when one group was to relieve another. The spray crews were listed as members of the U.S. embassy in Saigon.

Just weeks before Robby Robinson and Carl Marshall landed the first C-123s at Tan Son Nhut Airbase, a unit of thirty-three American helicopters and 500 crewmembers had arrived. This unit represented the first U.S. personnel sent to Vietnam for purposes other than training or technical assistance. When Robinson and Marshall arrived, they were assigned to a hut on the sprawling base. Before long, someone had nailed a plaque over its door with the motto of the Twelfth Air Commando Squadron: It pictured Smoky the Bear with the legend "Only We Can Prevent Forests."

From the beginning, the spray missions operated subject to a complicated set of instructions and procedures, called rules of engagement. Robby remembers that every mission had to be cleared through various levels in the Vietnamese and American command structure, up to, and including, the White House. "After all that," he lamented, "the enemy knew exactly what we were planning and was usually waiting for us when we got there." The complicated rules, called Project Farmgate, created problems. For example: Since it was impossible to tell which crops were, in fact, intended for enemy soldiers, crop destruction was disguised as a South Vietnamese activity, and

the planes were flown with South Vietnamese markings and
with a Vietnamese observer aboard.

The Ranch Hands were presented with an unusual mission
in that no country had ever conducted massive defoliation as
an instrument of war. "It was all new," Jack Spey remembers.
"That's what helped develop our unit's camaraderie and esprit
de corps; there weren't any manuals, we had to figure it out
for ourselves." So, with good ol' Yankee ingenuity, the small
band of pioneering aviators set out to accomplish what no
one had ever done before: systematically destroy millions of
acres of foliage from the air under combat conditions.

John Lemanski showed up at the reunion wearing a bright
purple jumpsuit that would have won the prize for most unusual uniform had one been offered. Large Chinese characters
which translated as "purple" (referring to the defoliant called
"Agent Purple") were stitched on the back in white thread.
Over his heart, John wore the Ranch Hand emblem. John and
several buddies had designed the uniform themselves and
then sent the patterns to a custom tailor in Hong Kong. John
described to us the standard operating procedures for defoliation missions.

("We'd take off while it was still dark. Arriving near the
drop area, we'd circle at a relatively high altitude until the sun
came up. Just at daybreak, we'd swoop down over the target.
We did this for two reasons: one, to try and keep the enemy
gunners off-balance; two, you had to dump early in the day—
later on, the intense ground heat would keep the spray from
settling properly. We'd return to base, reload, and often make
another run before it got too hot.)

"The spray operator was a recycled flight mechanic," John
continued. "He'd start the twenty-horsepower motor once we
were aloft; after checking the valve and hose pressure, he'd
radio the pilot that everything was ready. The pilot would
activate the spray mechanism once we'd arrived over the
target."

Like the other pilots at the reunion, John talked in a casual,
offhand way about what must have been some rather hairy
flying experiences.

"We'd fly with both cockpit windows and the rear cargo door open. We left the cabin windows open so that a stray round wouldn't shatter the Plexiglas in our faces. Also, the air conditioning didn't work well at low altitudes and it was hot as hell in there. The cargo door was left open so the flight mechanic could visually check the spray pattern. Also, he could throw out smoke grenades to mark 'hot' areas which were giving us fire."

Lemanski emphasized that the spray missions required some very demanding precision flying. "We'd come in over the target in tight formation, sometimes with as many as eight or ten planes flying just above stall speed." Another flyer estimated that the planes were often no more than fifteen or twenty feet apart during spraying.

As the C-123 was intended for cargo hauling, not combat, it carried no armament and had armored plating only in the pilot's cabin. Flying at about half its normal cruising speed— "low and slow" as the Ranch Hands call it—the craft was vulnerable to small-arms fire from the ground. John summed it up: "If the enemy had ever learned to wait and 'lead' the airplane before firing, we'd have been in big trouble."

Robby Robinson remembers flying the very first defoliation mission just a few days after arriving, as old Vietnam hands used to say, "in-country." They sprayed along both sides of Highway 15, which runs south forty miles from Saigon to Vung Tau on the sea. This route was chosen because it offered several different types of foliage as test targets, and also because the area had recently been infiltrated by National Liberation Front guerrillas. A few days later, scientists from the Army Chemical Corps visited the spray sites, taking samples and photographing the effects of the sprays.

A month or so later, the unit flew another series of test missions, this time spraying mangrove forests and nipa palm in the Ca Mau peninsula in the Delta. Just after the other four planes arrived in Vietnam, the squadron suffered its first loss when a plane went down in the Delta with all hands lost.

"They thought it was mechanical failure, but they never found out; given the terrain and possibility of 'unfriendlies,' you couldn't do the type of accident investigation you would in the States," Jack Spey observed without emotion. "In the early days," he added, "the program wasn't much. Both the ARVN [South Vietnamese] and the Americans had to learn that it existed and what it could do. You start slow, just like any new program that has merit."

Listening to Jack, one gets the uneasy feeling that he could be describing a sales campaign for a new type of aluminum siding, instead of a vast program for devastating the foliage of an entire subcontinent. In any case, the official figures confirm Jack's recollection. During 1962, only 4940 acres were sprayed, mostly in the Delta region in the southern part of the country. The following year, this increased to a total of 24,700. The air force estimated acreage sprayed by calculating the amount of ground area each sortie could be expected to cover if everything went according to plan.

From August 1965 onward, the air force maintained a computerized history called the HERBS file which logged missions of both spray planes and helicopters in considerable detail. Each entry lists the date, type, and quantity of herbicide used and it classifies each mission as to type—for example, crop, supply route, military installation, and the like. The exact geographical location, called a Universal Transverse Mercator Grid Coordinate, for each mission is also listed. The HERBS file, which runs 315 computer pages in length, could be a valuable document in tracing personnel exposures. At first, the spray mechanism was set to disperse at one gallon per acre, but Jack recalls that this had been increased to three gallons per acre by the end of 1963. Flying under ideal conditions, each plane could lay down a 250-foot swath over an eight-and-a-half-mile stretch in three and a half to four minutes. A special valve allowed the pilot to dump the entire load of herbicide in just thirty seconds. This was activated whenever a plane developed serious mechanical trouble or was badly hit by ground fire.

The Pentagon continues to minimize the frequency of such emergency dumping. Spokesperson Tom Dashiell stated in a September 1979 interview that, according to military records, only thirteen such dumpings occurred during the entire war. Based on the accounts of the small number of pilots we interviewed, his figure seems a gross underestimate.

The navigator was essential to the success of defoliation missions. It was his job to receive target orders from command, plan the mission, direct the planes to the target, and oversee the actual spraying. As already mentioned, he rode in the lead aircraft, with a backup navigator usually along in another plane in case the first one went down or had to turn back. We talked to one former navigator, Aaron Valenzuela.

Aaron is a Chicano who now practices law in San Antonio, Texas. Since returning from Vietnam, Aaron's had no contact with other Ranch Hands, although he was interested when we told him about the Ranch Hand reunions. Aaron flew as a navigator on the "spray birds" during the last half of 1969 and early 1970. He described his job: "It was a tough mission, all map reading at low levels; this was unusual work for an air-force navigator. I would ride astride the radio on top of an armor-plated box between the two pilots."

Asked about the process of preparing missions, he told us: "We would get target requests in from MACV [Military Assistance Command-Vietnam]. They would tell us what herbicides they wanted used and give us a target number. By the time I got over there, practically the whole country had already been targeted. So you'd go into the safe and pull out the folder for that particular target. There were a few new targets, and on these we'd have to fly out and recon it ourselves.

"After planning the mission, I'd conduct the briefing for the flight crews, giving them the flight time, geographical coordinates, airspeed, and details about the spraying itself. After the first drop, sometimes we'd put in at a satellite base where we'd pick up more herbicides and go out to hit another target."

Aaron remembers targeting spray missions around "friendly" base camps on many occasions. "We flew around their perimeters to destroy foliage—this would prevent guys from sneaking in. We'd also spray along likely avenues of approach to the camps."

The soft-spoken lawyer recalls having some second thoughts

about the safety of the chemicals while in Vietnam. "It was strange seeing loaders wearing protective clothing at one refueling base while I was flying this machine in a set of fatigues!" At the main base at Ben Hoa, he recalls, the Vietnamese loaders usually wore only shorts. "We normally flew with the plane windows open, so we'd often get hit with spray from the other planes in our formation."

Charley Hubbs, who piloted spray planes for two years, put it more graphically: "You could always tell a Ranch Hand—by the way he smelled. You'd get hit [through the windows] with four minutes of whatever you were putting out." According to Charley, the crew also could get doused if their plane's spray system got hit by ground fire. "If you open the rear window of a station wagon when the front windows are already open, where's the air going to go? It's the same in a plane, the spray in the cargo hold would get sucked up into the cabin. It was very common to get fogged out this way." Charley served as deputy commander of the Ranch Hands during 1966 and 1967. Now retired from the air force, he works as an aircrash investigator with the National Transportation Safety Board.

Navigator Valenzuela remembers one time he was acutely exposed to the chemicals. "They didn't get the top back on the tank and it came off just as we were taxiing for takeoff. The flight engineer and I got soaked before we could get it back on." Three years ago, Aaron was forced to retire from the Air Guard reserve when doctors found he had cryptococcus—a funguslike condition in his lungs. He wonders if this condition wasn't somehow brought on by his service with the spray birds.

Flight-crew members, other than navigators, apparently knew practically nothing about the chemicals they were dumping all over Vietnam every day. "Any evaluation of effectiveness was done by the army's Chemical Corps; we didn't get into evaluation—our job was to put the chemicals where they wanted it," Jack Spey summarized.

Lieutenant Colonel Dick Peshkin from Great Neck, New York, served as Ranch Hand operations officer during 1965 and 1966. He confirmed their ignorance about the chemicals:

"I never saw any technical data on 2,4,5-T [a compound that is a major ingredient of Agent Orange] or the other herbicides. It was strictly a 'You call, we haul' type of situation."

Hal Underwood, another Ranch Hand pilot, who flew his own small plane all the way from his Montana home to the reunion, agreed with Peshkin. "Before each mission we were briefed only on the geographical characteristics and coordinates of the target area. We were never told what was beneath the foliage, nor were we ever told what type of defoliant we'd be using on a particular day. You couldn't mistake rice crops, however. They were a bright green—almost chartreuse."

At the same time that Agent Orange was being routinely sprayed along Vietnam's canals and waterways, Dow Chemical, a principal manufacturer of 2,4,5-T, was affixing the following warning to each can produced for domestic use: "Do not contaminate irrigation ditches or water used for domestic purposes. Caution. May cause skin irritation. Avoid contact with eyes, skin and clothing. Keep out of reach of children." No one we've interviewed, however, has ever mentioned seeing any sort of warning on any herbicide used in Vietnam. It's apparent that no effort was made to educate any of the flight crews as to the toxic properties of any of the defoliants. Instead, it appears that the command constantly repeated the theme that they were harmless to animal life. To this day, many of the Ranch Hands seem to cling to this dubious assertion.

The defoliants were relatively slow to take effect. It took at least a week for highly susceptible mangrove trees to die, while it took nipa palm trees up to five weeks to lose all their leaves. Jack Spey remembers that, depending on the time of year and weather, you might begin to see a slight discoloration of the leaves of hardwood trees a day or two after spraying. If the trees were exposed during growing season, the defoliant's effects would register more rapidly than they would otherwise; but it took anywhere from one to three months for the full impact to take effect.

This meant that the spray program had no immediate tactical value to the military strategists: one couldn't spray a forest area in the middle of a battle hoping to unmask a concealed enemy. Its only value was as part of an overall plan for denuding areas over a long period. Of course, crops could be spoiled immediately by contact with the sprays.

Some of the Ranch Hand pilots expressed serious doubts about the value of the whole program. Hal Underwood, who flew in both World War II and Korea before Vietnam, told us that he noticed that "we were fragged [ordered] to return to the same area over and over." This caused him and others to doubt the effectiveness of the defoliating sprays, on both a short-term and long-term basis.

The history of the defoliation program can be divided into two distinct periods. The first phase, from 1962 to early 1965, consisted of relatively limited spraying of selected targets, mostly in the Delta region, by a squadron of about eight planes. The second phase, which coincided with the rapid buildup of U.S. combat forces in Vietnam, dwarfed the first period in both the size and scope of the spraying. Eventually the squadron grew to thirty planes which flew missions in all four military corps areas of South Vietnam, from Bien Hua, Phu Cat, and Da Nang, which the men called the "Mountain Range."

Jack Spey spoke nostalgically about the Vietnam he remembers from the early days. "Saigon had a very sleepy atmosphere; it was very much a Vietnamese city, not yet Americanized as it later became. I remember its tremendous restaurants and the French-colonial atmosphere of many of the buildings. Prices were very, very low, by comparison with later years. We were urged to wear civilian clothing downtown to maintain a low-keyed presence. We didn't want to look like an occupying army.

"At the time, most of the Americans were army; we had only a few air-force elements there, helping out in the air tower and doing training. . . . There was no security problem in any of the large cities or in most of the provincial towns. You could safely drive to Vung Tau, and the train was still running north along the coast. You could still go hunting around Ban Me Thout for lion, tiger, or peacock. The insurgency was at a very, very low level by 1965 or 1966 standards.

"Most of the officer corps was billeted downtown, while

the enlisted men were quartered in a tent city out at Tan Son Nhut Airbase. Three or four of us officers would find a building downtown and rent it from a local owner, just like you would in any city in the world. A lot of the houses were passed down through the same unit; when a guy would leave, his replacement would just move right into his bed."

Jack's recollection of a peaceful and "secure" South Vietnam would have surprised General Taylor, whose pessimistic situation report to President Kennedy triggered the U.S. buildup in late 1961.

Being a mountainous country in a tropical zone, Vietnam presented the pilots with many diverse flying situations for which the Ranch Hands had to develop or adapt techniques. Jack recalls: "When we first started to spray in mountainous terrain, I can remember going down a hill spraying a power line near Dalat. We tried to hold it to the proper airspeed, but we were doing a hundred and seventy knots by the time we got to the bottom. The second time down, we were able to hold it to a hundred and fifty; then we got smart and the third time kept it to a hundred and thirty. We were feeling our way along, devising various techniques on the spot."

One experiment that didn't work out was an attempt to fly defoliation missions at night. It was hoped that this would increase the element of surprise and make it more difficult for enemy gunners. Jack flew on one of the test missions and says, "It was very scary because you could see the muzzle blasts from gunners on the ground; during the day you didn't hear or see anything until the slugs hit the plane. The experiment was ended because it became very evident that a successful rescue would be almost impossible if a plane did go down. Also, navigation was a problem, because at such low altitudes you're doing it all visually . . . once you got into a target area at night, you could get so lost you'd have chemicals where you didn't want them—it would be a real bucket of worms."

As the rate of missions increased, so did the intensity of small-arms fire from the ground. The crews soon learned under what conditions they could expect hostile fire. "It depended on the area you were flying in," Jack noted. "If it's real dense jungle, you can't see them and they can't see you, and you don't get shot. If an area's unpopulated, like mangrove swamps, there's no problem unless you run across a military unit that's in transit. If you're working in or around populated areas, the probability of receiving opposition increases. Opposition also increased as you got into crop destruction; if you got crops, you got people who plan to harvest them."

Jack and the other Ranch Hands seemed strangely oblivious to the consequences of their action. Like many who've spent years in government service, they tend to lapse into a jargon that is utterly devoid of any real feeling. "Unfriendlies," "suppressing fire," "hostile-incoming," and "crop denial" are some examples of terms commonly used by Ranch Hands. They would talk about encountering "opposition" while they were destroying six months of a farmer's labor as if the problem were simply a banal fact of life, like rush-hour traffic on the Long Island Expressway. Perhaps in this way they insulated themselves from the human consequences of their actions, thus avoiding what might be a very painful accounting.

They quickly learned to expect ground fire if they were operating in an inhabited area, but apparently that never caused them to question their assumption that America's military effort had but one objective: to protect the Vietnamese from a ruthless invader.

According to Jack Spey, the Ranch Hand pilots developed tactics for evading ground fire as they went along. "We tried everything we could think of to get through the 'small-arms envelope' that can eat you alive. Above twenty-five hundred feet, you're relatively safe as far as small-arms fire; below that, you're vulnerable. Assuming we expected opposition on a run, we'd fly out there above that altitude and then, when we had the target in sight, we'd make a very rapid descent to spray altitude and start spraying. As soon as we were finished we'd make a rapid climb back above the twenty-five-hundred threshold.

"Another technique we used was much more difficult from a navigational standpoint. This was the 'pop-up' technique, where you'd make a rapid descent right onto the deck about five or six miles out from the target. You'd scoot across the ground just as low as you could go without knocking things down, at as fast a speed as you could manage. Then, at the pop-up point, which hopefully was easy to identify, you'd pop up to a hundred and fifty feet and flip on the spray switch. The problem was that if the terrain didn't have features that stood out, you were going to pop up and be way out in left field, with no choice but to abort it. Sometimes you could look at a map or aerial photograph and pick out approach aids, but a lot of targets weren't suited for it and it was easy to get lost and botch the deal."

Since the Americans enjoyed virtually total control of the air, the powerful jet fighters that accompanied the spray birds on many of their missions had a relatively easy time of it. Jack said that "if we expected any opposition, we'd normally request dust-off [rescue] helicopters to stand by in the area. Sometimes we'd also request an FAC [forward air controller] to come along and, if the navigation was difficult, to mark the start of the target.

"Our flight commander would decide if fighter support was needed, and, if so, how it was to be deployed. We'd always get fire in the Delta, because that's where the people and crops were. Sometimes the fighters would sit high and dry and would respond only if we threw out smoke grenades. Also, the FAC would try to pick out where hostile fire was coming from and he might employ fighters.

"Sometimes we'd even request that the fighters hit an area before we sprayed; this negated the element of surprise, but there were a few places where it was worth it. Sometimes, the fighters would strafe alongside us as we sprayed; they'd sit there and sparkle right in front of us. We'd have empty twenty-millimeter cartridges fall right through the holes of our fuselage as the A-1 fighters opened up above us."

When the massive buildup of U.S. forces began in March

1965, defoliation operations increased accordingly. Total acreage sprayed that year was more than double the figure for 1964. For the first time, significant stretches of croplands were destroyed—nearly 66,000 acres in 1965 alone. In 1966, the program again expanded, with the total acreage sprayed quadrupling. The 1967 program was the largest ever, with 1.5 million acres of foliage and 221,000 acres of croplands hit. The heavy spraying continued during the next two years at only slightly lower levels. That 19,000 sorties (one flight by one plane) had been flown by the end of 1968 gives some idea of the intense activity. By the time the spray program finally ground to a halt in 1971, an estimated 6 million acres, of which 10 to 15 percent was cropland, had been doused by a total of 107 million pounds of herbicide.

Herbicide manufacture became one of the "growth" industries spawned by the Vietnam War. Annual sales increased from $12.5 million in fiscal 1966 to $79.8 million in fiscal 1969. Eleven chemical companies shared the booming business: Dow, Hercules, Northwest Industries, Diamond Shamrock, Private Brands, Thompson Chemical, Monsanto, Ansul, Trans-Vall, Hooker, and Velsicol. Evidently Hercules, a huge multinational conglomerate, had good sources within the Pentagon, for it had the foresight to purchase a herbicide-manufacturing operation, Reasor-Hill, Inc., in December 1961, as the first C-123s were wending their way across the South Pacific. So great did the war-demand become, according to journalist Thomas Whiteside, who wrote the first articles questioning the safety of Agent Orange, that 2,4,5-T and 2,4-D (the principal ingredients of Agent Orange) became extremely scarce on the U.S. domestic market after 1968.

Two air force buddies who flew during those years of heavy spraying were reunited at Fort Walton Beach. At first glance, Jim Pochurek and Ralph Dresser couldn't be less alike. Jim is a mild-mannered forty-five-year-old who, in his polyester leisure suit, could easily pass for a real-estate salesman—which, in fact, he is. Ralph, by contrast, has "soldier" written all over him. Decked out in his black Ranch Hand jumpsuit, with the unit's purple scarf knotted around his neck and a thick stogie clenched between his teeth, Ralph still stands tall. A full bird colonel, Ralph was the only reunion guest who still takes jets up every day. But for two years, from 1965 to 1967, Jim and Ralph flew spray missions together.

Ralph and Jim fell to reminiscing about their years on the Ranch, and Jim couldn't conceal his delight when he told us about the day he took Dan Rather of CBS News along for a ride. It seems that journalists were forever visiting the Ranch Hands in search of a different angle for a story. As Jim tells it, Rather's first trip up was very quiet, but when they went out on a second run, all hell broke loose, with ground fire coming in from all directions. "You should have seen Rather's face," Jim recalls with a wicked grin. "He didn't make a peep until we finally set the gooney bird back on the ground."

Once safely back on the tarmac at Tan Son Nhut, Rather questioned them about National Liberation Front allegations that the defoliants were a hazard to health. Ralph took a sip of the herbicide to show Rather what he thought of such "commie propaganda."

The reunion we attended took place just two days after the House Veterans Affairs Committee had conducted the first congressional hearings on the growing controversy over whether defoliants may have impaired the health not only of the Vietnamese but also of many of the 2.8 million Americans who served there. We asked Ralph what he thought of this controversy. He recalled that on at least two occasions in Vietnam he was confronted by other American commanders who complained that his spray planes had made their troops sick. "I told them, 'Bullshit,' " he growled. "I'd grant that the stuff tastes bad, but I'd dip my hand in and drink it, for chrissakes, to show them it was harmless."

Like the Apostle Thomas the Doubter, Ralph Dresser is a man of the senses, and for him, personal experience is the final arbiter in the controversy over Agent Orange. Looking at Dresser, it's conceivable that he *could* drink poison, the way some people eat glass or chew nails. In his opinion, guys who now complain of health problems have been "psyched out" by communist propaganda.

"The Viet Cong charged that we were waging chemical warfare so they could turn international opinion against us. They told the Vietnamese that they could prevent maladies by putting plastic bags on their bodies when the planes came over," Dresser chortled. "They even had some crazy antidotes. They told people to rub onion and garlic mixed with urine on exposed parts. They thought this would bring the toxic chemicals to the surface!"

In the early days of the defoliation program, the Viet Cong weren't the only ones concerned about the possible health effects of these toxic chemicals. According to Dresser, the South Vietnamese also insisted that their workers wear protective gear whenever they worked around the herbicides. Eventually, the Americans' repeated assurances that the defoliants were harmless won the Saigon government over and safety precautions became very lax.

Asked if he believed that any of the Ranch Hands had been harmed by exposure, Ralph gestured toward his fellow cowboys: "Look at these guys. They lived and worked with the stuff every day; there's nothing wrong with them," he laughed.

As we talked further with Ralph, he grew more serious. Judging from the obvious respect the others accorded him, he must have been a good commander, a man others would trust with their lives. These reunions, he felt, took place only because of the uniquely high morale among the Ranch Hands in Vietnam. This, in turn, stemmed from the shared dangers and unprecedented nature of their mission. He acknowledged that since the opposition didn't have antiaircraft defenses in southern Vietnam, the odds of survival for his flight crews were much greater than they would have been, say, during World War II.

When he took command of the Ranch in 1965, Ralph recognized that the anomalies of the mission required a flexible command structure. He allowed responsibility to shift from person to person, depending on the needs of the moment. From Thailand he brought a carved wooden statue of a man with his head up his ass. This became the Master Magnet Ass Award, which was given to the pilot whose plane had taken the heaviest beating from ground fire the previous week. This crude barracks humor had a point: Rather than chew out the offending pilot, Dresser figured that the prizewinner would analyze his mistakes and take corrective action. "It made something positive out of something negative," Dresser explained.

One plane earned the name "Patches" because she'd taken so many hits. At the reunion we saw a home movie that recorded the homecoming of "Patches" at the previous reunion. It was strangely moving to watch as the Ranch Hands walked up and down the plane, fondly stroking her much-battered fuselage.

The elements of nature seem mixed in Colonel Ralph Dresser: part Dr. Strangelove stereotype of the macho, invincible career soldier; part man of human responses, warm and congenial to his friends, competent and effective within the limits of his mission. Ralph doesn't seem to have the Big Picture, however, and his scoffing at the thousands of sick vets who got caught in the prop wash of the cowboys' jungle hose-down seems self-serving and protective of his superpilot image.

The fact is, once the fateful decision was made to have Americans take over most of the war effort, troops, equipment, and armaments poured into Vietnam on a truly massive scale, and new means for conducting defoliation—principally helicopters, but also spray trucks, riverboats, and even backpacks—were rapidly introduced wherever U.S. troops were deployed. UH-1 "Huey" helicopters were converted for spraying by attaching 200-gallon fuel tanks and gravity-feed sprayers. Flying at fifty-five knots, they could lay down one and a half gallons per acre from an altitude of 100 feet.

Ed Kernea, who now lives near Rickman, Tennessee, served as an army chemical officer in the First Air Cavalry during the period 1969–70. Ed's not a member of the Ranch Hand Association and his views differ markedly from those of some of its members. When asked about the government's claim that the spraying was always done in remote areas where U.S. troops were unlikely to be exposed, he responded: "Completely false; we sprayed around the perimeters of our base camps on many occasions. I often did the spraying myself, using a backpack. We'd spray in real close to the bunkers; anyone in the camp could have been exposed."

Ed also went out on many missions where helicopters were used to spray crops suspected of belonging to the enemy. "Often we'd get splashed when we loaded the chopper's tank from the fifty-five-gallon drums. We never wore any protective gear or gloves. We'd often go back and hit the same areas again, especially where rice was growing."

Ed's job was not unique: "There were at least four or five other chemical officers in the division, each doing exactly the same thing I was, only in other areas." He remembers being told that the air cavalry also used tanker trucks for spraying, although he never actually saw them in operation.

Ed is one of the few handlers we encountered who seems to have allowed himself second thoughts about his actions in Vietnam.

"I think about the program now and wonder how the hell I ever did it. To see the whole countryside just dead from that stuff, it was very sad. I never wanted to do crops, but I had to do it—following the old orders, ya know."

Since returning from Vietnam, Ed has suffered from a chronic skin condition. He's furious that the VA director in Nashville responded to a White House query about his case by denying that Ed had ever worked with defoliants in Vietnam.

Gerry Cece and another enlisted man who attended the reunion privately confided to us that they had a series of personal health problems which could, conceivably, be related to acute exposure to herbicides. As flight mechanics, or loaders, they routinely rode in the cargo hold, where they were often doused with the chemicals in the course of performing their duties.

Jan Soroka of Dallas, Texas, had the same job in Vietnam as Ed Kernea, although he served with the army's Ninth and

Twenty-fifth Infantry Divisions. He confirms Ed's account of using army trucks to spray around "friendly" base camps. "We'd take barrels of the defoliants out on trucks and use a gas-driven pump to spray everything around a base camp. No one wore any protective gear—there wasn't any."

Soroka went along on many helicopter flights in which defoliants were sprayed along river banks. Since the helicopters had no doors, spray drifting back into the cabin was a constant irritant. He also remembered an incident which demonstrated the danger from spray drifting to the ground. "This pilot refused to fly low and he released the spray from about 500 feet; this killed everything for a mile back from the river."

Jan, who works as an industrial chemist today, has experienced some health problems since Vietnam. "I keep feeling congestion at the top of my lungs; I'm always trying to clear my throat." After an examination at his local VA hospital, he was told they could find nothing wrong.

Lee Jurney commanded a helicopter unit attached to the 199th Light Infantry Brigade (nicknamed the "Red-catchers") in Vietnam during 1968 and 1969. His unit's area of operations was a twenty-five-mile arc around Saigon. For six months, Lee flew spray missions for the brigade's chemical unit. "At the end of six to eight hours of flying, we'd have the stuff stuck all over us. It was a white creamy fluid and smelled like a horse lathered down real bad. Your eyelids, the fingers of your gloves, stuck together like glue. We inhaled it, yet we weren't provided with any type of mask; it was a real bummer. All eight pilots in my unit rotated on these spray missions, but I flew a lot of them because I was an experienced low-level pilot. I probably got in over a hundred hours with defoliants. A month or two after I started these missions, our choppers were refitted with 200-gallon tanks with very long booms protruding out each side. Before that, we had dumped the defoliant directly from the 55-gallon shipping drums.

"We conducted lawn-mower style spraying. When I returned to Vietnam for another tour three years later, I could still tell easily where we'd sprayed."

Lee remembers the names of two U.S. firebases (Stephanie and Pineapple) around which he sprayed within a hundred yards of the emplacements, but he says that there were several others that got the same treatment.

Lee Jurney is a bitter man today. He's convinced that a tumor, which doctors discovered in his pituitary gland, was caused by his massive exposure to the defoliant. His experience with herbicides has "raised his consciousness" about other environmental concerns. Asked where he works now, Lee says: "Babcock and Wilcox. But," he hastens to add, "not in their nuclear reactor division."

Paul Steinke lives in San Diego today, where he attends law school. His wife has suffered four consecutive miscarriages which her doctors cannot explain. Paul feels that he underwent what he calls a "personality change" after he came home from Vietnam. He'd flown a helicopter there in support of the 101st Airborne Division in the northern part of South Vietnam. On several occasions he flew defoliation missions during which "we sprayed around friendly hamlets and firebases." Steinke remembers that the rotary blades of his helicopter would sometimes suck the spray right into the doorless cockpit.

So, with each pilot we interviewed, the evidence accumulated that the possibilities for exposure for U.S. servicemembers was much greater than the U.S. government has yet been willing to admit. In keeping with the contention that only a small group (the spray pilots) risked any substantial exposure to herbicides in Vietnam, President Carter announced on Memorial Day, 1979, that the air force would launch a study of the 1200 Ranch Hands. Jack Spey pledged the Ranch Hand Association's full cooperation in conducting the study. Within a month, nearly half of the spray unit veterans had been located, and the search continues.

In a sense, the issue has come full circle. The men who followed orders and dumped the chemicals, now find themselves the subject of the *only* epidemiological study of GIs which the government has been willing to undertake so far. Even by the end of their reunion in October 1978, there were signs that many of the Ranch Hands were feeling more sensitive to the health allegations, despite their posture of indifference. As the long weekend of boozing and eating drew to a close, we went out to a farewell dinner of enchiladas and tostadas with Jack Spey, Robby Robinson, and Hal Underwood. Several stacks of tortillas and rounds of Dos Equis beer later, we said good-bye to our hosts. Still uncomfortable with us and our opinions, Hal Underwood called us aside in the restaurant parking lot. There was just a trace of a plea in his voice as he shook our hands once more: "Don't forget, be good to us, won't you fellas?"

CHAPTER
8
As Ye Sow ... Science Joins the Air Force

For ten years, the United States armed forces in Vietnam sprayed the forests and croplands, the banks of waterways, and the perimeters of friendly base camps with chemicals especially designed to kill a broad variety of vegetation. Although these biocides were used as weapons, military planners reasoned that their use in Indochina did not constitute chemical warfare because the defoliants posed no hazard to the health of humans. Even the environment so obviously violated, they argued, would suffer no long-term effects.

The specific military objectives of defoliation were: (1) to strip the triple-canopy jungle cover so that the elusive guerrilla enemy could be flushed from his safe haven and engaged in conventional battle; (2) to clear thick foliage running down to the edge of canals and roadways and thus reduce the danger of ambush; (3) to clear and maintain fields of fire around artillery and infantry base camps and landing strips to enhance security and provide added protection against sapper infiltration and surprise attack; and (4) to impose additional hardship on the enemy by denying them their food crops.

In sum, the decision to employ chemical defoliants in the Vietnam War was, according to official policy, a decision to save American lives by modifying an environment that gave a decided advantage to the indigenous inhabitant—our clever and unconventional enemy.

As is often the case, the position of the U.S. government and its military establishment on the issue of herbicide safety was hardly the last word. And, understandably, the first to take issue with the U.S. disclaimer were the Vietnamese enemy, who leveled the charge of "germ warfare." Defoliation was a weapon of mass destruction and ecocide, they maintained. Far from being aimed at the Viet Cong fighter, it would be employed against a whole people and their environment, poisoning both and causing widespread starvation.

The two extreme positions concerning the use of herbicides in warfare were stated by the adversaries from the very inception of the defoliation program. The controversy would swell and heave for a full ten years, never far from stage center. In the end, however, the tide of history and of world opinion turned against the U.S. herbicidal-warfare program as it did against the validity of the overall American adventure in Indochina. In fact, the final act for the U.S. defoliation program preceded by several years the ultimate defeat of American and allied ground forces. But before the final chapter was written on herbicides, there were ten years of struggle, beginning with the cautious reservations of a few ecologically-minded scientists who feared permanent damage to the land, and culminating with the renunciation by an American president in 1975 of first use of herbicides in warfare.

In the pages that follow, we retrace the steps of the fight against the defoliation program and Agent Orange in particular. It's a fascinating history, and one of the most remarkable facts to emerge from our research is that *nowhere* in the vast literature concerning herbicide's potential for causing biological harm to humans is it even vaguely considered that several million American service members might have been harmed by their often daily exposure to the chemicals in Vietnam.

Just as war has been viewed as a legitimate extension of a nation's foreign policy, so have soldiers been regarded as merely another form of firepower, as anonymous and expendable as so many bullets. As a national archetype, like The Cop, or The Star, the GI has a certain stature, but the soldier as an individual has few rights and fewer advocates. It isn't surprising, therefore, that even those in the American antiwar movement, alarmed by the disastrous health toll they suspected the herbicides of taking on Vietnamese civilians and combatants alike, would ignore the GI who occupied such an ambiguous position among both the prowar and antiwar leadership.

Herbicides and *defoliants*: These words are not common to the vocabularies of most people. They belong to a family of chemicals called pesticides, and if you weren't raised on a farm or a ranch, chances are you wouldn't know a pesticide from Ajax-the-foaming cleanser; 2,4-D or 2,4,5-T might as well be the nemesis of R2D2 and C3PO in the sequel to *Star Wars,* rather than two of the most popular herbicides used by American farmers, ranchers, and foresters since the end of World War II.

Yet suburbanites have used these and similar chemicals for years in their battle against crabgrass. They know them simply as "weed killers." The utility companies and railroads have also liberally applied these weed killers along power lines and rights of way. In the fifties, chemicals were fun. At dusk in the summer, suburban kids all over the country eagerly awaited the DDT truck and then ran or rode their bikes the length of the block, weaving in and out of the oily mist. It had a nice smell, like gasoline. Who knew?

In any event, the air force didn't have far to look when it wanted an effective weed killer for its defoliation program: 2,4-D and 2,4,5-T, along with several other popular herbicides, were made to order for doing a job on hardwoods, broad-leaved vegetation, elephant grass, and even food crops.

During World War II and the Korean War, vast numbers of scientists were mobilized into the war effort and developed whole new systems of chemical, biological, and radiological (CBR) weapons. We've already traced the genesis of nuclear arms, and there are many parallels between their development and that of other CBR weapons. Just across the leafy campus where the world's first atomic reactor was being built under the football stadium, University of Chicago botanists toiled to unravel the mysteries of phenoxyacetic acids, whose ability to profoundly affect the metabolism of growing plants had only recently been discovered. (Ironically, the word "defoliant" is a misnomer; the chemicals are actually plant-growth regulators. You can apply a little growth regulator to a grapefruit tree, for example; let it grow to a commercially attractive size, and then pick it for the marketplace. Or, you can apply a little more, and the fruit will grow itself to death, literally exploding from the inside out.)

Working under a top-secret military contract, these scientists tested and refined the powerful herbicides, which could strip trees and other plants of their life-giving leaves with a single dusting. The new herbicides were rushed into production, and by June 1945 were adjudged ready for combat use against pockets of resistance in the densely jungled Pacific islands held by the Japanese. Then came the A-bomb, ending the war before herbicides could be tested on the battlefield.

Fifteen years later, herbicides got their chance to prove themselves as weapons in another war. In Vietnam, pockets of resistance to a U.S.-imposed regime were everywhere; and since neither of the two rival superpowers wished to provoke a nuclear holocaust over a mere localized conflict, the defoliation scheme was revived and tailored for the new tactical situation.

For Vietnam, the herbicides 2,4-D and 2,4,5-T were combined in a fifty/fifty mixture and shipped to Vietnam in fifty-five-gallon drums color-coded with an orange stripe. This mixture became known as Agent Orange and was the most widely used all-purpose defoliant. There was also Agent Purple (an earlier form of Orange used before 1965) and Agent White, which combined 2,4-D with the chemical Picloram and was used mostly for forest defoliation. A Dow product, Picloram is such a persistent herbicide, so long-lasting in the environment, that its use was never authorized by the federal government to aid the cultivation of any American crop. One early critic of the Vietnam defoliation program, Dr. Arthur Galston, a Yale biologist, called Picloram "a herbicidal analog of DDT."

Finally, there was Agent Blue, which was particularly effective against grassy plants and was used primarily against rice fields in the crop-destruction program. This herbicide, a solution of cacodylic acid, was highly poisonous, containing 54 percent arsenic.

Today's health controversy concerning the exposure of Vietnam veterans to toxic substances during combat has focused almost exclusively on Agent Orange, and 2,4,5-T in particular. Initially, however, criticism was leveled at the concept of defoliation, regardless of the herbicide employed. And, as mentioned, the early critics were primarily concerned about the herbicides' effect on Vietnam's environment rather than about the long-term human health effects of the sprays. Vietnamese reports that the spraying was making people and animals sick were dismissed out of hand by U.S. military officials as "Viet Cong propaganda." Yet even in the early days of the defoliation program, reports like the following from a Saigon-area doctor were not uncommon. After a chemical attack on a 2500-acre area with approximately 1000 inhabitants in October 1964, the doctor reported:

"At first [the people] felt sick and had some diarrhea, then they began to feel it hard to breathe and they had low blood pressure; some serious cases had trouble with their optic nerves and went blind. Pregnant women gave birth to stillborn or premature children. Most of the affected cattle died from serious diarrhea, and river fish floated on the surface of the water belly-up, soon after the chemicals were spread."

So persistent were the reports of human poisoning in the embattled nation that the United States was forced to respond through diplomatic channels to the allegations. The use of diplomacy in Western civilization, one should note, is very akin to the role taboos play in other cultures: It is thought that if you repeat something often enough, people will believe you, regardless of the improbability or even utter falsity of the statement. Thus, in March 1966, the State Department issued a report stating that "the herbicides used are nontoxic and not dangerous to man or animal life. The land is not affected for future use."

Despite the growing crescendo of reports to the contrary from Vietnam, critical American scientists had to soft-pedal their allegations, due to a lack of firm evidence as to the biological effects of herbicides. One persistent and effective early critic, however, was E. W. Pfeiffer, a member of the zoology department at the University of Montana, Missoula. He was active in the American Association for the Advancement of Science (AAAS), which Philip Boffey described in his book *The Brain Bank of America* as "closer to grass-root opinion in the scientific community than the elite National Academy of Science [NAS]." In June 1966, Professor Pfeiffer submitted a resolution to the Pacific division of AAAS proposing that since the United States was using chemical warfare agents against enemy forces in Vietnam without knowledge of the effects of these agents on biological systems, the AAAS should launch an immediate fact-finding investigation in the field.

The AAAS acted quickly to establish a committee, which expressed its deep concern about the use of chemical agents, and then just as quickly tried to pass the buck to none other than the "elite" NAS. The defoliation issue was political dynamite, and while the AAAS was definitely interested in it and would entertain the passions of men like Pfeiffer, science costs money and is one product that the Defense Department loves to buy. You might nibble around the edges once in a while, but you didn't bite the hand that fed you if doing so could be avoided.

Pfeiffer, of course, opposed the NAS's involvement. The NAS played the role of principal adviser to the Pentagon on its biological-warfare efforts, and, in addition, sponsored a postdoctoral research program at the army's biological-warfare center at Fort Dietrick, Maryland. The *New York Times* often refers to certain foreign newspapers as "semi-official" because of their favored and uncritical relationships with the governments they serve, so the National Academy of Science could just as easily be described as a "quasigovernmental" agency in relation to the U.S. government.

Though the AAAS was reluctant to become involved, its president did send a letter to the Defense Department stressing the necessity of a field investigation as Pfeiffer had urged; the interest of the AAAS had its effect within the Pentagon. If domestic opposition to defoliation began to grow to proportions it already had reached abroad, the generals reasoned, the continued use of chemical weapons could be jeopardized. Instead of a field study, however, the Pentagon chose to commission the Midwest Research Institute (MRI) of Kansas City, Missouri, to conduct a review of all published and unclassified literature "related to the ecological consequences of repeated or extended uses of herbicides, particularly those being used in Vietnam," and to consult with experts who were knowledgeable in these scientific areas. There would be no field study. Studying possible ecological damage in a war zone would be too dangerous, the Pentagon maintained; there would be time enough to conduct field investigations after hostilities ceased.

Men like Pfeiffer, naturally, feared that there would be little left of Vietnam's ecology if nothing was done until the war was over. The Pentagon's attitude, on the other hand, illustrates the arrogant folly of official American thinking—the assumption that victory was assured.

To lend greater credibility to the results of the MRI survey—on the assumption, again, that it would come out in support of their herbicide policy—Defense sought and obtained agreement from the NAS to review the Midwest Research Institute report. To accommodate the Pentagon, the NAS created a committee which Philip Boffey reports was heavily weighted with scientists experienced in the production and use of herbicides. The committee even included a scientist who worked for Dow Chemical, by far the major profiteer in the combat-herbicide market. Not surprisingly, the

NAS did not see fit to include any scientist critical of the use of herbicides in its self-proclaimed review panel of "disinterested experts."

It took MRI exactly three months to complete the herculean task of reviewing 1500 pieces of literature and querying more than 140 scientific experts. The report was a voluminous 369-page document, whose conclusions have been summed up in a single paragraph by author Philip Boffey:

"The greatest ecological consequences of using herbicides in Vietnam or anywhere is the destruction of vegetation, with the result that the region is set back to an earlier stage of development. . . . Lethal toxicity to humans, domestic animals or wildlife was highly unlikely. Data were inconclusive with respect to chronic toxicity and many other issues."

There can be no doubt that the library is a safer place to study the ecological damage of herbicides in combat than the battlefield. But even the NAS, in its January 1968 review of the MRI report, was forced to concede that the scientific literature provides far less about the ecological consequences of herbicides than it does about vegetation management, the principal concern of farmers and other major herbicide consumers. This mild criticism was further tempered by NAS president Dr. Frederick Seitz in a letter transmitting the NAS review to the Pentagon. After all, he wrote, the MRI report is "only a first step in investigating further the ecological consequences of the *intensive* use of herbicides" (italics ours).

It seemed clear that the Pentagon's strategy for handcuffing its university critics and keeping the scientific community generally in step with official herbicide policy was succeeding handily, but when even the pristine Library of Congress described the MRI report as "somewhat uncommittal [*sic*]," it was apparent that Defense had merely won a battle, not the war.

A word should be said about our emphasis of the word "intensive" in NAS president Seitz's letter. When herbicides like 2,4,5-T are sold for U.S. domestic use, their packaging contains instructions for both the application and safe use of the products. Domestic buyers are warned, for example, to avoid body contact with the agents and to avoid contamination of water supplies likely to be consumed by humans or animals. The concentration of 2,4,5-T employed during routine spray sorties in Vietnam was *thirteen* times that recommended by the manufacturers, and in an emergency the spray planes could jettison their entire load in seconds, thus exposing small areas to even greater toxicity. It is this intensive—in some cases, torrential—saturation of the land and its inhabitants with these chemicals (chemicals that even their manufacturers warn should be handled with extreme care) that was ignored, or at least severely underplayed, by the Midwest Research Institute report.

Professor Pfeiffer and the American Association for the Advancement of Science were, of course, displeased with the MRI report and its National Academy of Science review. Pfeiffer kept his comments to the obvious—they had not dealt with the long-term effects of herbicides—and he reiterated his demand, echoed by the AAAS, for a field investigation of the defoliated areas. It should be noted that during the year that Pfeiffer and the AAAS had struggled to take positive action leading to the abolition of the defoliation program (1967), the air-force Ranch Hands had doubled the amount of spray used the previous year—more than they would spray in any subsequent year of the program.

Ultimately Pfeiffer grew tired of waiting for the various powers that be to initiate any appropriate action. Along with another zoologist, Gordon H. Orians of the University of Washington, Seattle, he obtained private funding for a field expedition to Vietnam. Pfeiffer was not only anxious to begin the lengthy task of gathering evidence to discredit the defoliation program; he also was determined to demonstrate that a worthwhile study could be performed under battlefield conditions and with limited financial resources.

Once in Vietnam, Pfeiffer and Orians found that herbicide damage to that country's ecology had been extensive. While they heard numerous reports of illness among humans and ani-

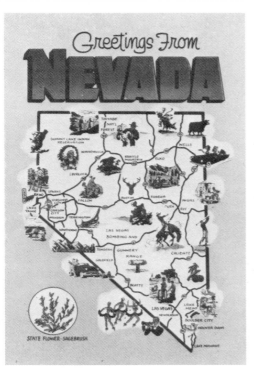

Greetings From NEVADA

STATE FLOWER-SAGEBRUSH

NO DANGER

Atomic Energy Commission officials declare there is no danger to travel over Nevada highways from radioactive "fall out particles." U S 95, The Bonanza Highway, courses nearest the Yucca Flat test site, 45 miles north of Las Vegas. General terrain, colorful panorama, and expansive solitude of the Nevada desert are strikingly impressive along that highway. No restrictions are in force, but security measures at Mercury, the post of entry to the test site, are in force at all times.

An atomic cloud as seen from Las Vegas, approximately 60 miles away.

The "Met" shot, April 15, 1955; part of the Operation Teapot series. The thin lines are ribbons of smoke from high explosive charges used to chart wind direction.

Above: A silent dinner party, part of a simulation of a typical American home. The house, specially constructed to show the blast's effects, was 7,500 feet from ground zero; Operation Doorstep, March 17, 1953. *Below:* Dinner's end.

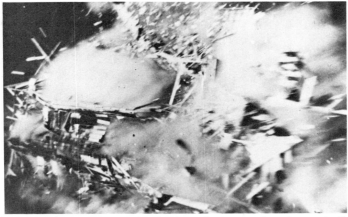

Going, going, gone . . . Again, a typical suburban house built on the test site for one purpose—to be destroyed. Operation Doorstep, March 17, 1953.

Troops huddle in the trenches in preparation for the "Turk" shot; March 1955, Teapot series. Often these open trenches were only a little over a mile from ground zero.

A few miles behind such trenches, men sitting in open fields shield their eyes from the "Hood" shot, the largest domestic detonation in United States history, on July 6, 1957.

Decontamination, army style: brushing away radiation with a broom.

An MP makes sure traffic runs
smoothly at the test site.

GIs watching the most publicized test shot, "Smoky," on August 27, 1957. U.S. public health officials are currently investigating the health of GIs present at this shot only.

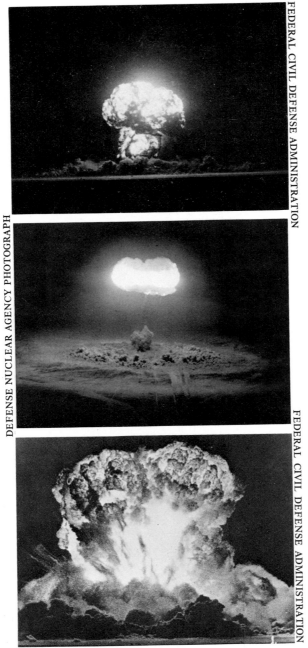

Almost all tests were detonated just before dawn. The blasts churned up the desert and created enormous irradiated dust clouds.

Corporal Jim O'Connor in 1954, at age nineteen.

Jim O'Connor (center) in 1979. The men of Wire Team B are reunited for the first time in twenty-five years outside a Philadelphia courthouse. Other Teapot veterans are, left to right: Howard Hinkie, Ned Giles, Jerry Dobbs, Nick Mazzuco.

MICHAEL UHL

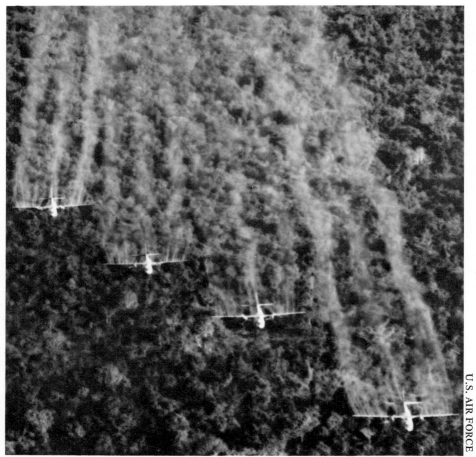

Vietnam: Air Force C-123s lay down a carpet of toxic herbicides across the countryside.

Above: The Ranch Hand insignia—a brown swath across a field of green. The Chinese symbol stands for "purple." *Below:* Loading the planes with Agent Purple, the first herbicide used in Vietnam.

THE PURPLE PEOPLE EATER

"Smilin'" Jack Spey, president of the Ranch Hand Association.

Pete Spivey and Charlie Hubbs model their custom-made shirts with the traditional insignia and brown swath at the 1978 Ranch Hands reunion at Eglin Air Force Base, Florida.

"Patches," the most decorated spray plane of the Vietnam War. It took over 1,000 hits from ground fire.

Unloading 55-gallon drums of Agent Orange. It was pumped from these smaller drums into one huge tank for storage and then transferred to the spray planes.

James "Peewee" Fortenbury.

Coauthor Lt. Michael Uhl, with the 11th Light Infantry near Duc Pho, Vietnam, 1968.

Low-flying C-123 spray plane lays down swaths of Agent Orange.

roops move through a defoliated rea 70 miles south of Saigon, arly 1970. Note dead mangroves 1 foreground, resulting in long-rm soil erosion; this area will re-ain devastated for years.

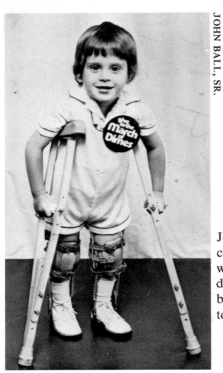

John Ball, Jr., national poster child for the March of Dimes. He was born with a congenital birth defect, which researchers fear may be linked to his father's exposure to dioxin.

Actor Martin Sheen, star of *Apocalypse Now*, makes a public service film short alerting GIs to Agent Orange dangers. Flanking him are Lee Meyrowitz and John Ball, both Vietnam veterans.

mals living in sprayed areas, they were unable to confirm these accounts scientifically. As environmentalists, however, they were able to confirm that defoliants had caused the near-permanent destruction of ancient forests and of much of the commercial timberlands and rubber cultures.

They also returned from Vietnam with a profound understanding of the deeper meaning of technological warfare and its ultimate consequences. Reporting on their trip in an article for *Science* magazine, they wrote:

> In Vietnam the chemical weapons of a technologically advanced society are being used massively for the first time in a guerrilla war. In this conflict, there are no battle lines, no secure territory and no fixed, permanent military installations which can serve as targets for attack. Rather, the military efforts are aimed at increasing the toll of fatalities, denying food to the enemy and depriving him of cover and concealment afforded by natural growth. This type of warfare is, therefore, extremely destructive, both of human lives and environment.

Following Pfeiffer and Orians's pioneering fieldwork accomplished in the midst of a shooting war, the AAAS finally was moved to create the Herbicide Assessment Commission (HAC) in late 1969. Matthew S. Meselson, a Harvard biologist, was named to head the commission and to direct a full-scale field investigation. The choice of Meselson to head the HAC was a brilliant political maneuver by the AAAS board of directors. A member of the National academy of Sciences with impeccable scientific credentials, Meselson was also a long-standing critic of chemical-biological warfare. He was, in fact, already on record as opposing the use of defoliant weapons in Vietnam.

Meselson is a man in whom politics and science hang in a delicate balance: Each has its own set of rules, one often based on instinct and the other dependent upon empirical findings. In the case of wartime defoliation, science had yet to produce definitive evidence to support the political conclusion to halt the spraying on the grounds of its measurable long-term effect on humans and the environment. This reality no doubt created a conflict for Meselson the man of science. Unlike the pro-herbicide scientists who often owed both their training and livelihood to the chemical manufacturers, Meselson believed that the lack of evidence worked both ways. The chemicals in question had never been properly tested by their producers as to their long-term safety. The political issue thus became for Meselson and other cautious men of science a question of who should shoulder the burden of proof. It was from this perspective that Meselson in 1966 had helped his colleague at Harvard, Dr. John Edsall to collect the signatures of 5000 scientists on a petition to President Lyndon Johnson. The petition had called upon the president to stop the spraying on the grounds that it constituted "a dangerous precedent" in chemical and biological warfare.

Meselson and his HAC team of three associates did not arrive in Vietnam for their study until August 1970. When they went, however, they were armed with some very powerful and shocking new evidence of the herbicides' potential danger to humans. In the political arena, this evidence led to the rapid winding down of the defoliation program in Vietnam and the first major restrictions in the domestic use of herbicides.

In mid-1969, before the AAAS announced it would send a research team to Vietnam, a member of Ralph Nader's Raiders, Anita Johnson, showed Meselson some data from a laboratory report that had been leaked to her from a friend at the Food and Drug Administration (FDA). The data showed that small doses of 2,4,5-T and slightly larger doses of 2,4-D cause birth defects in rats and mice. The significance of these data was not lost on Dr. Meselson. The question of herbicide toxicity had become a public issue after the publication and popular reception of Rachel Carson's book *The Silent Spring* in 1962, a plea for environmental sanity. Even the MRI report had hinted about the toxicity of 2,4-D, albeit from the great distance of a disinterested and neutral observer, urging the reader to "form his own opinion of the hazard associated with the use of 2,4-D compounds." As for 2,4,5-T, the MRI report noted only that it "resembles 2,4-D in its toxicity to animals and fish, but is a little more toxic."

This newly revealed FDA laboratory report, however, was hard data from a government-sponsored study—a study that had, moreover, been commissioned five years earlier and, in the case of its preliminary conclusions, been concealed for political reasons since 1965.

An account of these events from John Lewallen's eloquent paperback *Ecology of Devastation: Indochina* is worth quoting in its entirety:

> In 1964, the National Cancer Institute of the Health, Education and Welfare Department (HEW) commissioned the Bionetics Laboratory to test various widely used pesticides and industrial compounds for carcinogenic and teratogenic [fetus-deforming] effects on laboratory animals. By the summer of 1965, the Bionetics Laboratory had obtained results indicating that 2,4,5-T in small doses causes birth defects in mice. Late in 1966, Bionetics had completed a preliminary report on 2,4,5-T. Officials of the Food and Drug Administration (FDA) knew of this report by 1968 and officials of the Agriculture and Defense departments learned about it in 1969. No one else saw the Bionetics Report.

Lewallen states that a former White House staff member told the Nader group that "disclosure of the report would have fueled the antiwar movement and fed international criticism of American chemical warfare." Dow Chemical also applied pressure, according to FDA officials, to keep the public from knowing the truth. For Dow, this was merely another step in its long history of denying the toxicity of herbicides and distorting or concealing evidence that threatened its manufacturing interests.

In any case, the cat was now out of the bag and yowling for

attention. The results of the Bionetics study had been treated like state secrets instead of scientific information of vital interest to the safety and health of the public. Viet Cong "propaganda" alleging that herbicides had caused miscarriages, stillbirths, and gross birth abnormalities would now have to be reexamined in light of this "new" evidence.

Dow, of course, rushed to its own defense. According to Dow, the sample used by Bionetics was not representative of most 2,4,5-T; it had inadvertently been heavily contaminated with an impurity produced during the manufacture of the herbicide, which, Dow maintained, was ordinarily present in 2,4,5-T only in trace quantities. The official chemical name for the impurity is 2,3,7,8-tetrachlorodibenzo-para-dioxin— TCDD for short, or simply dioxin. TCDD, said Dow, was present in the Bionetics sample at a level of fifteen to thirty parts per million, whereas the then-current Dow product had been cleaned up considerably and contained less than one part dioxin per million.

Another 2,4,5-T producer, Hercules, subsequently commissioned Bionetics Laboratory to repeat its earlier study with what the manufacturers were now calling the "pure" 2,4,5-T. The results, at least temporarily, confirmed Dow's explanation. But these results conflicted with those of another replica of the Bionetics experiment conducted by the National Institute of Environmental Health Sciences (NIEHS). The NIEHS results showed that even "pure" 2,4,5-T caused birth defects in the lab animals exposed. The conflict between the Hercules-sponsored Bionetics study and the NIEHS results was soon easily resolved. Someone had misplaced a decimal point in the Hercules study, resulting in their rats being fed one-tenth the amount of herbicide fed to the NIEHS animals. The Bionetics results were also subsequently confirmed by Dow itself, and by the Food and Drug Administration. Scientists were still in the dark, however, on the question of *which* chemical compound was the potent fetus-deforming agent— 2,4,5-T itself, or its contaminant, dioxin. Ongoing experimentation, while not fully exonerating the herbicide, hastened to show that dioxin may be the most toxic and teratogenic chemical compound ever discovered.

In his book *Defoliation: What Are Herbicides Doing To Us?* Thomas Whiteside gives an account of an interpretation of one remarkable dioxin experiment. Whiteside, staff writer for *The New Yorker* magazine, has become the veritable Tom Paine of American journalism on the dangers of herbicides and the insidiousness of dioxin, sounding the alarm in numerous excellent books and articles over the past decade.

Whiteside says that an FDA researcher, Dr. Jacqueline Verrett, discovered extensive defects in chick embryos she had treated with one-part-per-trillion dioxin per gram of egg. The results showed the dioxin was a million times more potent a fetus-deforming agent than the dreaded thalidomide had been found to be in similar tests on chicks.

Whiteside goes on to put this study into a perspective that is difficult to dismiss. "Even if, for theoretical purposes, we reduced the teratogenic power of the dioxin, as shown in Dr. Verrett's chick-embryo studies, approximately a million times, we would *still* have to consider that we are dealing with a substance as teratogenically potent as thalidomide."

Now, it is true, as Whiteside points out, that "chick embryos are far down the biological ladder from human fetuses." Still, Verrett's study showed that there was ample reason to be concerned about the potential hazard to human health, especially in Vietnam where the 2,4,5-T used in herbicides contained as much as *47 parts-per-million dioxin.*

Since the end of World War II, the introduction of toxic chemicals into the American home and work environments had increased geometrically, and the public had tended to view this increasing use of chemicals as a step in the never-ending forward march of technological progress. It would take a war where chemicals like herbicides were employed overtly as weapons to awaken us to the reality that we were using these same weapons (albeit to a far lesser degree) against ourselves. Ailments for which previously there had been no known cause began to be understood by many to stem from the unperceived and untested side effects of "technological progress."

The political heat of opposition to the defoliation program was turned up considerably after the Bionetics study became public. As a result, on October 29, 1969, President Richard Nixon's science adviser, Dr. Lee Du Bridge, issued a statement announcing a series of actions, including the restriction of the use of 2,4,5-T in Vietnam "to areas remote from the population."

The White House response to the Bionetics findings seemed decisive, but it became obvious the very next day that it would bring about few changes of essence in the military's use of herbicides. The *Washington Post* reported that "the Defense Department feels its present policy conforms to the new presidential directive." The meaning of this was clear: The military was claiming that the spray program had *always* been restricted to remote areas.

Accounts from Vietnamese villages indicated that this policy had certainly *not* been followed in the past. In addition, it was standard operating procedure for the C-123 spray aircraft to lay down herbicides on enemy base camps and training and regroupment centers, areas almost certainly populated some of the time. But the piece of evidence that perhaps most damningly gives the lie to the Pentagon statement was the relentless spraying of American base camps and landing zones "populated" by millions of American GIs during the course of the war. The spraying of *these* population centers continued even beyond the last defoliation missions aimed at the enemy and the people of South Vietnam.

In 1970, the public already was beginning to feel the thorns in what had been presented as a harmless bunch of roses. By March of that year, responding to mounting political opposition, the Pentagon was forced to announce a 25-percent reduction in its spraying operations in Vietnam.

A month later, Senator Philip Hart of Michigan held hearings where evidence was introduced to further discredit defoliation. It was during these hearings that confirmation of the Bionetics experiments was demonstrated with samples of 2,4,5-T containing the new low levels of the dioxin contaminant.

At an earlier set of congressional hearings in December 1969, Dr. Arthur Galston, the Yale biologist, summarized what was perhaps the key political point to be made concerning the widespread use of herbicides. He said that in "some twenty-five years after the first introduction of the chlorinated phenoxyacetic acids like 2,4-D and 2,4,5-T . . . there have not been published before this year adequate toxicological data to support their extensive use in agriculture."

It must be emphasized that 2,4,5-T was only one of ten compounds Bionetics Labs found to be teratogenic in the small sample of pesticides tested; the other primary ingredient of Agent Orange, 2,4-D, also was found to cause birth defects in animals. But, 2,4-D was not really under political fire, perhaps because it was one of the most popular pesticides in use by American wheat and corn farmers. In fact, the discovery of this synthetic had so excited the scientific establishment that the original pound of 2,4-D is enshrined in the Smithsonian Institution. In 1969, U.S. sales of 2,4-D reached $25 million. Thus, when the Defense Department finally announced on April 15, 1970, within a week of the Hart Senate hearings, that it was suspending the use of Agent Orange in Vietnam pending review, its purpose was to halt the spraying of 2,4,5-T, not its companion component, 2,4-D. Agent White, the other defoliant containing 2,4-D, would continue to be sprayed.

At the same time the military moved against Agent Orange in Vietnam, the newly created Environmental Protection Agency (EPA) issued an order banning further use of 2,4,5-T on croplands and for home weed killing. However, under the EPA's rules, Dow and the other 2,4,5-T manufacturers were allowed to continue production while the issue was being fought in the courts. Dow, fearing a "domino effect" against chemicals in general, was determined not to lose the 2,4,5-T battle. And, at the time, it didn't. Firm evidence linking human health problems to herbicide exposure was lacking and ultimately Dow prevailed on narrow legal technicalities. In June 1974, the EPA was forced to withdraw its ban. The chemical manufacturers had managed to win the courts as allies in shifting the burden of proof on the issue of herbicide safety from themselves to their critics, including the fledgling EPA.

In the meantime, although the American critics of chemical warfare were scoring some impressive victories, they were dealing with the most tenacious of foes, the U.S. Pentagon, which by now was more committed to defoliation than ever. While field commanders were increasingly disillusioned with the tactical value of the spray programs, high-level military officials in Vietnam had found a new rationale—an unforeseen strategic purpose—for continuing it. The denial of cover and concealment and the destruction of foodcrops, they said, had little effect on the enemy but did have a telling impact on the civilian population living in the countryside under the political control of the National Liberation Front.

A 1967 government-financed study by the Rand Corporation "think tank" had estimated that more than 325,000 Vietnamese villagers had been affected by the spraying. Millions of peasants, tied to their ancestral villages for generations by tradition and religious custom, were being bombed and sprayed into urban areas controlled by the government of South Vietnam and secured by American military presence. From a battlefield perspective, the air force viewed removal of people from the countryside as one of the real gains of crop destruction.

On a more lofty—some might say demonic—strategic plane, the "generating" of refugees was not only forecast as the path to victory in Indochina but was seen to have vast global implications for American power. Such was the view of one of the war's architects, Samuel P. Huntington of Harvard. Huntington was considered an archvillain by the American antiwar movement, a reputation well deserved. His capacity to reduce human suffering to the banal prose of strategic thinking was unsurpassed, as illustrated by the following infamous passage from an article for *Foreign Affairs* in July 1968:

> In an absent-minded way the United States in Viet Nam may well have stumbled upon the answer to "wars of national liberation." The effective response lies neither in the quest for conventional military victory nor in the esoteric doctrines and gimmicks of counter-insurgency warfare. It is instead forced-draft urbanization and modernization which rapidly brings the country in question out of the phase in which a rural revolutionary movement can hope to generate sufficient strength to come to power.
>
> Time in South Viet Nam is increasingly on the side of the Government. But in the short term, with half the population still in the countryside, the Viet Cong will remain a powerful force which cannot be dislodged from its constituency so long as the constituency continues to exist.

The spirit of this statement is not unlike the bland conclusion drawn by the authors of the Midwest Research Institute report that one consequence of defoliation would be to return Vietnam's ecology to "an earlier stage of development." Air Force General Curtis LeMay was perhaps the crudest articulator of this devastation model for total victory regardless of the means. He had advocated introducing battlefield nuclear weapons to bomb the Vietnamese "back to the Stone Age."

What can account for the viciousness with which these unprecedented chemical weapons were hurled against this tiny nation of warriors?

Policies like defoliation reflected more than a national obsession with victory in Vietnam at any cost; in their brutality, they reflected an unconscious knowledge that defeat was inevitable. If Vietnam could not ultimately be held by the United States, then there was no limit or accountability to preclude the devastation of the countryside by U.S. weapons.

A Vietnamese poem by Ngo Vinh Long gives us an exquisite portrait in miniature of whom the United States was fighting and what was at stake from the point of view of the enemy.

> On this land
> where each blade of grass is human hair
> each foot of soil is human flesh
> where it rains blood
> life must flower

There were, of course, critics of the program within the government. The 1967 Rand study already mentioned painted a dim picture of defoliation's effects on the campaign to win the "hearts and minds" of the Vietnamese peasantry. A Rand survey found that 88 percent of the villagers interviewed blamed the United States and the South Vietnamese government for the destruction of their crops, and 74 percent expressed "outright hatred."

But the top staff at headquarters, Military Assistance Command Vietnam (MACV), had long abandoned the "hearts and minds" notion to outcommunist the Communists. This attitude of the brass was reflected as frustration in the attitude of the typical American foot soldier, as expressed in the following GI homily: "There's only one way to win the war in Vietnam. Separate all the good Vietnamese from the bad Vietnamese. Put the good Vietnamese on ships and sail them into the South China Sea. Nuke all the bad Vietnamese. Then, sink the ships."

And so, defoliation would roll merrily along for more than a year after the Pentagon's self-imposed ban on the combat use of Agent Orange.

In the meantime, however, Matthew Meselson and his company, Herbicide Assessment Commission, were preparing to arrive in Vietnam to finally accomplish the field investigation that Pfeiffer and the AAAS had been calling for since 1966. The Herbicide Assessment Commission was able to secure an enormous amount of logistical support from the U.S. Agency for International Development (AID) and the South Vietnamese army once the team arrived in the country. In addition to food and lodging, they were provided transportation, within reason, to wherever they wanted to travel. They were barred only from areas being hotly contested by the opposing forces at that moment.

But the most significant piece of support Dr. Meselson and HAC had sought was denied by the Pentagon. Before leaving, Meselson had requested that the military declassify data giving the location and dates of the spray missions and the identity and amount of the agent applied. The Defense Department refused. The HAC scientists had wanted to compare sprayed areas with those that had not been defoliated, and Meselson considered his inability to obtain this crucial information a major detriment to the success of their investigation.

Nevertheless, Meselson and his associates were able to prepare a preliminary report for presentation to the annual AAAS convention, held in December 1970. Like Pfeiffer and Orians's report of the previous year, the HAC tended to concentrate on the damage that defoliation had caused the environment, but they also uncovered certain disquieting (though generally unsubstantiated) reports of adverse health effects. One heavily sprayed province had reported a disproportionately high rate of stillborns, and at a large Saigon hospital there was a reported increase in two types of birth defects during the years of intensive spraying. One of the birth defects was spina bifida, an abnormality that apparently is showing up—perhaps in epidemic numbers—among the children of Vietnam veterans. . . .

John Ball is a Vietnam veteran whose son was born with spina bifida. John did thirteen months and one day with the Twenty-sixth Marines in I Corps, the northern war zone of South Vietnam. The Twenty-sixth hit the beach near Da Nang in 1966, in an invasion that was hyped back home in the style of the great World War II battles.

But this wasn't World War II. It was Vietnam. And for all their over-the-top, charge-the-hill bravado, these tactics were not suited to a guerrilla war. The marines were linear while the Vietcong threw nothing but curves. During their first sweep, the Vietcong really put the hurt on "C" Company, John Ball's unit. Twenty were dead and wounded. That was half the company.

"From the first time someone got killed, I knew this was bullcrap. I didn't belong here," John said, wincing perhaps unconsciously. "But, I had a very positive attitude. From the beginning, I said to myself, I'm going home and that's it."

As a squad leader, John tried to protect himself and his men as much as possible. One evening, the squad was sent out to spring a night ambush on some NVA (North Vietnamese Army) units operating in the area. Rather than lead his men to the designated map coordinates, when he spotted a rundown pagoda he suggested they go in and spend the night there. To hell with the ambush.

When they filed into the base camp the following morning, John learned that the position they were to have staked out had been heavily mortared throughout the night. His squad had been given up for dead. John gave his commanding officer some bull story about being pinned down the whole time, having lost their radio to an incoming round.

"You're fulla crap," said the commanding officer with a shrug, dismissing his young corporal. The officer took the long view. After all, the easiest thing you could do in Vietnam was die. Staying alive could take real imagination. On the minus side, Ball's squad didn't come back with any kills; on the plus side, no GIs bought it either. Charlie nothing, jar-heads nothing. Tomorrow would be another day.

For John Ball, there were thirteen months and one day of tomorrows, all of them in the field. And most days on patrol, danger couldn't be skirted. It was either you or one of your buddies, he felt. The whole country was booby-trapped, and a trip wire was always lying around to spoil someone's day. *Wham!* A toe-popper would take off the point man's foot as though it were clay, and off in the distance an old papa-san ploughing his rice field wouldn't even turn around.

"VC here, old man. Where VC, you old fucker?"

"Khong biet, khong biet! Khong Viet Cong."

"You no bik, old man? Don't know Viet Cong, huh, shit-for-brains . . ."

It made you want to kill the old man. Charlie must have been nearby in his spider hole, laughing his ass off just waiting for the next GI to hit the next wire.

Ball is matter-of-fact when he recalls, "I came close to getting killed many times. One time, it was the guy just in front of me, another time, the guy right behind."

When Ball describes himself in Vietnam, he sounds a little like Cacciato in Tim O'Brien's novel, *Going after Cacciato.* Cacciato snapped his gum at night when his squad dug in. Sometimes, he'd sit for hours fishing on the edge of a bomb crater filled with monsoon rain and completely disconnected from any sea. In Nam, Ball felt, you had to keep going through the motions or you'd forget how to live in the world across the great pond. Ball carried a transistor instead of extra ammo and listened to rock 'n' roll on the armed forces station. "Hang on Sloopy, Sloopy hang on . . ." Hang on to that New York savvy as though it were a talisman against that one bullet someone was making in Hanoi with his name on it.

Today, even after thirteen years, John Ball sometimes feels bitter about the war. Other times he feels that one could just look at it for what it was and try to write it off, let it go. Ball's feelings about the war have now become facts.

"The war was a big ripoff," he says, "a waste of time. People were dying for nothing. You'd always get the feeling you were fighting the wrong people. Now, the NVA, you could respect them. You couldn't love 'em but you could respect 'em. But, I hated the South Vietnamese. We were fighting their war. So, when you heard of things like My Lai, you thought, 'Sure, it's wrong.' But you understood where it came from. The South Vietnamese deserved it."

These are not the words one expects to hear from John Ball.

Reason seems to rule his exterior; but these words represent the dark side where many vets store their painful memories.

In the medical questionnaire he filled in for the organization Citizen Soldier, Ball checked "yes" to the question that asked: "Do you ever have violent rages?" He works the late night shift on an obscure New York subway line and rides empty trains to avoid the dangers of too many people crushed into too few trains. He has complained of a host of chronic physical and nervous problems since coming home from Vietnam.

Didn't the GIs say it every day? Write it on their flak jackets? "When I die I'll surely go to heaven 'cause I've already spent my time in hell!"

John Ball is a gentleman, a family man, a solid citizen and a trade union American; he also may be a victim of Agent Orange poisoning. Everywhere his team operated had been defoliated; many times they ate the fruit or drank the water where the herbicide had come down.

Five parts Agent Orange, twenty parts brutalization: it's hard to sort out the causes from the effects you see in so many vets. What does a twenty-year-old kid know about brutality? Back home on the streets of Queens John Ball had thought brutality was a few snarls at some sap who didn't belong on the block.

But Ball got a bellyful of real brutality from the war and from those glorious marines. First, they tried to beat the New York "fuck it" attitude out of him. In Basic, he spent his first two weeks in the Corrective Custody Platoon for refusing to be punished for somebody else's screw-up.

For two weeks, it was up at dawn. "Strip, on your belly, on your back, on your feet." Running the perimeter of Parris Island with a rucksack full of rocks. Ball didn't want the marines like they wanted him. He was part of the first group drafted by the marine corps in 1965. They never won his respect or his submission. But he was cool enough to take his attitude underground and survive.

The marines may have been brutal, but they weren't "bad." "The 'baddest' man I ever saw," says Ball, "was an NVA lieutenant with his leg blown off who spat in a dude's face when our squad captured him." While the Americans, he said, did chicken shit things like throw prisoners off helicopters and took their frustrations out on the peasants because they almost never got their hands on Victor Charlie (the Viet Cong).

In the end, it was just a hard war for vets to bring home. There's a truth to the war that's never been grasped, only dimly perceived. Part of the answer is in the vets.

All in all, though, John Ball is doing well. But the parts of him that aren't all right, he thinks can be traced to Vietnam. And he believes that the war and Agent Orange also have made a victim of his son. He may be right.

When Carol Ball went into labor, John rushed home from his job and drove his wife to the hospital. Their doctor, seeing that delivery was not imminent, told John to go home; he'd be called as soon as anything began to happen. (This was the Balls' first child, born almost ten years ago; the natural-childbirth phenomenon, with the father participating fully in his child's birth, had yet to penetrate the thickly traditional skin of New York working-class culture.)

Later that night, John passed the time with his brother in the husbands' room, which he remembers as dingy and impersonal. Finally, he was called to the phone; it was the doctor calling from upstairs outside the delivery room. He got right to the point. "Come up here, John," he said. "We have a problem."

John rushed upstairs and found that Carol had delivered a baby boy who was in great distress. The doctor wasn't sure the infant would pull through. To complicate things, the baby had an open wound in his tiny spine.

Suddenly, while they talked, John heard the strong crying of an infant from within the nursery. They entered the room, and the doctor was shocked to see the weakened baby, whose life he had feared for just moments before, screaming and full of life. But there was still that strange open wound. A specialist was called in who immediately diagnosed the problem as spina bifida. The baby would have to be operated on within eighteen hours and the spine closed by surgery.

Today, John, Jr., is a handsome and alert nine-year-old.

Both his size and his sense of presence suggest an older boy. When we saw him last, he had come down with chicken pox, an unwanted gift from his kid sister, Melissa, so he sat around in the backyard of the Balls' suburban Long Island home in his wheelchair. Normally, he would be on his feet, walking with the aid of braces and crutches.

Young John has no feeling in his legs from the knees down. Still, Carol Ball says they were lucky that their son's condition was as benign as it is. Spina bifida is a developmental birth defect in which the baby's spine fails to fully join. Eighty percent of the babies thus afflicted also develop water on the brain (hydrocephalus) within the first three months of birth.

John and Carol Ball are now members of the Spina Bifida Association of America. One board member gave us an extraordinary account of a meeting of the non-profit group's Nassau County, Long Island chapter. This woman, who has been the mainstay and president of the suburban New York chapter for many years, told of a Spring 1979 meeting in which the relationship of Agent Orange to spina bifida was discussed.

Of those attending, mostly mothers of children with the birth defect, the question was asked, "How many of you are married to Vietnam veterans?" Of the fifty people present, thirty-five were reported to have raised their hands!

This was in fact extraordinary. If we were able to show that in one segment of this grassroots organization 70 percent of the fathers served in Vietnam and were at least potentially exposed to herbicides, a giant leap forward would be taken in the quest to prove a cause and effect relationship between birth defects in humans and contamination by the highly suspect defoliants.

Unfortunately, after tantalizing us with this scientific blockbuster, our source later refused to help us contact any of the meeting participants, so we might verify her story.

Her reason was that the fathers of the afflicted children already felt "enough guilt," and their wives were reluctant to "get involved" in any public discussion of their "personal tragedies," preferring instead to protect their husbands from further pain resulting from the knowledge that their experience in combat may somehow be connected to their child's genetic damage.

This is certainly an understandable, if somewhat backward attitude concerning the reality of birth defects, considering the incredible pain all parents of such children must certainly feel. But there can be pain without guilt; pain is not synonymous with responsibility. The parents of spina bifida children should not feel personally responsible for the host of environmental insults that constantly bombard and weaken human genetic material. Responsibility for these violations of humanity can and must be located firmly in a social and economic system where the powerful are often allowed to pursue their destructive private interests at the expense of the public safety. The defoliation program and the continued irresponsible domestic uses of chemicals like 2,4,5-T and 2,4-D are cases in point.

Much more is to be gained by pinpointing rather than ignoring the causes of human afflictions like spina bifida. Some parents of such children might even be heartened by this knowledge. John and Carol Ball, for example, who belong to the Nassau group, but did not attend the meeting in question, were also unsuccessful in their attempt to get fellow members to come forward and corroborate this powerful information. John Ball believes that by knowing the cause of his son's spina bifida, he'll actually take the monkey off his own back. Not only that, but his family might then receive some modicum of justice from the responsible parties. And, he says, of even greater importance, each cause of these genetic birth defects that can be isolated will help us protect future generations from the affliction he and his family have suffered.

Not wanting to let the matter simply rest at this point of impasse, we appealed to the president of the national Spina Bifida Association to push for further investigation around the startling allegations. Our request was met with polite but unresponsive disregard. One association member speculated that the organization leadership was afraid that by getting spina bifida involved in a political controversy, especially one connected to Vietnam, it might hamper ambition to upgrade the group on a par with the gargantuan March of Dimes. Traditional "health" organizations shy away from connecting their particular disease or condition with any government policy, depending as they do on public funds for survival.

The meeting anecdote told to us may have been the embellishment of an extremely committed mother and health activist to gain publicity for the almost unknown number two birth defect in America. Or it may be disturbingly true. It certainly is frustrating not to be able to provide proof of this account, which if accurate would mean such an important advance of knowledge for science and Vietnam veterans alike. For the time being, the matter must remain open-ended; here is a lead that surely will be picked up with enthusiasm by subsequent investigators, be they scientists or journalists.

Evidence of a possible high incidence of spina bifida among the children of Vietnam veterans is trickling in through other sources, as well. In the health follow-up studies being carried out by Citizen Soldier and other veterans' groups, a large number of spina bifida cases already have been logged. And while the hard statistical evidence that children of Vietnam veterans suffer disproportionately from this abnormality is lacking, many indicators are pointing toward this conclusion.

When the question of spina bifida among the offspring of Vietnam vets is juxtaposed with the findings of Matthew Meselson's herbicide assessment team in 1970—which suggested that this birth defect increased sharply in at least one region of South Vietnam coincident with the time period defoliants were sprayed—we see how the subtle signals from the prophets of the opposition, whether in science or politics, are conveniently overlooked. Policy makers are more committed to the justification rather than the truthful evaluation of their programs. Even when proven false and dangerous, a policy like defoliation already has gathered such ideological momentum that by the time it is discontinued, it still must be justified as correct. That this is particularly true for defoliation is obvious, since the case against herbicidal warfare carried vast implications for the domestic use of herbicides. The chemical industries, along with the farm, range, and lumber interests, would close ranks with military professionals to perpetuate the guarded myth that herbicides pose no danger to human health. Every effort would be made to ensure that the lessons of the military experience with defoliants would have little impact on the domestic herbicide market. Massive doses of government and industry public relations rhetoric have been endlessly available to drug the public awareness. In the Vietnam war, truth, as Aeschylus first noted, was the first casualty.

Because of the prestige and scientific reliability of the Meselson report described earlier, its publication was a source of great discomfort to officialdom despite the outpouring of government propaganda supporting defoliation. It put Washington in a bad light and some officials evidently decided it now would have to be placed in perspective. In 1970 Congress, under heavy pressure from the military establishment, appropriated funds for "a comprehensive study and investigation" on the effects of Vietnam defoliation, by the National Academy of Sciences. The Defense Department would administer the contract.

The idea of an academy, especially an Academy of Science, is enshrined deep in the tabernacle of sacred national myths. The NAS was to the AAAS as a full house is to three of a kind. The Academy was the precise instrument needed to blunt the edge of the report of its grassroots rival.

The National Academy of Sciences therefore was mustered out to regain some ground for a national ego bruised by both the charge and the reality that the U.S. was engaged in chemical warfare in Vietnam. The Academy sent a team of investigators to Vietnam for a "thorough" investigation—one which essentially only retraced the steps of their AAAS predecessors. The NAS final report concluded that the AAAS findings, while having some short term validity, were exaggerated. The presence of Matthew Meselson on an in-house panel chosen to review the final NAS report seems to have ensured after considerable struggle that his team's findings were not completely dismissed out of hand.

On the issue of human health effects, the NAS report has this to say: "The Committee was unable to gather any definitive indication of direct damage by herbicides to human health." And, "no evidence substantiating the occurrence of herbicide-induced (birth) defects was obtained." The question of human health effects, was, however, left open-ended. The NAS cautioned that the persistent reports from Montagnards living in heavily sprayed regions, "albeit largely secondhand" or from observers who were not "medically qualified," could not be completely ignored. "The Committee considers it important," wrote Academy President Philip Handler to Congress, "that this matter be pursued at the earliest opportunity."

It is likely that the "earliest opportunity" referred to an American victory in Indochina, a vision that was rudely shattered the following year by the sight of American military and embassy personnel scrambling on to helicopters in Saigon, just a few steps ahead of the arriving North Vietnamese troops.

With the publication of the NAS report and the decision by President Gerald Ford in 1975 to renounce American first use of herbicides in any future war, the domestic controversy surrounding the defoliation program and its potential damage to the health of exposed humans, was believed to have been finally laid to rest. Subsequent allegations by American Vietnam veterans that they and their children are victims of herbicide poisoning not only have reopened this issue, but have sent interested investigators like ourselves back to the official records such as the NAS report in search of clues to important questions that were left unanswered or even unasked.

Toxicological information on the biological dangers of dioxin, for example, has advanced steadily since 1974. Still, we wanted to know just how much was already known at the time the defoliation program began; might there have been a more cautious policy, we wondered, if human safety had been placed before the needs of the "military mission"?

"At the time the program began, it was not known that preparations of the herbicide, 2,4,5-T were contaminated with the extraordinarily toxic compound, TCDD . . ." Philip Handler made this point in his letter accompanying the National Academy of Sciences' final report. This comment suggested that any subsequent issue of negligence, whether on the part of the chemical manufacturers or the federal government, was moot. How could either the herbicides' producers or the agencies sponsoring defoliation be held accountable for side effects that the scientific state of the art had yet to discover? After all, wasn't it only after the Bionetics Laboratory's report was published in 1969, warning of 2,4,5-T's potential danger to the unborn, that Dow first suggested the real problem might be dioxin, not the herbicide? By that time, "pure" 2,4,5-T containing less than one-half part dioxin per million was being produced. And anyway, Agent Orange spraying soon was suspended in Vietnam following the Bionetics Lab revelations.

We have discovered, however, that NAS President Handler may have been mistaken or misguided in his statement of disclaimer quoted earlier. In fact, the chemical companies almost certainly knew that 2,4,5-T was contaminated with dioxin at least as early as 1957—*four full years* before Vietnam defoliation even began! Furthermore, it already was known that dioxin was a serious hazard to human health.

In his doctoral thesis for Harvard, Dr. Robert Baughtman sketches the history of dioxin, hitting the high points along its dirty trail beginning in the late nineteenth century. Baughtman is a uniquely qualified source: The year before his thesis was completed in 1974, he and his mentor, the ubiquitous Matthew Meselson, pioneered a novel analytical technique for measuring dioxin in the minute parts-per-trillion range.

Baughtman writes that the Dow Chemical Company introduced the chlorophenols—the base compounds from which 2,4,5-T is manufactured—in the mid-1930s. Almost immediately, workers producing the new "Dowicides" began to experience an aggravated skin condition called chloracne. Dow missed a chance in 1937 to determine the cause of this worker ailment when it refused to support a company physician who wanted to test the chemicals on laboratory animals.

Twenty years later, however, two German scientists unraveled the secret. As the result of an accident in a German 2,4,5-T factory in 1953, many workers developed chloracne and other more serious conditions including chronic liver ailments. By 1957, the German researchers had isolated what they believed to be the cause: 2,3,7,8 tetrachlorodibenzo-para-dioxin. An earlier accident in 1949 at a Monsanto 2,4,5-T factory in Nitro, West Virginia, before the positive identification of dioxin, is illustrative of the seriousness of the symptoms observed among the exposed workers. According to Baughtman, "228 workers developed chloracne. . . . Other symptoms observed included severe pains in skeletal muscles, shortness of breath, intolerance to cold, palpable and tender liver, loss of sensation in the extremities, fatigue, irritability, insomnia, loss of libido, and vertigo."

Not coincidentally, this list of symptoms is disturbingly similar to the complaints of Vietnam veterans today. The same dioxin that has poisoned chemical workers for more than three-quarters of a century, probably also poisoned the Vietnamese and the American combat soldiers during the ten-year span of the defoliation program. Dow could have known about the effects of dioxin in 1937, *should* have known, along with the other 2,4,5-T manufacturers, by 1957, and *did* in fact know the truth about dioxin by at least 1964, before the defoliation program really went into full swing.

Baughtman reports a piece of evidence that must certainly condemn Dow and the numerous other herbicide producers. "In response to the greatly increased demand for 2,4,5-T which resulted from the U.S. military herbicide program in Vietnam, facilities and schedules were put under great pressure in an effort to increase production. Several outbreaks of chloracne occurred. In 1964, about the time the major phase of the herbicide program was getting underway, one such incident involving over seventy workers occurred at a plant operated by the Dow Chemical Company. An investigation was conducted which not surprisingly led to the conclusion that TCDD was the source of the problem. Although these results were not published, they were communicated to other manufacturers, including Diamond Alkali, Monsanto and Hercules."

Philip Handler's statement was vague on the question of exactly when it was known that the herbicide was contaminated with the awful toxin. "At the time the program began, it was not known," his comment reads. Yet the legal standard for negligence is that a manufacturer has a *duty* to know the current scientific state of the art on the properties and effects of a given product. Obviously the reports of the German scientists, published in 1957, were reasonably available to Dow and the other chemical companies in the small world of herbicide manufacturers. Sometime between 1957 and the beginning of the defoliation program in 1961, it must be assumed that Dow and the other companies became aware that their own workers' health problems often resulted from exposure to the dioxin-contaminated herbicide. Americans are indeed xenophobes, but certainly some chemist or physician working in the field must have been aware of the international medical literature. Whether or not the chemical industry knew about dioxin in 2,4,5-T in 1957, legally they had a duty to know.

In any event, what was Dow's excuse in 1964? And furthermore, did the possibly disingenuous NAS president Handler know that Dow attributed health problems among workers resulting from its 1964 accident to herbicide poisoning? Why did Dow wait until 1969 to speak publicly about what many scientists believe is the most toxic synthetic chemical compound ever created? How could Dow have informed the other herbicide manufacturers about dioxin in 1964 and yet not have shared this information with the U.S. armed forces who were laying down tons of 2,4,5-T on the South Vietnamese population and American GIs alike? Or did U.S. Air Force toxicologists know all along about dioxin and merely choose to ignore the dangers in favor of continuing a popular and militarily strategic program? These questions are far from being rhetorical. For the time being, they remain unanswered only because the truth is monopolized in the minds and the vaults of the corporate and government elites who profited so heavily from the chemical warfare they inflicted on their victims. It is to be hoped that these herbicide philanderers soon will be held accountable for their despicable actions.

It is easy to see why "Dow" has become a dirty word in the vocabulary of American politics. But a day of partial reckoning is fast approaching. The scientific evidence needed to prove that herbicides cause damage to humans is increasing daily; so too is the popular movement opposing the continued use of these chemicals.

In addition to causing birth defects, dioxin-contaminated herbicides are now believed to be cancer-causing agents as well. Recent evidence from Sweden indicates that workers and farmers exposed to chlorophenols have a much higher cancer mortality than unexposed populations. One of the world's eminent authorities on dioxin, Dr. Ton That Tung of Vietnam, reports that liver cancer, virtually unknown before the defoliation program, is now the second most common type of cancer in Vietnam. In the laboratory, researchers at the University of Wisconsin found that, among rats fed with a diet containing only five parts per trillion dioxin, half the animals developed malignancies.

The earlier claims among Vietnamese women—in part substantiated by Meselson's AAAS report—that herbicides may increase the incidence of stillbirths and miscarriages, has also been buttressed by alarming new evidence. In March 1979, the Environmental Protection Agency ordered an immediate suspension of some continued uses of 2,4,5-T, primarily the spraying of forests to retard hardwood growth. The agency based its unusual order—only the second one issued in its history—on studies of pregnant women in Alsea, Oregon, who reported increases in miscarriages following periods of defoliant spraying in their region.

Dioxin contamination apparently is not limited to exposed

workers or those who live in the vicinity of spraying operations. Thomas Whiteside's latest book, *The Pendulum and the Toxic Cloud*, is largely about the town of Seveso, Italy, which was contaminated by a giant plume of dioxin vented as the result of an industrial accident in a nearby factory producing 2,4,5 trichlorophenol (the chemical precursor of herbicide 2,4,5-T). He lists other chemical compounds and common products derived from chlorinated phenolic compounds, often during the production of 2,4,5-T itself. These include products used as "slime killing agents in paper-pulp manufacture, and as stabilizers of fungicidal agents that are incorporated in a wide range of consumer products, including adhesives, water-based and oil-based paints, varnishes and lacquers and paper and paper coatings." The antibacterial compound hexachlorophene, whose use is highly restricted in the United States, is also commonly contaminated with dioxin. A 1978 study among female medical personnel working in six Swedish hospitals revealed a much higher rate of birth defects in children born to those women who washed repeatedly with hexochlorophene every day compared with women who never washed with the agent.

The greatest insult to humanity, where the manufacture of chlorinated phenolic products like 2,4,5-T is concerned, may be the fact that dioxin is now in the human food chain. Traces of dioxin have been found by scientists in the mothers' milk of women who live in the vicinity of sprayed rangelands. It is also in beef fat from cattle that grazed in the same regions.

It is a cruel twist of fate that the veteran who went off to war in Vietnam may have received a "double dose" of dioxin. He may have been poisoned while fighting a war which politicians told him was to preserve our way of life, only to return home to an environment in which a dioxin time bomb ticks more loudly each day.

CHAPTER
9

So Shall Ye Reap . . . War-torn
Vets Are a Nonrenewable Resource

There can be no doubt that to date science has provided volumes of convincing evidence that 2,4,5-T, its contaminant dioxin and 2,4-D—which together formed the ingredients of Agent Orange—are highly toxic and dangerous substances. Dioxin itself has disabled thousands of chemical workers over the years as the result of industrial accidents. All three chemicals appear to cause cancers and birth deformities in laboratory animals.

It has become the opinion of thoughtful and well respected scientists, government officials, and environmentalists that the use of these herbicides should be totally banned; this opinion in effect asserts that the risk to human health far outweighs the economic benefits derived from the commercial, public, and private application of these biocides.

Vietnam veterans, taken as a group, most certainly manifest every imaginable symptom that medical and public health specialists ascribe to chemical and in particular herbicidal poisoning.

Does this mean that the case for Agent Orange poisoning has been firmly established, that a cause and effect relationship exists between exposure to Agent Orange or other herbicides or toxic chemicals employed by the U.S. military for over a decade in Indochina and a clearly defined illness? No. Scientists, even those who would have these chemicals banned yesterday, cannot say that human health effects *definitely* result from exposure to 2,4-D and 2,4,5-T. Dioxin is the exception because of the vast record of afflicted industrial workers chronicled for years in the medical literature. But these workers were directly exposed to quantities of pure dioxin in acute doses. Veterans were exposed years ago to dioxin in combination with 2,4,5-T where the impurity was present in the parts-per-million range. In addition, the soldiers' exposure was chronic, not acute, since they may have been exposed to repeated spraying operations and may have consumed unspecifiable amounts of contaminated food and water where the relatively stable dioxin had entered the food chain of Vietnam.

It is precisely this long term effect of minuscule particles of dioxin resulting from chronic and indirect exposure to the herbicide that has stirred such a controversy in the scientific community, even among those scientists who do not require that veteran affliction be proven to justify a complete ban on these chemicals.

Nevertheless, while the causal link between Agent Orange and ill health among vets seems far from certain, it is almost irrefutably apparent that Vietnam veterans are sicker and more ill-adjusted to society than their peer group who did not serve in the combat zone during the late war.

In September 1979, the *New York Times* reported, "The first Government-sponsored study of Vietnam veterans has tentatively concluded that more than 40 percent of them suffer major emotional difficulties, such as alcoholism and narcotics abuse, and that more than 75 percent of them complain of nightmares, marital discord and job problems."

And it is equally true that Vietnam veterans will continue to suffer from certain maladies—social and biological—regardless of the outcome of the Agent Orange controversy. For better or for worse, this controversy will come to some practical resolution in the years ahead through a combination of political, legal, and scientific action. In the process, millions of Americans and others will learn invaluable lessons concerning the underregulated and wanton use of toxic chemicals and their inevitable contribution to the increase in technologically associated illnesses such as cancer and the heartbreaking genetic damage suffered by the as yet unborn.

But whatever finally is determined about the relationship of herbicide exposure to the health problems of Vietnam vets and their children, the entirety of the Vietnam veteran postwar phenomena of disease, crime, drugs, emotional numbing, and general alienation from the American dream can only be understood within the context of the war itself and the brutalizing way in which it was fought, within which the defoliation program plays an undeniably important but by no means disproportionate role.

Among sophisticated observers of world affairs, there were a few who could see disaster coming as far back as the early Fifties when the reins of colonialism passed in Indochina from the French to the Americans. Graham Greene was such an observer. In *The Quiet American*, Greene describes a character who, in reality, began to appear throughout the world, engaged in Uncle Sam's missionary task of nation-building. Greene's novel, which is set in Saigon, subtly portrays the exterior of this new Yankee persona: quiet yet aggressive, studied but not scholarly, sincere but overbearing in point of view. And very white and middle-class. These young Americans who patrolled the decomposing former colonies of the nineteenth century exploiter nations were motivated by a new idealism appropriate to the ascension of the U.S. as a victorious world power after World War II. They inevitably took jobs with agencies whose devious functions were masked with the bland initials by which they were known: AID, CIA, CORDS, etc.

But Greene was most deeply concerned by the darker side of the protagonist's soul, not with his appearance. Greene foresaw that a new style of exploitation was on the horizon—one that would attempt to integrate all the underdeveloped nations rich in the natural resources that fueled modern industry in the West. He recognized, in the calculating idealism of the quiet American, the advance man for a new system capable of transforming every peasant into a consumer of space-age "necessities" such as Coca-Cola, Enfamil, and polyester. And indeed, in due time, a legion of such men was unleashed among the backwaters of the world. The men were apostles of the new order: the Great American Global Shopping Mall.

For the West, the mission of these young men was the ideological opposite and yet the equivalent of world communism, the one force that threatened to inhibit the accomplishment of their goals. The quiet Americans were, however, doomed to failure. They mistakenly viewed the principal opposition to their schemes—to remodel societies like Vietnam according to American specifications, for example—as outsiders like themselves. The Communist agitator was conjured up as a servant of the godless Soviet monolith. Wars of national liberation—like that in Vietnam, which spanned decades—were in fact homegrown. The indigenous Communists were successful primarily because they were willing to join and lead a struggle for freedom from foreign domination.

With money to burn and a full inventory of modern weapons to "ensure security," our earnest counter-insurgents could nevertheless either seduce or frighten their Vietnamese counterparts into the anti-Communist crusade. Regimes came and regimes went. They all shared a total lack of popular support, fashioned as they were from among a French and then American-educated military elite; and they were each in turn constitutionally incapable of accomplishing even the most minimal of social and economic reforms.

By the mid-1960s the savants in Washington acknowledged with regret that the battle for the hearts and minds of the Vietnamese was being badly lost. Political victory was abandoned in favor of military victory. If we couldn't out-Communist the Communists, we could sure as hell out-gun them. The quiet Americans merely exchanged their briefcases for commissions as field grade officers, shifting gears from the CIA and AID to MACV, the Military Advisory Command Vietnam. And by 1965, with the first big landing of marines on the shores of Danang, the conscripts and volunteers of an entire generation were drawn into the fray.

From the ghettos and the farms, the suburbs and the inner-city neighborhoods, the sons of World War II veterans were summoned to fight a war whose ends and means had been fashioned by men who never did make sense of their aims to the vast majority of Americans. To stage center came the American fighting man, but the drama was not the same as that of past wars.

The rest is history. And like most history for Americans—even an event as momentous and painful as the Vietnam War—it already has been filed away in some dusty archive of the national consciousness. Still, the war continues to influence our society, a fact that is nowhere more evident than in the destroyed lives of many Vietnam veterans.

While half a generation has grown up since the war heated up in the mid-Sixties and the soldiers started coming home, a great many veterans have not yet readjusted to civilian life. Some say the explanation lies in the nature of war itself. And it must certainly be true that all war is hell. But it also is true that each war has its peculiar hell. The Vietnam War was not a war for terrain, where large conventional armies pushed each other from point to point on vast territorial battlefields. It was a war lost before it even began. And perhaps from the frustration born of fighting a losing cause, a plague of technological destruction was visited upon Vietnam without analogue in modern warfare: napalm, cluster bombs, torture, random harassment, and interdiction artillery-shelling of populated areas, chemical defoliation, and crop destruction, all staged in free-fire zones. A body count mania turned Vietnam into a turkey shoot. The American combat GI became a modern bounty hunter, whose slogan was:

"Though I walk through the valley of death, I fear no evil.
For I am the meanest motherfucker in the valley."

The hunt for the enemy constantly turned up civilians. If they lived in free-fire zones, they were "unfriendlies," so they could be bombed or shelled or shot. And the bodies were piled up under the assumption that the number of dead would some day add up to victory.

Fighting in such a war with such tools and measures, one had to become mean. The technologies of destruction, the strategy and the tactics of counter-insurgency led inexorably to an ever-widening free-fire zone in which the face of an entire population was turned to the fire; these elements built a kind of brutalization of skill and instinct into the very conduct of the war. And it is likely that the underlying cause of many of the illnesses borne today by veterans is traceable to the brutalizing effect of that meanness—it isn't just the surrender and suppression of basic human instincts, but the substitution of a meaner-than-thou posture behind which the frightened and disoriented recruit might hide his horror. One way or another, thousands and thousands of combat veterans are left stranded with this internalized brute, this creature of the war— a bastard product of a society which resists, under pain of too hard a truth, acknowledging its paternity.

From among the hundreds of Vietnam veterans the authors have known personally, or have interviewed in the course of our organizing and writing, we have chosen to present only one man's story in great detail. We feel the tortured yet icy memoir of James "Peewee" Fortenbury cuts through to the heart of what it was like to fight the Vietnam War.

Co-author Michael Uhl conducted a lengthy interview with Fortenbury in July 1978 and had a very personal reaction:

"Peewee Fortenbury fascinated me. It wasn't his violence— though he probably was the most unambiguously violent person I've ever known. There were killers in my unit—unrestrained bullies with an obscenity of excess firepower. They would beat old men and boys with pistol butts and break their arms trying to get combat intelligence—a form of plunder. But those slobs couldn't engage Victor Charlie where he lived with smokeless fires and the feet of small animals like James 'Peewee' Fortenbury.

"I headed a small intelligence team attached to the Eleventh Brigade, Americal Division. We were analysts, spooks and interrogators. By the time I arrived, the unit had a reputation because of its productivity; its riches were counted in bodies, weapons and rice caches, and its grail was the elusive 'prisoner of war'—an enemy soldier in uniform with a weapon. We abused the Vietnamese with our tongues and our fists—we all did it to one extent or another. Sadism is a logical weapon in a war fought among civilians in hamlets and rice fields. Choppers descended like locusts on anything that looked healthy—and anything that looked too healthy was Charlie's—and so for us a target of opportunity. Jews in Poland and Russia could not have feared the pogroms of the Don Cossacks more than the Vietnamese, who would sink to frightened silence while a unit of American boys swept their hamlet, burning, pillaging and shooting people like hired thugs.

"Peewee is a natural storyteller. He tells one everything about his war experience without the slightest second-guessing as to motive or morality. It is not that he doesn't know the difference between right and wrong, but rather that he is so convinced of the evilness of his past that he believes himself to be damned. This despair has lessened his own chance of survival. Like so many Vietnam veterans, he carries the burden of the war's vileness on his shoulders alone, thinking that no one can share or understand so morally repugnant an experience. This aloneness leads him to relive Vietnam every day, and there is only one way out when a person is so isolated with such pain: some form of self-destruction.

"Unfortunately, while there presently is some renewed interest in Vietnam veterans, most of the organizations and individuals involved are trying to deal with the war-related pain of vets without understanding its true source. They'd rather try to change the way veterans feel about their war experiences from the outside in than to deal with the society capable of creating such brutalizing and dishonorable war machinery. Here's how Americans might understand the real meaning of the domino theory: If average Americans could grasp for one instant the meaning of body count and apply it to an American child; if they could see a little Yankee girl aflame with napalm running naked down some suburban asphalt street, or imagine their own community transformed into a free-fire zone beyond the protection of any convention of war, they might gain deep insight into the darker side of American power and glory. How many well-guarded myths and assumptions about American purposes at home and abroad might fall like dominos? And might not Americans then embrace the Vietnam veteran and share and understand his pain and disaffection? Military budgets might begin to crumble, and real disarmament could be accomplished in a mood of peace. What a burden might be lifted!

"But the stakes of the global sweepstakes have not changed. Americans have not become introspective about the Vietnam war. They do not identify with the pain and fear of the Vietnam veteran; instead, they themselves fear another 'foreign' enemy to repel. So if you can't raise the bridge, lower the water.

"Not only does the average American not want to think about Vietnam at all, but these aforementioned organizations have come up with a new message for the Vietnam vet: 'What you did in Vietnam was right. So win, lose, or draw—it doesn't matter anymore. Besides, Vietnam wasn't a fucked-up war; it was only a prolonged "conflict." '

"So we only lost the world's longest battle, not a war. Vietnam veterans are now invited to join hands with American warriors of yore and are offered full membership in the national war mythology. Nothing new will be learned, and the numbing of America will be complete. Nothing is easier to rewrite than history—and nothing is harder to outlive."

James "Peewee" Fortenbury

The only game I played when I was a kid was soldier. I was always the ringleader in the neighborhood. I was always the boss. Yeah, I loved the military. I saw a lot of war movies, and I used to imitate people like Audie Murphy. He was my hero, the real thing.

I've always had a quick temper, but I've been a mellow person too. I've always tried to shy away from trouble, but I couldn't wait to get to Nam. I couldn't wait to get there. When I first got there, things were different, maybe a little confusing. Scary. But, ya know, after a month you're there, you're not a "newbie" anymore, and you pretty well know what's going on.

I thought, well, this is my patriotic duty. I'm an American citizen. This is something I have to do. I definitely felt like it was my war for my generation. So I fought a war when I was young. I never got to go out and party like young people do. I joined the army when I was eighteen years old. And from then on, it's been one fast trip.

I had ROTC [Reserve Officers Training Corps] in college and I enjoyed it; the Vietnam war was going strong. They were taking people right out of college and stuff. Naturally, I was losing interest in college. I felt like I couldn't study because of the things that were going on around me. So, I just went ahead and joined. Go to Vietnam, do my part . . . be an all American boy. Come home to apple pie.

When I went and had all my tests they told me that I had such high scores that they offered me Officers Candidate School. They said you can have anything you want. I didn't want to be an officer 'cause that would take too much time. I felt like I had a mission. I wanted to get there as soon as possible. Even my leave, before I went to Nam, was an inconvenience. I felt I was sitting, getting physically out of condition; in top form I could run thirty miles without even getting out of breath.

I was a LRRP [pronounced "lurp" for long-range reconnaissance patrol]. Every time we blew an ambush we gathered intelligence. We'd strip their fatigues, their uniforms, weapons, their maps, anything they had . . . believe it or not, you could tell a lot. You could tell if they were fresh troops or if they'd been there a long time. You could tell by what they had for food . . . anything like that. We'd kill 'em, strip 'em down, bring everything back and then piece it together in base camp.

A lot of times we'd either grab one and zap the rest of 'em or we'd just grab one and take off. You know, it really depends on the size of elements we were going up against. But what you'd do is wait for the tailman to come through. You'd run up behind him and slip that piano wire over his neck, turn it back around and lift him up on your shoulder. See, with that piano wire he won't be able to mutter a sound. Then you carry him off in the bush and take him back. Very seldom did we bring anybody back alive. We didn't take prisoners. They send us out to take 'em alive, but by the time they got back, they'd be dead. My job was to kill. I killed.

The only way to keep yourself alive is to never leave any loose ends. When I killed, I made sure they were dead. Various ways. Our favorite way was getting them up in choppers; we'd have that chopper pilot go up to 1200 feet and hover. We'd take one and drop him out right away. We'd ask the next one some questions, but before you give him a chance to open his mouth, you just drop him down. By the time you get to the third one they'd tell you about their girlfriend and anything else you want to know. Then you drop him. No loose ends.

I know it sounds cruel about over there, but we had no one to depend on. We carried everything we needed on our backs: food, water. We couldn't call for backup or have a company over here or a battalion over there. When we'd go out and spring an ambush, it was just us. Sometimes we could call in artillery, but a lot of times we'd be in an area where we couldn't get artillery.

One time, I had an airstrike pulled on me by the South Vietnamese Air Force. They dropped 250-pound bombs just fifty meters away and were blowing trees down on the other side of the river. We had been looking for a high speed resupply trail that the North Vietnamese were using across the Saigon river corridor, and we'd been out there for seven days straight. See, when we go into an area, "friendlies" are supposed to stay out. There's no friendlies, right? Well, for some reason, something had got crossed up. All day long, I heard lots of 'em flying back and forth over the river, and I kept thinking, wouldn't it be something terrible if they thought we were gooks down here and called an airstrike on us? My God, it wasn't two minutes later when I hear this "eeeeeeeeyaw" [imitates diving plane], and this jet took a dive. Ya know, everybody was a gook to me. But they say that the ARVNs [South Vietnamese] were friendly gooks. A definition of a gook is a foreigner. OK, we were the gooks in their country. But to me, *they* were gooks, 'cause they were a foreigner to *me*. They were different than me. I was sent there to exterminate them, ya know. Once you see a few GIs laid out across the jungle, no longer do you have feelings or conscience. Automatically, you have no conscience.

When I first came back from Nam, I'd have dreams. I wouldn't dream about the dead gooks, I'd dream about GIs. That's what hurt me. Not the dead gooks, 'cause I feel like a gook is an insect. And I'm very hostile toward our government right now for letting 250,000 of 'em into my country.

Our Ranger company (only about 120 men) killed more gooks than the whole Twenty-fifth Infantry Division, and let's face it, we're talking about twenty to thirty thousand soldiers. I don't know how many I killed. I never took time to count. Sometimes you blow an ambush and then take off. I couldn't tell you if it was hundreds; I couldn't tell you if it was thousands. Just definitely a lot of dead ones. That was my job.

I never killed "friendlies" over in Nam. Like I said, they'd send me into a grid square, and they'd say, "no friendlies." So, anything that was in that area *wasn't friendly*, ya know what I mean? Women, men. There were NVA [North Vietnamese Army] women fighting the war over there. There was kids that did things, run satchel charges up on GIs. So, when I go into an area—ya know I don't like to admit that I killed a kid or a woman—but when I went in an area, there were no friendlies, right? They were all considered to be enemy. The civilians are enemies.

See, I never felt that the Vietnamese people were on the same level with us. I felt like we were more civilized, more educated. 'Course, we were doing the killing. But we were brought into a situation where we thought we were going over there to stop a war, stop Communism. And what happens? We gave it up and gave it to them. After all the GIs that were killed over there. That's another thing that makes me hostile is giving it away. We should of at least taken it and used it as an airstrip or something, ya know?

No, I do not like gooks. I tell you, when I'm driving down the street—we have some Vietnamese families living in this neighborhood—I drive down the street, and I see a Vietnamese kid in the street, my instincts tell me to pull the wheel and run over the kid. But my conscience tells me—well, not my conscience, but my intelligence tells me—that if I run over this gook and exterminate him, which is something that I was bred—not taught, but bred to do—that they would prosecute me and send me to prison for the rest of my life.

About kids: One time over in Nam we got this fourteen-year-old kid who was an NVA regular. Fourteen years old, and he had been south for three years already. We knew that they were sending kids down there to fight. I guess it was because supposedly we had killed off the whole population of the North and only kids were left.

So we get this kid, we blow his elbow off, and all he's got is this piece of skin hanging there. And he's got tears, and he's crying, and I start flashing things through my mind. I start relating to this kid as my little brother back home. Automatically I changed the battle scene to America, and this is my little brother that's coming out of the bush. And I ask myself: Well, how would I want the enemies to treat my little brother? And this goes through my head and so we wrap his arm up, give candy, comfort him. We guarantee him we're not gonna hurt him.

This is a new thing for me. All along I'm killing everything I could kill, water buffalos, elephants—anything we could get, we killed. Which is very confusing at the time to me. I still look back, and I ask myself why did I do this? That's just one more gook I could've added to my body count. I hate gooks, but I can relate to the sense that it's their country—we are the gooks there. I think about this, but I can't get over this drive that I hate them . . . I hate 'em.

We took the kid back and gave him to S2 [intelligence]. They took him, gave him medical care, treated him. I wanted to find out what happened to this kid, if they tried to rehabilitate him, or what they did with him. But over in Nam you lose contact with things. You can lose contact in lots of ways.

Once I did liquid opium for a week. That's the only time I did drugs there because I'm a strong believer that in a combat situation you should be in full control of your senses. So, I didn't do drugs over there, but when I'd go back to my hootch [billet] at night I'd be scared because I'd think of all the cooks and clerks that would be out on the perimeter guarding me and toking up, all spaced out.

But see, that *was* the war for them. The war for me was fear of getting killed in the bush. So, I don't think they really felt the same thing I did. When you're in Nam there's nowhere that's safe; nowhere, man. During the day, I'd see these gooks that were working in our base camp, and they'd be stepping off things, man; counting in their heads. That night, mortar rounds would come into the area they'd been stepping off. So, nowhere's safe over there. I've seen it all.

And no one's safe here, either. There's too many crazies in this world, and a lot of crazies are vets, which is a shame. Vets that are snapping out, going out and get them a body count, right? A lot of GIs flipped over the killing. I'm not at that point. I don't think I could ever be at that point because I think I'm more intelligent, more capable of grasping things around me.

I'd never flip out and start doing things like that. I'm not a threat to anybody, unless I'm pushed. I'm just an individual that wants to live my life and not be ignored. I like to feel I'm humane too. I enjoy life and don't like to see useless killings. I used to love to hunt, and I will not hunt now. I will not kill anything unless there's a purpose behind it. If I'm very very hungry, I'll kill for food. And I don't like to hurt people, but it's a reaction.

That's the reason I stay away from people. I try to stay to myself so people can't push me. Some want to beat me up or take me on, build up a reputation. But I don't feel like I have a reputation. I'm just an individual who wants to live my life peacefully with no hassles.

When people came home from Korea and World War II, they were accepted with open arms. When I went to San Francisco, I was met by a bunch of hippies calling me "baby killer" and shit like that. Then, two minutes later, they turn around and ask me if I got any spare change. I felt like, here I am a conquering hero coming home, that people were going to shake hands with me, and tell me, it's so nice to have you home. You know, it's cool to be against the war, but why put down the GIs? We're all the same; we're all Americans; we're human beings; why put us down? I don't like war any more than anyone else; even more so with me experiencing it. . . . I hate it, I never want to experience it again, you know.

I should rephrase that; I don't want to totally forget it because there are things that I learned from Vietnam, believe it or not. I learned a lot about life there. I learned what it is to enjoy life to its fullest. My mom says: "I know you're very sick, but you don't have any ambition; isn't there more to life than just enjoying life?" I tell her, there is nothing more important than enjoying my life, because life is too short. I have these views because I've been so close to death. I've seen death, you know.

I smoke dope now; I'll admit it. Dope makes me relax, 'cause I'm really hyperactive all the time. You can ask my family and people who know me; when I came back from Nam I was very short tempered. People got on my nerves very quickly, and I would explode and hurt people badly. People are scared of me. When I came back from Nam, I put my own brother in the hospital for two weeks, and all I wanted was peace and quiet.

My brother comes up—he's in the marine corps—with all of our friends that ran around in high school together. Everyone's in the service, and they talk him into picking a fight with me 'cause he's a marine and I'm a Green Beret. All marines eat this up. Well I took just so much of it, and then I just pounded him into the ground. Broke four ribs or something like that, and he's in the hospital . . . my own brother!

After my time in Nam I beat up lots of people. I was in the reserves here in Albuquerque. Then I joined up again and went to Fort Carson, Colorado. I was supposed to go to A Company, Seventy-fifth Rangers, right? This is what they promised me. I got up there, and ya know what they did? They put me in there with seventeen-, eighteen-year-old kids. OK, I went into the army when I was eighteen, but I felt I was more mature. Here I was, a non-commissioned officer, and they had me training the infantry.

I would get so frustrated that I would take people in my room and beat 'em. They wouldn't listen to me, so I would take 'em in there and bang their heads on the walls. And the officer would come and stand outside my door, the platoon leader. He'd stand there, and he wouldn't come in, 'cause he knew my temper. After I'd beat 'em and throw 'em out, he'd come in, and he'd say, "Sergeant Fortenbury, you can't do things like that anymore. This is the Volunteer army. You can't hit GIs. You'll get court-martialed. You'll get drummed out of the army."

And I would tell him: "Look, you can't teach an old race horse new tricks. This is how I was trained."

I lived in Nam, so I felt like I went through the right type of physical and mental training for something like this. When they said, OK you're going to train the infantry, I did the best I could, ya know, to my potential. I had to teach 'em what I knew. If they got out of line, I did them the way the drill sergeants did me. Special forces phase one training was the most strenuous thing that I have ever done in my life, physically and mentally. They worked on my mind bad, man. It wasn't something where they'd just say, "kill, kill, kill, kill." It was the things they did, man. They made your mind real tired to the point where you gave up, and you started listening to their propaganda, or whatever you want to call it.

I have a UD [undesirable discharge] from my second hitch, but I have two Honorables before that, and I can collect on my VA benefits at any time. That UD is just more or less degrading, that was the VOLAR [volunteer] army. I didn't fit in because I believed in the old army. The old ways of training troops, discipline, rules. However VOLAR was real big in order to stop the draft, and I just didn't fit in. Still, everybody up there wanted me as a platoon sergeant for training purposes.

I went AWOL for thirty days and they sent me to Fort Sill, Oklahoma, where they were sending people to let them out. When I got there I was really treated bad. See, I was still an NCO, but I was treated like a private there. They promised me a general discharge because of my military record, but when they gave me my discharge it was a UD.

I almost flipped out two years after I came back from Nam. I had gotten into a hassle with this girl and her parents. I had me a 30-6 rifle with a scope. I was gonna zap their family, and I thought, what the hell, once I zap someone, they're gonna come after me. So I was gonna plant myself on a mountain peak where there was a cave, and I was gonna zap every pig I could get. But I was intelligent enough to handle it myself, and pull myself out of that depression with my family's help.

My mother has been through hell since I've come back from Nam. Not things that I've done to her but with worry about me. My father died two months after I came back from Nam. He and I were never really close when I was a kid. We never embraced, never hugged. My mother and I never kissed. We've never really been a real close family. But just before I went to Nam my dad broke down and started crying and hugged me and all; like he just knew I was never gonna come back.

Yeah, I cried too, man. I came back from Nam, and my father and I sat, and we talked and, oh god, it was heaven then. I think the best part of my life is the period right after I came back from Nam. My father understood what was bothering me, he understood my feelings about things, but he was very scared of me going out places. He was afraid of me hurting someone bad; he knew I had the capabilities of hurting someone if I wanted to.

I'm a trained killer. I've had people call me who want me to take hits; I've had 'em call me to make explosives for 'em. I don't know how people get my name. I know that that's what I'm best trained at, what I can do better than anything in the world. If I want you, I'm gonna get you, but I don't want to do

that no more. I don't want to kill anybody no more. I just want
to live my life to its fullest. I want everything I can get. I wanna
sit outside at nighttime . . . I'll lay on my roof and look at the
stars and wonder.

I am in pain, man, and not from my disease; I have a
pain in my head. I tell my mom and I tell my brothers that I
have a lot on my mind. I have things that they could never com-
prehend because they've never experienced anything like I've
been through. I used to go and talk to my uncle. He was a
World War II vet, and he saw a lot of action in the islands in
the Pacific. I'd go and ask my uncle: "Tell me, how can I forget? I can't forget it; it bothers me all the time." He says, put
it out of your mind. He tells me this, but I know better, because
my uncle has a Jap grenade and a German grenade that he
keeps in a box. He keeps 'em around and looks at 'em and stuff
like that. I've been told that he cries in his sleep. So, I can't
talk to my uncle anymore because he tells me lies.

My uncle tells me we lost the war in Vietnam. I tell my uncle,
don't ever tell me that. I don't want to hear it. You're not going
to tell me we lost that war over there. We lost sixty thousand
GIs, and you're not going to tell me we lost. I say we pulled out.
We might a gave it to 'em, but we didn't lose it. Because I feel
like there isn't a country in the world that can beat the United
States in a war. Not a true war. Vietnam wasn't a true war.
Vietnam was a political war. It was something for the politicians to play with.

If there was a declared war right now, I would never, ever
go back into the service. I think that I've done my part. It's
time for me to collect the fruits. Let me be one of the people
that stays behind, get the good jobs, ya know.

War has no rules. War is something that's terrible. War has
to be something that people never, ever want to experience
again. Something people never want to see, never want to happen in their country. It's got to be something that's horrifying,
terrible. That's the only way you're going to eliminate war.

Fantasies? I dream a lot about being in a field of gooks and
blowing them away and things like that. Sleeping or awake, I'm

a daydreamer. Sometimes, people will be talking, and I'll just drift off. They say that they talk to me for an hour and they'll never get a response.

I'll tell you one fantasy I've had this past year. I was gonna get about ten guys together and get some M-16s. We were gonna find a prison in Mexico where they're holding some rich Americans, and we were gonna kidnap the people who were in there. I was going to get their names and contact their parents, and ask them how much it was worth to them to get their sons and daughters out of prison. We make 'em pay, and then take off for adventures. Maybe go to Nam. I've had a lot of dreams about going back to Nam, a lot of 'em.

What am I doing in Vietnam? I don't know; sometimes I'm just looking around. I'm cheering during the day, and at night I'm out in the bush doing my old thing again. These are my fantasies [laughs].

I never really thought that the American people would turn away from the GI that went to Vietnam. The one thing that really hurt me and really put me down the most, is the way I've been treated. Like they say "job preference for the vet." Bull. I don't believe it. I've been to the unemployment office where they've had state jobs and they'll say "Hire the vet." But I'll go for an interview, and they'll say: Well, we've got to see all these other people that we're interviewing too. And then you come to find out that somebody's got the job that's not even a vet.

The people that I know in this town that's been to Nam, maybe one out of five is working. And most of them have been unemployed most of the time since they've come back from Nam because the good jobs were taken while we were there. They're young people who went to Nam right out of high school; they don't have job training. And a lot of people now don't want to take you in and give you the training because they say you're too old. Or a lot of people say, "Hey, you're a Nam vet," like it automatically means you're a heroin addict or smack freak. Something they want to keep away from the kids.

You want to know how much I've worked in the last seven years? Maybe a total of eight months. I've worked as a carpenter, laborer, whatever I could get. Plus, I'm a mechanic. But I like to be outside. I love the outdoors; I like to do anything physical. Running, hiking up a mountain. But it seems like in this last year it's really getting hard for me. The lifting makes my stomach really hurt a lot. Up to two weeks ago, I was working up in the mountains as a carpenter, building log cabins for my brother's construction company. I did all the hard work and I hurt every day. I lost weight continuously; I never had an appetite because of the physical strain of lifting. My stomach hurt bad, and it drains all my energy out and makes me real hard to get along with. My muscles are deteriorating too. The exercises I used to do hurt. And I have a hard time remembering things now. So I snap at people. But, I would do the work because I pushed myself. I don't really want to accept this. I'm not the type of person that likes to lay over and just die 'cause someone says, "Hey you're sick and you're never going to be the same." And I'm only twenty-seven years old. I'm not old.

They tell me, "You can go to work." And I say, "What can I do?" They say, "Well, you can't do anything physical, no lifting or anything like that." I say, well, what you're telling me is I can't work. Because to me that's what work is all about, doing something physical.

I'm a man; I'm not some girl or lady. I'm not a secretary that pushes a pencil all day. And I can't take an office job and be cooped up in a building all day. I have to be outdoors. Maybe all this stems from my training in the service, because I was trained for the outdoors. But I feel like I'm a labor man, someone that has to do physical labor. You take this away from me, then I no longer feel like a man. I feel like somebody just shriveling up to nothing.

Then I said, no, this ain't gonna happen to me—it can't happen to me, because I'm America's best [laughs].

You know, a lot of times, before I heard of this Agent Orange poisoning, I used to think, maybe it's my mind trying to shut out everything. Maybe I've had too much for my mind to handle, maybe it is mental. But I don't want to believe that. I know that my liver disease and my enlarged spleen isn't mental.

Maybe something's got to cause my slowing-down process. Like I said, I don't like to accept things. I don't like to think things happen to me because Mother Nature made it happen. It's because somebody did something.

Like these guys who say they have Agent Orange poisoning, and they have liver cancer or a liver disease. I have things like that eating away at *my* liver, and that makes me wonder am I gonna live or am I gonna die from this? I don't know what to do. I'm really confused because I'm in the woods right now about this Agent Orange poisoning. I didn't even know anything about it until I read it in the paper; all I knew is that I have a liver disease, I've been very depressed. Of course the depression could be caused by things that's happened to me in Nam. But is it causing sleeplessness, liver disease, enlarged spleen, high fevers?

I ask myself, when am I gonna get out of it? When am I gonna try and straighten my head out and finally live my life peaceful? That's what I've been trying to do, and then I come down with this sickness. The doctors tell me they don't know what caused it. They can't even diagnose what kind of disease I have in my liver. And they're doctors; they're supposed to help people, treat you, try to cure you. . . .

I guess they don't want to look stupid or—I don't know what the problem is. They act like they don't wanna treat me anymore. They haven't given me medication to try to treat the disease. They say your spleen is three times too big and your liver is being ate away by a disease, but they never give me any medication. They never called for me or set up another appointment. I only went back for a liver screen scan and that's it. I went back a month ago, and they said that my spleen was still three times too big and my liver disease hasn't progressed any further. But they don't know how long I've had it, when it started, and at what rate of speed it's progressing. You would think they'd try to find out, wouldn't you?

My mom keeps telling me to go to the VA, but I won't go because I know what's going to happen if I go there. They're going to turn me away. They're going to say, "What's Agent

Orange? It hasn't been proven it's in somebody's system, you know; Agent Orange only causes rashes."

I tell you I have gone through hell in the past seven years. Sometimes, I'll sit in my house all day long, no TV, no music, and I would just withdraw and think about the world. I would think about the way I was being treated and others were being treated the same, and I'd go crazy to the point of snapping. This police department here is lucky I didn't snap out, because I know I coulda took out fifty cops before they got me. I planned to barricade myself in a cave. The only way they would have got me out is my armor-piercing rounds; blow me out of there. So they would have had to come up the hill at me . . . I would've got 'em [laughs]. I'm glad I didn't do it. But at one point I was at that slim barrier to where I could've fallen on either side, and that scared me. You know, I almost did it. If it hadn't been for my brother and my mother I would probably either be dead or in prison somewhere, labeled a mass murderer. I wouldn't be here today talking with you [laughs].

It scared me that I almost did something like that. But, my mind is always on, thinking of maneuvers; like I'd be watching war movies on TV and I'd be sitting there thinking, that dude's full of shit, man, you can't do it that way. You do it *this* way, man. I feel like I'm still fighting a war right now. I'm very depressed. I'm in Nam. But I'm . . . I'm fighting something I can't see.

The reason I'm doing it now [the interview] is because somebody will read something that I said and maybe understand how I feel. Maybe understand that I'm just not some crazy Vietnam Vet drug addict . . . maybe they start to realize that I have feelings just like everybody else and it hurts being treated like shit. Not just me but all of us have had a great injustice done to us right now. We went to Vietnam for a legitimate reason. I felt I was trying to stop Communism in its tracks, which was what was taught, you know . . . stop it there so it'll never be here where we live.

It would kill me if something like what I saw happen in Nam went on here. How would you like to see your little kid running around in rags, begging? My God, I could never stand that.

I had pity for the Vietnamese people. I hate 'em, but I do have pity for 'em. I feel sorry for 'em. I don't want to see anybody have to live in an environment like that. Where all your life you never really know when somebody is going to run in your hut and blow you away or you're gonna get hit by a friendly or unfriendly rocket or artillery piece. I feel for 'em.

It's terrible, man . . . it's terrible. That's what I'm trying to tell you. My life is confusing . . . I have deep depressions. I used to sleep with a pistol underneath my pillow, because I was afraid someone was gonna come in—you hear about all of these crazy people killing people—and see, I thought someone was gonna come in my house and kill my family. It's my duty to protect my family, so I'd kill them first. I'm a very light sleeper; I could hear a leaf drop out of a tree, and I'll wake up—so I don't get very much sleep. But I live, I try. I don't go to parties. . . . I don't go to bars anymore because I always get into trouble when I go to a bar.

The only thing that I really care about more than anything is my little girl. You know it's like a craftsman who's going to die, but they make a masterpiece; you know what they leave behind. That's how I feel about my little girl. I think she's beautiful, and she's like my masterpiece I'm gonna leave behind. But my wife . . . I think my wife and I need time to get away from each other. She doesn't understand a lot of what's happening to me. Sometimes I wonder what love is.

I believe in God strongly and all that stuff. You have to believe in God, or how can you say how all this came about. People say evolution. Well, how did evolution start? Well, I believe in God. I believe that I won't never go to heaven. I think I'll go to hell and you know what I think hell is? I think hell is reincarnation. I think earth is hell and nothing could get any worse than this.

But I would like to see some GIs be helped. If it is this Agent Orange poisoning, this defoliant that's causing depression and other things to GIs, medically, mentally, then something should be done. Not for me, 'cause I'm not one to go and ask for help.

I've already gone to the VA one time; I'd never go there anymore. I don't look for handouts. I don't ask for things. I feel like if I'm not worth the American government helping, then, OK, I'll help myself. I'm not going to give up. But I know there's a lot of GIs out there who maybe aren't as strong as me or maybe don't have the drive, ya know. They need help, not just medical help, they need financial help, man. There's GIs out there going hungry. They're trying to make a living. Maybe they can't find a job that they can do; they don't have the training. Maybe they're not physically capable of doing the job. I'd like to see something be done.

Oh, it makes me feel good. It makes me feel like maybe I'm not just a radical or someone that's spouting off a lot of nothing. I've never really done anything in a radical sense, to burn something down or plant a bomb; I think that's useless. That's not gonna accomplish anything; blowing something up or killing someone. I almost went to the veterans' march in Washington. I thought that was dynamite, man. Because that's letting the people know we're not just any ordinary person against the war. We're people who fought over there, so we should be listened to.

But I'm not the one who's yelling. No, I'm not sitting here crying. I accept what's happened to me. I'm just trying to make the best of it. I could die tomorrow; I could die a year from now. They don't know what's going to happen to me. They don't know if it's going to be a slow process or a fast one. They just don't know. That's the reason I stay to myself. That's the reason I like to go to the mountains and stay away from people. Because I don't really feel like I'm a human being, ya know. I feel like I'm an animal.

But the thing is, am I an animal to be overlooked or am I an animal to be coped with? That's what I feel the question is, ya know. Should I be helped? Or should I be overlooked?

I've been overlooked.

10

The VA Fiddles While Agent Orange Burns Vets

Maude DeVictor works behind a gray steel desk in the benefits section of the Veterans Administration in Chicago. Maude, a thirty-nine-year-old black woman, had never heard of Agent Orange when she took a telephone call in the summer of 1977. Mrs. Charles Owens was on the line. Her husband, she told Maude, was dying of cancer, and he blamed it on "those chemicals" in Vietnam. Charley Owens, a black man from Chicago's South Side, had made a career of the air force, spending twenty-seven years on active duty, including a tour of Vietnam. He had retired and returned to college when his doctor gave him the bad news—terminal lung cancer. Maude gave Mrs. Owens what information she could, although she knew that the VA had no disability rating for exposure to military herbicides.

In October, Ethel Owens called again, in tears. Charley had died, and the VA had denied her claim that his death was service-connected. Maude was confused and angry. Could it be that some weapon used in Vietnam *could* cause cancer? she asked herself. She decided to do a little investigating on her own.

When Maude called the office of the air force surgeon general, she was told that they didn't know what she was talking about. The next morning, however, she was called by Captain Alvin Young, an air-force plant physiologist who knew plenty about Agent Orange. Young gave her a full run-down on the defoliation program, including descriptions of the health symptoms that scientists have attributed to dioxin exposure. Maude didn't know it at the time, but she was being briefed by one of the air force's resident experts on herbicides and their long-term effects. A claims worker in an obscure government niche, she must have felt a little awed by the attention which her innocent inquiry had generated.

She began to prepare memos for her supervisors, sharing her newly acquired information about this mysterious issue. At this point, it should be noted, Maude was no longer merely following the bureaucratic routine of her job; her unusual curiosity had a personal basis. While serving in the navy's medical corps during the 1950s, she had attended women with uterine cancer who were undergoing experimental chemotherapy with radium pellets. Some years later, she herself had developed breast cancer and had undergone a mastectomy. Since then, she'd lived in the shadow of a cancer she suspected was induced when the navy exposed her to dangerous levels of radiation.

Armed with some basic information about herbicides and their potential for long-term health effects, Maude went to her supervisors and obtained their permission to conduct an informal investigation within her VA facility. Working in the intake office, she talked with sixty or so veterans over the phone on an average day. She also conducted personal interviews with an additional ten to fifteen claimants. Whenever she encountered a vet who'd served in Vietnam, she began asking questions. "Ever had a persistent skin rash?" "Have any kids born with deformities?" "Do your arms and/or legs tingle and go to sleep?" Often the vets would answer, "Yeah! How'd you know?"

During Christmas, Maude was temporarily assigned to the VA's West Side hospital for a few days. Just checking records informally, she identified eight patients whose symptoms indicated they could be suffering from dioxin poisoning. In the first two months of 1978, she identified twenty-seven other Vietnam veterans through her own sleuthing at the benefits office. Then, suddenly, without explanation, her boss told her to stop logging cases. Apparently, the VA higher-ups were becoming concerned with her findings.

Angry at what she calls "bureaucratic ass-covering," Maude decided to tell what she knew to Bill Kurtis, a respected anchorman with WBBM-TV News in Chicago. Kurtis, at first, wasn't too impressed. "Frankly, I had filed away the herbicide problem as no story," he remembers. But when he saw Maude DeVictor's research, "it just hit me between the eyes like no other story."

On March 23, 1978, WBBM telecast a one-hour documentary which focused on the allegations of several Chicago-area veterans that they or their children were suffering from dioxin's long-term effects. Kurtis interviewed scientists who had demonstrated dioxin's toxic effects on lab animals, and also spoke with government representatives and with scientists employed by the herbicide manufacturers. On camera, the air force's Dr. Young was less forthcoming than he had been earlier with Maude DeVictor. Asked about alleged dangers from 2,4,5-T, he stated, "I don't think there's any supportive evidence."

Response to the broadcast was immediate. Several hundred Vietnam veterans called or visited the VA's Chicago facilities, complaining of ailments like those discussed on the program and seeking information and examination. Predictably, Dow Chemical issued a statement denying any connection between their herbicides and the veterans' health problems. And on the day of the broadcast, the VA issued a press release which emphasized that out of a total of 2.5 million claims decided annually by its fifty-eight regional offices, only twenty-seven were based on herbicide poisoning, and these all had been filed in one office—Chicago. The VA's logic was clear: No health problem existed since only a handful of people had complained and these probably were stimulated by an individual or group in just one city.

Two veterans located by Maude were featured on the show. Their Vietnam experiences were typical of the experiences of many of the vets who later came forth in response to publicity. One was Michael Adams, twenty-eight, of Evanston, Illinois, who served in Vietnam as a combat engineer with the Twenty-fifth Infantry Division in the Central Highlands in 1968. One of his jobs was to clear brush away from U.S. bases, using a backpack spray pump. He also remembers watching as C-123s sprayed defoliants near his unit on several occasions. After he returned to the States, large pimplelike sores began to appear on Mike's face. An army medic told him they were "razor bumps" that would go away. But the sores have persisted and are probably chloracne, one of the most common symptoms of dioxin exposure. Chloracne is similar to the acne which plagues many teenagers. It appears on the face, neck, shoulders, and upper part of the arms as festering pimples and blackheads that periodically erupt. All scientific authorities agree that exposure to dioxin can produce a chloracne condition in those exposed.

After he was discharged in 1972, Mike's shoulders and arms began to go numb for periods of time. He had difficulty sleeping and in the past two years he's lost more than sixty pounds. He believes he's undergone a personality change as well. "Before I went to Nam, I was an easy, cheerful guy; now, I often feel wound up real tight, and I'll blow up over just any little thing."

Agent Orange may have affected not only Milton Ross, thirty-four, of Matteson, Illinois, but his son, Richard, as well. Milt served with the Fifth Special Forces in Vietnam's Central Highlands, and he told us, "Although I wasn't involved in spray operations, I was sprayed upon. They sprayed a lot around our defense perimeter at Kontum to keep a clear 'field of fire' open. Often the wind would blow the spray right over our camp."

Milt's son, Richard, who was conceived after Milt returned from Vietnam, was born with the last joints of his fingers and toes either malformed or missing. Milt and his wife consulted a genetic counselor who took a detailed genealogical history from both parents. Her study uncovered no genetic disorders in the family history which might explain Richard's condition.

Despite the hundreds of new claims, the VA hadn't formulated any criteria for rating disabilities possibly brought on by the herbicides. According to Maude DeVictor, "Nothing was done with these new cases, since they didn't have any standards for evaluating them. Some were denied outright, but most were 'diaried'—that is, placed in a computer which was programmed to print them out every sixty days for re-review."

A few weeks after the show, Maude got her "thanks" from a grateful employer; she was transferred to a back office and given the job of answering telephone inquiries about missing disability checks. Such is the fate of government "whistle blowers."

Ralph Metcalfe, a black congressman from Chicago's South Side, became interested in the controversy and asked the General Accounting Office (GAO), Congress's investigative arm, to probe both the Pentagon's use of herbicides during the Vietnam war and the VA's handling of disability claims based on Agent Orange exposure. The GAO published the first half of its report three months later, just prior to Metcalfe's untimely death. It basically just repeated what the Pentagon already had said: that no scientific testing of the chemicals was done prior to use, since the herbicides already were widely used in the U.S. It passed along, without comment, the Pentagon's conclusion that, despite several studies done after 1967, "no firm link has been made between long-term adverse health effects and exposure . . . in Vietnam." The report ended by noting that the Defense Department has no plans to conduct epidemiological studies on military personnel who may have been exposed. This would remain the Pentagon's position until May 1979, when President Carter directed the air force to conduct a study of 1200 men who served with Ranch Hands in Vietnam.

As staff members of Citizen Soldier, a GI and veterans' rights organization based in New York City, the authors were contacted by friends in Chicago who knew we'd be interested in this emerging controversy. Based on a decade's organizing among GIs and veterans, we suspected that the problems being reported in Chicago were not unique to that city but probably were shared by veterans across the country. On May 5, 1978, Citizen Soldier held a press conference in New York to announce its "Search and Save" campaign (to be contrasted with "search and destroy"), which would alert and identify ailing Vietnam vets, by offering a toll-free "800" phone service. The distinguished environmental scientist, Dr. Barry Commoner, who directs the Center for Biology of Natural Systems at Washington University in St. Louis, joined several Vietnam veterans who were suffering from ailments associated with dioxin poisoning. Dr. Commoner drew the broad implications of the fight for Agent Orange victims: "My knowledge of the industrial accident in Italy two years ago, when a cloud of dioxin vented from a factory and settled over Seveso, convinces me more than ever that all dioxin-contaminated pesticides and chemicals should be immediately banned from further use."

As wire-service stories and the broadcast media spread the word about the toll-free "hot line," the calls began to pour in from across the country. An article in the *National Star*, a tabloid weekly with over two million readers, stimulated many calls. Soon, the phone lines were jammed beyond capacity. In just five weeks, 2000 calls were taken from worried veterans and their families. Unfortunately, the huge phone bills and the crushing burden for a small staff of handling so many calls caused the service to be terminated, but not before an important point had been made: There apparently were tens of thousands of Vietnam veterans who were suffering in silence from a common set of symptoms.

Although Agent Orange was rapidly evolving from a local to a national issue, the VA's policy makers continued to act as if they thought the issue would go away if they minimized its significance. On May 18, a policy memo by Dr. Gerrit Schepers, deputy chief of Health and Medical Services, was circulated to all one hundred seventy-two VA hospitals and fifty-eight regional offices. After providing a brief history of the defoliation program in Vietnam, Dr. Schepers drew the following scientific conclusions: "The herbicides have a low level of toxicity . . . they appear to be rapidly absorbed and completely excreted in both humans and animals." (He also states as fact that dioxin is eliminated from the body "fairly rapidly" and that "all available data" suggest that it's not retained in the body tissue after contact.) "Humans exposed repeatedly may experience temporary and fully reversible neurological symptoms, however the only chronic condition definitely associated with exposure . . . is chloracne." (A few weeks earlier, the VA had issued a new rating memo stating that only chloracne was to be recognized as a basis for a granting of disability.)

Dr. Schepers' memo dismisses fifteen years of research by Dr. Ton That Tung, a Vietnamese scientist who has received numerous international awards for his work on dioxin, by stating that comprehensive animal studies "failed to confirm the [Vietnamese] suggestion" that liver cancer, miscarriages, and birth defects can be caused by exposure to dioxin.

In cases where a veteran manifests health symptoms that cannot be explained by reference to defined disease, Schepers instructs the staff to take a detailed medical history, including any exposure to herbicides. "If [he] has no objective symptom or sign, simple reassurances should be offered. The veteran should be told that a record will be kept . . . but if [he] doesn't have symptoms and didn't previously experience any, the likelihood of herbicide poisoning is virtually zero."

The medical staff, however, is cautioned not to make any entry in a patient's file which suggests "a relationship between a veteran's illness and defoliant exposure, unless unequivocal confirmation . . . has been established." If such a case is found, it is to be reported immediately to VA headquarters. On the subject of conducting outreach for ailing veterans, Schepers is adamant; under no circumstances is a VA facility to initiate examination of any veteran for dioxin poisoning.

Field staff is also warned not to make any public statements about Agent Orange unless they're first "reviewed" by head-quarters.

The good doctor then waxes philosophical about this whole problem, lamenting that "a great deal of concern has been engendered among veterans and their families . . . by media presentations." His implication seems to be that this issue has been created by a sensationalist press which has been bombard-ing the public with "scare" stories.

The underlying message which permeates Schepers' memo must have been clear to all but the densest bureaucrat: This whole controversy is probably a hoax, but we're getting some heat, so we've got to appear to be doing something. If you can find *any* other explanation for a veteran's health problems, use it. If you can't, send the case to Washington immediately!

As the Schepers memo was being distributed internally, the VA continued to issue statements to the press which minimized the problem. A United Press International dispatch quoted an unidentified Veterans Administration spokesman as claiming that there was no proof of any long-term effects from herbicide exposure. He added that the toxicity of Agent Orange was "no higher than that of aspirin." This phantom spokesman pointedly observed that the "primary source" for reports of herbicides causing birth defects was "North Vietnamese propaganda." Some of the armchair warriors at VA headquarters were still using the old Johnson/Nixon formula that any criticism of America's involvement in Vietnam must originate in Hanoi. Like the Japanese soldiers who occasionally turn up on isolated Pacific islands, maybe they haven't yet heard that the war is over.

A few weeks later, the administrator of the VA, Max Cle-land, attended a Fourth of July celebration in Indianapolis. Cleland has made much of the fact that since he's a paraplegic due to Vietnam war wounds, he wants the truth and nothing but about Agent Orange. According to a VA worker who was present at the patriotic wiener roast, Cleland immediately bristled when someone asked him if he thought the agency was doing enough for the vets who may have been exposed. He intoned the litany about how no scientific studies have established any long-term health effects, and he added his opinion that the issue was largely the creation of irresponsible environmentalists.

As the phone calls and letters poured into Citizen Soldier, the media continued to follow the story, often conducting in-depth interviews with hometown veterans who'd called in response to previous stories about the "hot line." It is probably part of the legacy of Watergate that daily newspapers in cities large and small have reporters who are eager to write articles about an important issue of public policy. From the Lawrence, Massachusetts, *Eagle-Tribune* to the Albuquerque *Journal*, to the Seattle *Times*, the story of Agent Orange was told.

By the end of summer in 1978, Citizen Soldier had logged over 3000 calls and letters from veterans. Working with the help of environmental scientists like Dr. Susan Daum of Mount Sinai's Environmental Sciences Labs and Drs. Jeanne and Steve Stellman of the American Health Foundation, Citizen Soldier designed a six-page self-administered medical questionnaire (see Appendix). The survey form asked veterans detailed questions in five areas: military-service history, herbicide exposure, personal health history, past medical history, and family history, with emphasis on stillbirths, miscarriages, and congenital birth defects. A questionnaire was sent to every veteran who called in, and copies were distributed in bulk to hundreds of veterans groups, trade unions, and counseling centers across the country.

About this time, Paul Reutershan, 28, of Lake Mohegan, New York, read the allegations about Agent Orange in his local newspaper. Paul had flown a helicopter in Vietnam, and his chopper had passed through defoliant mists being laid down by C-123s. Back home Paul found a job as a conductor on ConRail commuter trains and was planning to be married when doctors gave him terrible news: he had less than two years to live. When Paul first learned that his abdominal cancer was terminal, he was incredulous. He'd always been a bit of a "health nut," and he neither drank nor smoked. So, when he read over the symptoms some doctors associate with dioxin exposure, it hit him with enormous force. Thinking back to Vietnam, Paul remembered that he'd developed chloracne on his back just before coming home.

Bitter at the fading of the light, Paul threw himself into a frenzy of activity, speaking about Agent Orange wherever and whenever someone would listen. Starting off with late-night cable TV in New York, Paul before long was being interviewed on the "Today Show" and other national programs. It was painful to listen as Paul exposed his deepest feelings at being used callously by the U.S. military. In his rage at the cruelty of his fate, Paul was disturbingly eloquent: "I got killed in Vietnam; I just didn't know it at the time."

With the help of his sister, Joan Dziedzic and other Vietnam veterans, Paul formed an organization for those most affected by defoliants, calling it Agent Orange Victims International. It was his dream that this group would unite victims of U.S. spraying in Vietnam with civilians who had been harmed by the domestic use (for crop and brush control) of the same herbicides.

On Capitol Hill, as constituent mail from "back home" increased, Congress slowly stirred. Since the veterans' affairs committees in both the House and Senate tend to be dominated by conservative partisans of the military, there was not much enthusiasm for prying open what might prove to be another can of military worms. However, when the traditional veterans' groups such as the Veterans of Foreign Wars and the Disabled American Veterans began to make inquiries about Agent Orange, even the most reactionary lawmaker had to pay some attention. Some of the more liberal members of the House committee circulated a joint letter to their chairman, asking that the Veterans Administration furnish the panel with a detailed report on its handling of Agent Orange claimants, as well as a summary of the scientific research being performed on the issue within the federal sector for the VA.

Nothing more was heard publicly in Washington until early October 1978, when the leadership of the House Veterans Affairs Committee announced that it would hold a one-day hearing on Agent Orange the following day. The witness list was no surprise, however; spokesmen for the Veterans Administration, the air force, and the National Cancer Institute dominated the proceedings.

Major General Garth Dettinger, the deputy surgeon general of the air force, set the tone for the day's proceedings; he offered the reassuring news that four times as much dioxin was dumped on rangelands and forests in the U.S. as was used in Vietnam from 1962 to 1971. Taking the hard line, he flatly asserted that the use of herbicides in the Vietnam or the U.S. "has not resulted in a documented increase in illness among users or the general population."

The general then turned to the risk faced by GIs during the Vietnam defoliation program: "The potential for exposure of U.S. military personnel is *highly* [his emphasis] unlikely." This, he explained, is because Vietnam's dense canopied cover would have prevented all but 6 percent of the total herbicide applied from actually filtering through to the forest floor. This level of exposure would be the same, he reassured us all, as that routinely encountered by persons entering sprayed rangelands in the U.S. Besides, Dettinger explained, ground combat troops would be unlikely to enter a sprayed area for several weeks after treatment, because "defoliation didn't occur until three or four weeks after treatment." The general apparently thought that because defoliation was not used as a *tactical* weapon, as artillery or an air strike would precede a ground assault in a target area, soldiers would not enter a recently sprayed area. But since Vietnam was primarily a guerrilla war, characterized by hit-and-run assaults and constantly shifting battle lines, GIs were required to pursue the enemy anytime and anywhere.

Regarding what portion of the 2.8 million U.S. troops might actually have been exposed, Dettinger demonstrated even greater rigidity and even less knowledge. According to him, only insecticides and smoke screens were aerially applied in areas where U.S. ground troops operated. "I want to stress," he declared, "that herbicides were *not* [his emphasis] used in this fashion."

As was shown in chapter 7 about the Ranch Hands, there are many eyewitness accounts of routine spraying of defoliants around "friendly" base camps and firebases. Perhaps it is the spirit of interservice rivalry which prevents the good general from taking any notice of what the army and marine helicopters and spray trucks may have been doing with their supplies of herbicides, but at least one account claims that air force C-123s themselves gave large numbers of U.S. troops an unwanted bath with Agent Orange. John East, of Santa Rosa, California, never will forget a morning in the fall of 1967 when he was standing with five hundred other marines on a hillside firebase in the northern I Corp sector. "Three planes were flying abreast as they came right over us. They were flying into the winds and as they released the spray it blew back over our base. I felt it dampen my shirt and I was quite upset that it blew onto me. Everyone on the hill got a shot of it. None of the officers said anything about it; it was just shrugged off." Further refutation of Dettinger is found in a GAO report, which we summarize below.

Dettinger offered one further argument why the spray poses little danger: "Photodegeneration has been shown to destroy dioxin within a [few] hours." Photodegeneration is defined as "chemical degradation in the presence of light." In other words, Dettinger was saying that a few hours of sunlight rendered dioxin harmless.

This argument seems dubious in light of a number of studies which found that dioxin resists decomposition and is soluble in human body fat. One study found that after one year, approximately 50 percent of the dioxin still was present in two moist soil samples, regardless of the amount applied or the type of soil.

The deputy surgeon general did acknowledge that a relatively small group, the spray handlers, could have encountered significant exposures; but he argued that "closed transfer systems" [for fuel loading] and the "use of *protective equipment* [his emphasis] employed during ground loading" would have kept such risk to a minimum. To buttress Dettinger's testimony, the air force released an extensive 247-page report which had been written for the surgeon general by Captain Alvin Young (the plant scientist Maude DeVictor talked to) and three other air force scientists. It echoed Dettinger's claims: "[Handlers] were indoctrinated in appropriate safety precautions, including gloves and face shields. . . . [they] were encouraged to take normal safety precautions . . . and to avoid skin and eye contact with the material. Contaminated clothing was to be washed before re-use. Spillage on skin was to be rinsed copiously . . ."

While the Veterans Administration and Congress continue to regard this report as authoritative, the surgeon general's office seems to have backed away from some of its assertions. In an interview with the authors in August 1979, Major Phil Brown, an official spokesman, stated: "I'm not aware of any directions to the men [in Vietnam]: 'Thou shall wear protective gear.' " Brown also injected a note of skepticism about Dettinger's claim that a "closed-transfer system" for loading would have kept risk of exposure low. "There was a fairly long period of time when they did hand pump from fifty-five-gallon drums into the fuel trucks," he stated.

Ranch Hand Charley Hubbs, quoted previously in chapter 7, served in Vietnam until the end of 1967. He sat in on our interview with the surgeon general's staff. When we asked him if the men actually hand pumped each plane's 1000-gallon tank, he nodded and laughed, stating that "we had some pretty tired folks." Charley feels that the Ranch Hands were poorly equipped. "You could sum up what they did for us over there in a word—nothing! Other squadrons had all kinds of planes and support units; we just had to live hand to mouth."

The air force's recitation of precise regulations mandating the use of protective gear and safety procedures reminds one of policy statements that the Pentagon issued whenever evidence surfaced of war crimes like My Lai. A whole list of instructions that each GI was given regarding the Geneva Convention and Rules of Land Warfare would be rattled off, as though such training shifted all responsibility for what might happen on the battlefield from the commanders to the individual soldiers. It's easy to imagine that in the early days of the spray program someone in the air force legal office foresaw the need for some "boilerplate"—as it's called in the legal trade—whose sweeping language could be used to cover any future situation in which a claim for damage might arise.

Charley Hubbs was very candid about the total disregard for safety measures in Vietnam. "They may have said, 'do these things,' but I can guarantee you that over there no one used any such gear. Loading, flying, getting shot at, spraying, we all wore the same thing, a T-shirt."

One fuel supervisor who worked at Phu Cat in 1970, Donald Martin of Tampa, Florida, told us that the American GIs who loaded the planes got "drowned" a number of times while transferring herbicide from storage barrels to the loading tanks. "No one wore gloves or protective gear, just combat fatigues; most guys didn't even wear shirts 'cause it was so hot. When a guy got splashed, he just kept on goin'." Don Martin doesn't remember any training in the proper handling or use of herbicides. Although he served in Vietnam after the Pentagon publicly had announced spray restrictions due to concern about the use of the herbicides, this concern doesn't seem to have resulted in any increased concern for the handlers' safety. Don today suffers from a severe arthritic condition which has rendered him unable to work. Several doctors have given him statements that his disability may have been brought on by his daily contact with the chemicals.

Dr. Paul Haber, the Veterans Administration's chief medical director for professional services, also testified at the House hearing in October. His testimony basically echoed that of the air force. He stated that "the only human disorder linked to herbicide is chloracne." Temporary symptoms such as nausea, diarrhea, headaches, and the like "disappear after a short period of time." But apparently the VA brass had had some second thoughts about the accuracy of some of Dr. Schepers' scientific opinions because Haber now acknowledged in his statement "a main scientific concern is whether . . . dioxin may persist in body tissue for protracted periods." To seek answers, he announced that the VA would conduct a study to compare fat tissue taken from a small number of Vietnam veterans with vets who hadn't served in Indochina.

Preliminary results from this study released at a VA scientific meeting in December 1979 confirmed that measurable levels of dioxin were present in some of the exposed veterans. Fat tissue was taken from thirty-three veterans, including a group of ten who hadn't served in Vietnam. Among twenty-two samples already analyzed, dioxin has been found in ten cases.

Haber then presented a newly revised medical circular that was being sent to all VA facilities. He explained that its purpose was to "insure that each veteran who alleges exposure will immediately receive proper administrative and health care management." Obviously, something had happened between April and September which accounted for the changed attitude at the Veterans Administration. That "something" was likely the fact that thousands of veterans had come forward to complain of health problems. They were proving impossible to sweep under the bureaucratic rug.

This September 14 circular ordered all VA facilities to submit quarterly reports to headquarters detailing all Agent Orange claims filed, along with copies of medical files in any case where disability for herbicide exposure was granted. This reporting was a dual-edged sword, however. While it could help the VA headquarters stay abreast of national developments, it also made any disability grant subject to the immediate review of headquarters brass. This would likely have a chilling effect on even the most dedicated VA workers. To no one's surprise, the VA announced later in the year that not a single claim for herbicide-related disability had been granted in the entire country. While the VA had altered its policy to create the appearance of greater sensitivity to the issue, the net effect of its *de facto* policy of discouraging all such claims continued unchanged.

Dr. Haber also told the committee that the Armed Forces Institute of Pathology had begun to receive and store body tissues that were taken from Vietnam veterans who underwent operations at VA medical centers. He also described a review

of in-house data on cancers, skin problems, and other medical
categories which the VA staff was conducting.

Dr. Haber's statement also contained a reference to a request
that the VA had made of the Pentagon "to furnish us with complete maps of each herbicide mission, the dates they were
carried out, units performing the spray missions, the unit
present in the area at the time of the mission or those units
entering that area after they were sprayed."

In his testimony, Dr. Haber referred to an "informal group"
that had been meeting to collect scientific data on herbicides
and formulate health care policy. It included representatives
from every federal agency with regulatory responsibilities concerning toxic chemicals, as well as "consultants" from Dow
Chemical Corporation and various universities. He neglected
to mention that the VA had been threatened with a lawsuit,
since Haber's informal panel violated the Federal Advisory
Committee Act. Enacted a few years ago, this legislation is an
attempt to deal with the problem of "stacked" committees
which produce predetermined conclusions and recommendations. The National Veterans Law Center in Washington, D.C.,
demanded that the Veterans Administration comply with the
act, which specifies procedures for the organization and com-
position of such bodies with an eye toward encouraging reasonable diversity. Apparently Haber's lawyers advised him to scrap
his informal panel and start over, which is exactly what he did.

No independent scientist—much less a potential victim or
group of victims—was invited to testify before the committee.
The one veteran who represented the Veterans of Foreign Wars,
issued a cautious statement politely asking for more outreach
and treatment.

The one-day hearing was over.

By November, over a thousand Citizen Soldier questionnaires had been completed and returned. The American Health
Foundation coded the responses to the first 536 and then analyzed them by computer. Volunteers from Citizen Soldier then

spent many hours checking each reported case of cancer or birth defect with local physicians or medical records. In an open letter to the veterans, Drs. Jeanne and Steven Stellman of the American Health Foundation summarized their findings:

"There were 35 cases of cancer reported, which included three cases of kidney cancer, a very rare disease for this age group; three testicular cancers, and a number of cancers of the lymphatic system. There were 77 children reported born with defects, ranging from missing or deformed fingers to heart defects to unusual skin and hearing disorders. One of the most unexpected findings was the large number of veterans who complained of changes in skin color and sensitivity to light, as well as nervous system difficulties."

Just a week before Christmas, Paul Reutershan succumbed to his abdominal cancer. Just before his death he was granted a service-connected disability for his condition, but dioxin exposure was never mentioned. The day after he was buried, his sister received a phone call from a VA official. He warned her not to cash the disability check they'd sent Paul, since his claim against the government expired when he did. Bureaucratic duty performed, he hung up.

In early 1979, two network shows, ABC-TV's "20-20" and Public Broadcasting's "For Your Information," both aired programs featuring the Agent Orange controversy. When Geraldo Rivera described Citizen Soldier's questionnaire and read its address on "20-20" he stimulated over 1500 calls and letters from veterans.

The avalanche had started.

11

To Move America

In less than a year, the question of Agent Orange poisoning had evolved from a localized concern to an issue which concerned the country as a whole. By winter in 1979, it must have been clear to the government and the chemical manufacturers that they were facing a problem that no amount of bombastic disclaimers would dissolve. Thousands of veterans, armed with the knowledge that their chronic ailments may be related to herbicides, were insistently knocking on the Veterans Administration's door demanding care and compensation. The VA had reported the previous September that only 600 vets had requested physical exams; by October 1979 this number had grown to 4800 veterans. In November 1979 Citizen Soldier released a series of public-service television advertisements that feature Martin Sheen (star of *Apocalypse Now,* Coppola's Vietnam war epic) advising veterans about Agent Orange symptoms and urging them to contact Citizen Soldier for information. These spots were sent to all 750 commercial TV stations and many of the 3000 cable TV systems in the United States. The response has been staggering; by January 1980 over 190 commercial stations had requested spots for previewing. They will motivate thousands of veterans to come forward; doubtless the courts, Congress, and the federal agencies will feel ever-increasing heat from this growing movement.

The Courts. The first lawsuit on behalf of exposed veterans was filed in federal district court in Westbury, New York, in January 1979 by Victor Yannacone, an environmental lawyer who played an important role in the successful litigation to ban DDT. The complaint was a novel class action suit which asked the court to certify as a "class" all 2.8 million veterans who served in Vietnam. It asked for $4 billion for damages not only to compensate the individual veterans but also to provide a fund to reimburse the affected governmental agencies for costs they would incur in caring for these men. In addition to allegations that the military's use of herbicides violated the constitutional rights of all veterans, Yannacone offered several other legal grounds for holding the manufacturers liable for damages, including breach of implied and express warranties to make safe products, failure adequately to test products and warn of hazards, and failure to remove such dangers from interstate commerce. As a separate count, he asked the court to order an immediate ban on any further spraying of 2,4,5-T in this country.

As expected, the defendant-manufacturers, Dow, Hercules, Diamond Shamrock, Monsanto, and North American Phillips, have waged a spirited defense against this suit. Herbicide sales account for only a small part of these manufacturers' total revenues—in Dow's case less than 1 percent of its total sales of $6 billion in 1978. However, since approximately hundreds of new chemical compounds are now being placed on the market annually, the manufacturers have an enormous stake in preventing legal precedents which would sharply increase their product liability. Among a battery of legal motions and maneuvers, they asked the court to issue a "gag" order on Yannacone, claiming that pretrial publicity about Agent Orange would make it impossible to obtain a fair trial anywhere in the United States. This motion was eventually denied, but in August 1979, Judge George Pratt also denied the plaintiff's request that domestic use of 2,4,5-T be halted, finding that the Environmental Protection Agency had primary jurisdiction over such an order.

During this same period, Citizen Soldier began working with a team of experienced trial lawyers led by Benton Musslewhite and Newton Schwartz of Houston and Mel Block of New York. After examining the legal alternatives, this team decided that the best chance for recovery lay with third-party products liability lawsuits, which would be filed on behalf of individual veterans or their survivors. "Third-party" refers to the fact that the veteran in this situation is really an innocent party, who was harmed by conduct between the two principal parties, the government on one hand and the chemical manufacturers on the other. In the lawyers' opinion, a class action lawsuit was likely to result in less actual money damages for ailing veterans than individual lawsuits. Musslewhite and Schwartz filed complaints in the federal district court of Texas on behalf of over a hundred individual veterans. Their complaints charged that the manufacturers had breached both implied and express warranties by making products that were "defective and unreasonably dangerous." It further alleged that their reckless refusal to take care constituted "gross negligence" which entitled the plaintiffs to punitive as well as actual damages.

In early October 1979, the federal judge in Texas granted the manufacturers' motion and ordered that all cases which had been filed in his court (125 in all) be transferred to the New York federal court in which Mr. Yannacone's lawsuits are being heard. This means that all pretrial motions and discovery will be consolidated into a single proceeding under the Multi-District Litigation Act. By January 1980 over 2000 lawsuits on behalf of individual veterans and their families had been filed in U.S. district courts throughout the country. All of these cases have been duly moved to Judge Pratt's court in Westbury, New York, for at least the pretrial discovery and motion stages of the lawsuits. Eventually, individual plaintiffs may "opt out" to conduct separate trials on the issues of causation and damages. At press time Judge Pratt had still not ruled on the plaintiff's request that he certify all ailing Vietnam veterans as a "class."

Congress. Practically every member of Congress runs in a district where the vote "swing" never amounts to more than eight percent of the total vote. This means that a small, well-organized bloc of voters can substantially affect the outcome of a given election, as proponents of gun-control legislation, for example, have learned to their regret. Hence, if a member of Congress avoids controversy and is reasonably adept at locating missing social security checks and mailing out Medicare pamphlets, he or she can expect to be returned to Washington time and again. Given this mentality, an issue like Agent Orange is about as welcome to most congressmen as a case of cholera. It is a complicated scientific issue which will likely be resolved only after a long and bitter struggle. Rare is the politician who looks kindly on renewed debate over the Vietnam war, so most congresspeople have tried to duck any serious involvement with herbicide debate.

In April 1979, the General Accounting Office (GAO), the congressional investigative agency, published the second part of its report on Agent Orange. This part focused principally on the VA's response to herbicide poisoning claims by veterans. However, a careful reading raises serious doubts about the investigative zeal of its authors at GAO. At several key points, the authors accept as gospel what they were told by the VA and the Pentagon. For example, the report states that "the VA's general policy is to examine and treat all veterans claiming toxic effects from exposure . . . all veterans who are currently being treated [or will be treated] in VA facilities, will be asked if they've been exposed to herbicides in Vietnam."

Contrast this with a survey conducted in May 1979, among 1000 veterans who had completed the Citizen Soldier medical questionnaire. Ninety-one percent of those responding described the VA's handling of their Agent Orange complaints as "unsatisfactory." Many of the six hundred respondents attached notes or letters describing their personal experiences at VA facilities across the country. For example, a veteran described his examination at the Philadelphia VA as follows: "The doctor told me to stand facing a wall, then he pushed me three times. 'You don't have it,' he told me." A vet from Manchester, New Hampshire, writes about his visit to the local VA:

"Before I could say a word the doctor told me, 'You don't have Agent Orange.' After looking down my throat with a flashlight, he reminded me that the clinic did not treat throat and sinus problems." A New Jersey veteran wrote that he was examined by a VA doctor who asked him nothing about Agent Orange exposure even though he knew that the vet had recently had a cancerous testicle removed.

After conversations with at least fifty different veterans, we've concluded that many Veterans Administration facilities have not been using the VA questionnaire (prescribed in the September 14, 1978, national memo and superseded by a similar memo dated April 16, 1979) despite the VA's claim that the questionnaire is being used to collect accurate exposure data at all facilities.

Despite its half-hearted investigation, the GAO report did point out two deficiencies in the VA operation. First, it noted the lack of a system to ensure that veterans who file claims are actually given physical examinations. Secondly, it cited the GAO discovery that VA regional offices were not using the military records of veterans to obtain information about herbicide exposure.

Turning to the Department of Defense, the GAO recommended that it conduct a comprehensive study of the long-term effects on military personnel from all branches of service. Also, it pointed out that only the air force medical services had any procedures for handling the health problems of active-duty personnel that might be related to herbicide exposure. In response, the Pentagon agreed to create such medical services in all branches, but it rejected the proposal to conduct a broad study. Richard Danzig, the military's spokesman, argued that "it is extremely doubtful that a retrospective epidemiological study of that population would produce reliable results." He cited as reasons the lack of precise data on exposure concentrations, the intervention of other causative factors in the years since exposure, and the impossibility of identifying an appropriate "control" group.

In November 1979 Senator Charles Percy (Republican-Illinois) released a GAO report which repudiated the Pentagon's claim that ground troops were unlikely to have been exposed to herbicide spray.

The GAO identified marine units consisting of 5900 men who were within a mile of spraying on the day it took place. It placed another 16,000 marines the same distance from spraying during a period of up to four weeks after it occurred. The investigators also found that army units were proximate to spray operations but could not identify individuals because of deficient army records.

The report concluded that "large numbers of U.S. Army and Marine Corps ground troops were in, and close to sprayed areas during and after spraying . . . we now believe that . . . personnel most likely to have been exposed could include ground troops, as well as herbicide handlers and aircraft crew members."

The GAO also noted that despite the Pentagon's claim to the contrary, it could find no mention in any army manual of an order restricting personnel from entering sprayed areas for four to six weeks after spraying; nor could any chemical officers it interviewed remember such a rule. While U.S. ground commanders were routinely told of spray missions forty-eight hours in advance, this was done, the GAO concluded, only to "prevent troops from being wounded or killed by fighter aircraft, which often protected spray aircraft."

On the issue of spraying around U.S. defense perimeters (which the DOD has consistently minimized), the GAO stated that the first three hundred yards around any U.S. base camp was considered a "free spray" area and the local commander could order it sprayed without seeking any approval from higher authorities.

Whether this report has dislodged the Pentagon from its previous positions remains to be seen, however. When coauthor Tod Ensign asked Colonel J. W. Thiessen, the Pentagon's representative on the VA's Agent Orange Task Force, what information had been assembled about spray operations from helicopters, trucks, and backpacks in the month since the report's release, he responded, "I have nothing new on this."

One small band of congresspersons (who call themselves the

Vietnam Veterans in Congress) has tried to stimulate congressional interest in this issue. Led by David Bonier (Democrat-Michigan) and Albert Gore, Jr. (Democrat-Tennessee), their success so far has been limited to a one-day hearing in May 1979, at which some Vietnam veterans were heard.

As the Agent Orange case load steadily grew in their district offices, members of Congress decided that new legislation was needed to accelerate the government's research effort. In November Congress passed two bills, one directing HEW to study "various populations" (except veterans) and the other mandating the VA to conduct a similar study among Vietnam veterans. In both bills the Office of Technology Assessment (an arm of Congress) was empowered to approve or reject the protocol (or design) of the proposed study. Under the HEW bill the agency had two years before it had to report any study results.

To avoid being upstaged, the White House announced in December the creation of yet another intra-agency task force which was to review and coordinate all federal efforts in this area. In January 1980 Carter surprised many when he used his first veto of the current Congress to reject the bill mandating the HEW study. He argued that giving a congressional agency the power to approve or deny agency study plans violates the constitutional concept of separation of powers. He failed to mention that the VA study bill which he signed a few weeks earlier contained the same restriction.

At press time confusion seems to reign in Washington. Just *what* studies of what populations are to be commissioned by what agencies is not at all clear.

The federal agencies. The Veterans Administration's public posture on Agent Orange underwent a perceptible change in early 1979. For the first time it began to issue public statements of concern and even began urging veterans who thought they might have been poisoned to come in for examinations. Of course, they still didn't post large signs in VA clinics or insert information about dioxin's symptoms in their regular mailings. For example, they sent eight million pieces of mail to veterans in late 1978 reminding them that their GI Bill benefits would soon expire, but no one bothered to include any information about Agent Orange.

In another shift, VA doctors actually met with Dr. Ton That Tung, the Vietnamese scientist, during his goodwill tour of the U.S. in April, to discuss his research. One VA press statement quoted Dr. Tung (whose work they had disparaged only a few months earlier). However, their reference to him quoted a remark that the possibilities of veterans passing birth defects through their sperm was "remote."

As we mentioned earlier, President Carter used the traditional veterans' celebration on Memorial Day to announce two new studies: a study by the Department of Health, Education, and Welfare of 288 Monsanto workers who were exposed to 2,4,5-T when a factory making the chemical exploded in 1949, and a six-year study by the air force of 1200 men who served in Operation Ranch Hand. This latter study encountered snags, however, and the air force announced in September 1979 that it wouldn't get underway until January 1980 at the earliest. At this rate ailing vets may have to wait until 1986 for any answers from the government.

A week after the president's announcement, the VA finally unveiled its long-awaited Advisory Committee on the Health Related Effects of Herbicide. Chaired by VA's deputy chief of medical services, Dr. Paul Haber, with another VA doctor, Gerrit Schepers, serving as vice-chairman, the fourteen-member panel included one scientist from each of the following federal agencies: the Environmental Protection Agency, the National Institute for Occupational Safety and Health, the Center for Communicable Disease (HEW), the Department of Agriculture, the National Cancer Institute, and the National Institute for Environmental Health Sciences. Two nongovernment scientists, Dr. James Allen of the University of Wisconsin and Dr. Sheldon Murphy of the University of Texas at Houston, were also named. Colonel J. W. Thiessen of the Army's Environmental Hygiene Agency was the sole military representative, while Dr. Irving Brick of the American Legion and Robert

Lenham, a program officer with the Disabled American Veterans, were named as "constituency" representatives.

If the type of detailed questions which were proposed for discussion at the group's first meeting are any indication, the panel seems serious about looking for answers. Two examples: "Can criteria be established for determining levels of exposure of [GIs] based on the HERBS [spray mission] tapes and unit histories? What medical tests should be utilized to help establish a diagnosis of chronic herbicide-induced toxicity among Vietnam veterans?"

The panel's diverse membership is quite an improvement over the semisecret advisory panel which the VA had quietly assembled the previous summer. No doubt the harsh criticism which that maneuver evoked bore on the VA chiefs' decision to come up with a reputable panel the second time around. While many hope that the panel will insist upon scientific work of the highest quality, it is, of course, too early to tell. For one thing, it's not clear just how much time the individual scientists on the panel will be able to devote to its work. This could mean that decision making might gravitate toward the VA constabulary. Secondly, the panel has no staff or budget of its own; all administrative support is to be provided by the regular VA staff. This causes concern in light of some correspondence one of the authors uncovered at VA headquarters.

While conducting an interview with Stratton Appleman, the VA's chief of news and media liaison, coauthor Tod Ensign was given permission to look through the press office's files. While leafing through stacks of yellowed press clippings, he chanced across a thick packet of materials which apparently had been misfiled. Atop it was a letter dated May 17, 1979, from Dow Chemical's public information director to Mr. Appleman. It was clear from the letter's tone that the two men were on very friendly terms. The Dow official, Mirrell Kephart, began by referring to two film "treatments" (outlines) which Dow was planning to make for free distribution to television stations across the country. He asked his friend "Strat" to review the treatments and to provide Dow with his suggestions and comments.

In the letter's second paragraph, Kephart referred to an attached report which had been prepared by a "PR consultant" after visiting Citizen Soldier's offices in New York. The report consisted of a two-page summary of a personal interview with Michael Uhl and copies of materials which Uhl freely gave the mysterious visitor. Ensign was alarmed when he learned about the interview since he knew that no one identifying him- or herself as a Dow employee or representative ever had visited Citizen Soldier. Looking over calendars and office logs, he and Uhl tried to figure out who the "consultant" might have been and when he had visited. The authors couldn't pin down any likely suspect as there had been many visits and calls by news and TV reporters in the three-month period prior to the Dow letter.

Dow's surveillance tactics disturbed us for two reasons. One, we need a mutual trusting relationship with the press in our efforts to bring the plight of the GI to the public at large. So, if Dow sent someone posing as a member of the press to our office, it will tend to make us suspicious of *all* reporters in the future. Secondly, we are concerned that Dow's agent may have obtained privileged information concerning litigation being prepared in concert with the Texas attorneys mentioned earlier. Tod Ensign is one of the lawyers representing over a hundred veteran plaintiffs, and an attorney-client relationship exists between him and each of them.

Citizen Soldier released a press statement on August 15 which included a summary of the Dow letter (which Ensign reconstructed from memory) and charged them with "corporate espionage." Kephart admitted to *Chemical Week* magazine that it had sent F. Leonard Shearer who works for Burson-Marsteller, a large public relations firm, to collect information. Although he didn't explicitly deny that Shearer posed as a journalist, Kephart stated that "there was no cloak and dagger involved." When the enterprising *Chemical Week* reporter tried to interview Shearer he was told that he had left for a European vacation. His employer, Burson-Marsteller declined to comment "until we get more information."

In the last part of his letter to the VA's press chief, Dow's

Kephart renewed what apparently had been a standing invitation to both Appleman and Dr. Gerrit Schepers to "visit Midland soon." He advised them that Dow would be setting up interviews for them with the Saginaw Valley media during their visit. Dr. Schepers, it will be recalled, is the vice-chairman of the newly created advisory committee mandated to conduct a thorough and honest investigation of the whole controversy. Stratton Appleman is a member of a Veterans Administration steering committee which is the sole source of administrative and logistical support for the advisory committee. Shortly after we released the contents of the Dow letter, Appleman was removed from his post and "promoted" to a new position.

In its press statement, Citizen Soldier asked the VA the following questions: Why is Dow inviting Appleman and Dr. Schepers to its plant and arranging media interviews on their behalf? What is the precise nature (if any) of the relationship between either man and Dow Chemical? What is official VA policy as to contacts between employees and manufacturers of Agent Orange? What is the Advisory Committee's policy as to contacts between its panel members and the chemical manufacturers?

As this book went to press, these questions still were unanswered.

Citizen Soldier also addressed a formal letter of complaint to Dow General Counsel I. F. Harlow, asking him to investigate whether Dow's agent may have violated the sanctity of the attorney-client relationship. He responded curtly that since Dow hadn't known of any pending litigation in which Citizen Soldier was involved, he could see nothing which required investigation. Apparently, Nixon-style "dirty tricks" still raise no ethical concerns at Dow Chemical.

A Veterans' Movement Grows. One legacy of the Vietnam War has been the appropriation of millions of federal dollars to provide educational and job counseling to many of the 8.4 million veterans who served during the war period. Hundreds of colleges and universities across the country have used these funds to employ veterans as counselors to other veterans. Many local social welfare and United Way agencies also have created similar programs.

As mentioned earlier, "old line" veteran organizations, such as the Disabled American Veterans, the American Legion, and the Veterans of Foreign Wars, have also tried to address the concerns of the Vietnam veteran. These groups enjoy a "special relationship" to the VA in that their claims workers occupy office space on the VA premises. In recent months, they have demonstrated increased concern about Agent Orange, although many in their ranks still believe that an "antiwar" taint is attached to the issue.

The 600,000-member Disabled American Veterans, however, jumped into the issue with both feet in July 1979 when its National Service Director Norman Harnett announced that it would provide free claims counseling. Harnett explained the obstacles: "It will be extremely difficult to show that disabilities result from exposure to Agent Orange for purposes of VA benefits. That's why it's so important that . . . a benefits expert, who doesn't get his paycheck from the government, represent the client." While the American Legion and VFW have made *pro forma* statements of concern, they've been much less active than the Disabled American Veterans on the issue.

Many of the college-based counselors mentioned above banded together to form the National Association of Concerned Veterans (NACV) in the early 1970s. Unlike other organizations of Vietnam-era veterans, this group never played an active role in opposing America's continuing military involvement in Indochina. In 1974 one of the authors attempted to convince NACV's officers that they should support universal amnesty for all resisters to the Vietnam war. Again, they refused to become involved in "politics," explaining that they could be more effective by sticking to the "bread and butter" issues of veterans' benefits.

In 1978, two other groups of Vietnam veterans were launched: the Council of Vietnam Veterans, a Washington-

based group concerned primarily with lobbying for govern-
ment programs, and Concerned American Veterans Against
Toxins (CAVEAT; "beware" in Latin), which was formed at
Columbia College in Chicago to work exclusively on the Agent
Orange issue. These two groups along with Agent Orange
Victims International met at the NACV annual convention in
Kansas City in May 1979 and decided to launch a Task Force
on Agent Orange to coordinate and unify the effort.

Although Citizen Soldier had implemented the first national
work on the issue and had initiated earlier meetings in an attempt to stimulate just such a coalition, it was not invited to
join the Task Force nor informed of its plans. Ron De Young,
Task Force chairman, later stated that "it was the consensus
of the group present that we did not wish to involve ourselves
with your organization." In an open letter which was circulated
to veterans' organizations across the country, Citizen Soldier
pointed out that some of the Task Force organizers were be-
having as though they thought a political coalition was a private
club. Citizen Soldier argued that a coalition should be open,
without condition, to all organizations which endorse its goals;
any other policy would weaken the overall effort to win justice
for victims of Agent Orange.

The exclusion of Citizen Soldier seems to be motivated by
two factors. One is that the coalition's organizers are uncomfortable with Citizen Soldier's beliefs and prefer not to air
possible differences in the open forum of coalition meetings.
Again, this discomfort stems from a fundamental misconcep-
tion about the nature of single-issue coalitions; there always
are differences between autonomous groups in any coalition,
but as long as there is agreement on coalition objectives, these
differences are irrelevant.

The second factor appears to be the sort of personal jeal-
ousies and ego conflicts which lead to petty empire-building.

An important political difference is the fact that Citizen
Soldier and its two predecessor-organizations, Safe Return
Amnesty Committee and the Citizens Commission of Inquiry
into U.S. War Crimes in Vietnam, grew directly out of the

movement against the war in Vietnam. Unlike the other groups, our work has had one consistent theme over the past decade: support for the right of low-ranking soldiers to resist illegal orders of an often autocratic military command. We created the Citizens Commission of Inquiry after the My Lai massacre was disclosed in 1969 because it became obvious that the nation's political leaders had no stomach for probing the effects of their military policies in Vietnam. These policies, such as "free fire zones," "search and destroy," and "body counts" made atrocities such as My Lai virtually inevitable. Instead, the leaders apparently hoped that by prosecuting a few low-ranking GIs such as Lieutenant William Calley, they could reinforce their contention that My Lai was an isolated incident caused solely by (in Vice-President Spiro Agnew's phrase) a "few rotten apples."

The Citizens Commission of Inquiry began to interview and organize Vietnam combat veterans to document evidence that the criminal policies the veterans had been compelled to execute in Vietnam were genocidal in effect, if not by design. The commission conducted numerous public hearings throughout the country, at which veterans spoke out against the Pentagon cover-up.

As the combat role of the U.S. troops declined after the Paris accords, the emphasis of our work shifted to support for amnesty for hundreds of thousands of GIs who were being punished for their resistance to "business as usual" in Vietnam. We created the Safe Return Amnesty Committee which became the first group in the U.S. to actively organize for amnesty for military resisters. These "self-retired" veterans were quite different from their mostly white and middle-class brethren, the draft resisters, many of whom had attained exile status in Canada or had escaped prosecution through legal maneuvering. While Safe Return supported amnesty for *all* categories of resisters, its priority was always on building support for a soldier's right (and duty) under the Nuremberg precedents, to resist complicity in illegal military policies. In 1976, we organized Citizen Soldier, believing that an organization which could become involved with the problems of active-duty GIs in the "all volunteer" military was needed; we then worked on the legal defense of GIs who've been victimized by fraudulent recruiting practices and military racism.

It appears that several of the Task Force on Agent Orange members are uncomfortable with Citizen Soldier's view that the issue of Agent Orange cannot be separated from the broader issues of the war in Vietnam, as some of them suggest. It's not just another "problem" that can be resolved without having reference to the specific historical context in which it was created.

Citizen Soldier's tactical emphasis has also differed considerably from that of some of the other groups. As the antiwar and civil rights movements of the 1960s demonstrated, Congress and the federal government generally *respond* to, rather than *shape*, popular opinion, particularly where controversial issues are at stake. Therefore, Citizen Soldier stresses independent mass actions, such as rallies, marches, and demonstrations, instead of polite lobbying in the bureaucratic and legislative corridors in Washington.

As this book went to press, Citizen Soldier still had not been admitted to the Task Force. The infighting among the various veterans groups is hardly unique in the arena of politics— which is not to say that the issues at stake don't often range far beyond the petty forms in which they are expressed. In a sense these squabbles are a microcosm of the dilemma facing the nation, and, indeed, all nations of the world caught up in the problems of scarcity and the loss of control over the engines of national growth—over the supply, distribution, and pricing of food and fuel. These are indeed tumultuous times.

The United States today is a country foundering in a sea of amorality, lacking any clear standards with which to measure its virtues and its vices. During the Fifties, political apathy was to some degree offset by a spirit of rebelliousness against the stagnation of the culture. In the Sixties, the yardstick of our national righteousness was perceived by many to be the relative distance between national policy and the vaunted ideals of

American democracy. Here politics exposed the hypocrisy of America's self-proclaimed benevolent intentions toward the nonindustrial nations.

In the Seventies, however, both art and politics have been reduced to mere stratagems for fighting a rearguard action against the tyranny of scarcity. There is a Depression mentality which shields the eye from power, nursing wounds instead of opposing wrongs. So, the rich get richer and the poor get poorer. It's an old story, but in details of its application to the present, as fresh and elusive as ever.

In our fight to defend the needs and the rights of the GI victims of radioactive and herbicide poisoning, we reject the pragmatists' argument that the pie has shrunk, therefore our demands are unrealistic or utopian. Regardless of the pie's circumference, it is the relative size of the slices, we respond, that is the point of contention. Veterans must reach across the generation that separates the victims of nuclear war from the victims of chemical war. Together they will find a power in numbers and in understanding to make their interests count, not just with a derelict authority like the Veterans Administration, but with the larger society which has heretofore ignored them.

APPENDIX

Radiation*

What Is Ionizing Radiation?

The type of radiation emitted from nuclear power facilities is called ionizing radiation. It has the energy needed to remove one or more electrons from an atom. The ionization of an atom creates an ion which is chemically reactive and can damage living tissue. Ionizing radiation includes X rays, gamma rays, and alpha, beta, and neutron radiation. Cosmic radiation and naturally occurring radionuclides (radioactive elements) such as uranium, radium, and thorium are all ionizing radiation and are referred to as natural background radiation. Ionizing radiation is also the type used in medical X rays, and the type found in atomic weapons fallout and all phases of the nuclear fuel cycle from mining and milling to waste storage. The radionuclides are unstable and eventually decay through a decay chain to a stable element. Radiation is emitted during this process. The half-life of a radionuclide refers to the time necessary for one half of a given amount of it to decay.

What Can Radiation Do to a Person?

When radiation strikes a person, one of four events may occur:

1. It may pass through the cell without causing any damage.

* All the information in this section was released by the Sagebrush Alliance, 704 W. McWilliams Avenue, Las Vegas, Nevada 89106, and based, in part, on information provided by the Environmental Policy Institute, 317 Pennsylvania Avenue, SE, Washington, D.C. 20003.

2. It may damage the cell; the damage may be repaired.
3. It may damage the cell, but the call may divide before being repaired.
4. It may kill the cell.

The last two events have an impact on human health. Cell killing is often harmless unless enough cells in a particular tissue are killed. Medical radiation therapy uses the cell-killing effect of radiation to kill cancerous cells. The third event may eventually result in delayed ill effects such as cancer, or be passed on to a future generation as a genetic defect.

Total body radiation involves the exposure of all organs. Gamma radiation is a highly penetrating form and creates the most damage as it passes through the body. This is also true of X rays and neutron radiation. Alpha and beta radiation, which have low energies and are not serious external threats, can be extremely harmful if inhaled or ingested.

Many types of cancer are known to result from radiation. The most common is leukemia, but recent studies have shown that bone marrow and soft tissues like the pancreas, brain, kidney, lung, and large intestine also develop radiation-induced cancers. The general risk of radiation-induced cancers to the population has been calculated with a formula developed by the National Academy of Sciences' Committee on Biological Effects of Ionizing Radiation (BEIR Report) in 1972 as being 0.5 cancer for every 1000 man-rems of exposure. Dr. John Gofman believes the formula should say that three cancers are caused with the same amount of exposure. This formula, he points out, does not take into account that fetuses, preschool children, and the aged are far more sensitive to radiation than the average adult.

How Can Radiation Reach People?

Radiation emitted from nuclear power plants and as a result of atomic testing occurs in the form of several radionuclides.

Routine operation of a nuclear reactor entails occasional releases of radionuclides that have built up within the reactor system. Once radiation has been released it is dispersed by the wind and brought down by gravity, rain, snow, and fog. If winds are calm, the radiation will just deposit near the base of the stack. If the radiation drifts over a city where it is raining, most of it will be deposited there. After radionuclides reach the ground, they can be absorbed by plants and people. It is possible to receive direct radiation from the nuclides at ground level and to receive a radiation dose through the inhalation or ingestion of contaminated materials. Many plants and animals which are important human food sources are known to concentrate several radionuclides. For example, iodine is concentrated in milk; strontium is concentrated in milk, root vegetables, and animal bones.

The following material describes how ionizing radiation is concentrated in the human body. All this radiation is harmful to normal tissues because it damages cells of the body. Generally speaking, alpha and beta rays are harmless to you as long as you don't breathe or eat them, but if you ingest them they set up permanent business next to the marrow of your bones and in your reproductive organs or vital parts.

The effects of ionizing radiation are not immediate. Exposure to radiation can cause cancers many years later. Exposure to very low levels of radiation can be equally dangerous over time.

The times listed next to the type of ray emitted are the half-lives: how long it takes for half of the radioactive material to break down.

THYROID
    Iodine-131: beta (gamma), 8 days.
SKIN
    Sulfur-35: beta, 87 days.
LIVER
    Cobalt-60: beta (gamma), 5 years.

OVARIES AND TESTES

The reproductive organs are attacked by all radioactive isotopes emitting gamma radiation. In addition, the deadly Plutonium-239 is known to concentrate in the gonads. The radiation it emits can cause birth defects or mutations and miscarriages in the first generation and/or successive generations after exposure.

Iodine-131: gamma, 8 days.

Cobalt-60: gamma, 5 years.

Krypton-85: gamma, 10 years.

Ruthenium-106: gamma, 1 year.

Zinc-65: gamma, 245 days.

Barium-140: gamma, 13 days.

Potassium-42: gamma, 12 hours.

Cesium-137: gamma, 30 years.

Plutonium-239: alpha, 24,000 years.

MUSCLE

Potassium-42: beta (gamma), 12 hours.

Cesium-137 (and gonads): beta (gamma), 30 years.

LUNGS

Radon-222 (and whole body): alpha, 3.8 days.

Uranium-233 (and bone): alpha, 162,000 years.

Plutonium-239 (and bone): alpha, 24,000 years.

Krypton-85: beta (gamma), 10 years.

SPLEEN

Polonium-210: alpha, 138 days.

KIDNEYS

Ruthenium-106: gamma (beta), 1 year.

BONE

Radium-226: alpha, 1620 years.

Zinc-65: beta (gamma), 245 days.

Strontium-90: beta, 28 years.

Yttrium-90: beta, 64 hours.

Prometheum-147: beta, 2 years.

Barium-140: beta (gamma), 13 days.

Thorium-234: beta, 24.1 days.

Phosphorus-32: beta, 14 days.

Carbon-14 (and fat): beta, 5600 years.

The Baneberry trial resulted from a lawsuit brought on behalf of three workers who had died from leukemia/cancer. All three men were working as security guards at the Nevada test site on December 18, 1970, when an underground blast ("Baneberry") accidentally "vented" through a 315-foot crack in the earth's surface, sending radioactivity 8000 feet into the air. Although they'd had no training in rad-safety procedures, the men had been ordered to remain in the "hot" area to assist in the evacuation of several hundred people who were working nearby.

Summary of the Testimony of Dr. John Gofman, Baneberry Trial, April 4, 1979, U.S. Federal District Court, Las Vegas, Nevada

1. The shorter the half-life of a radionuclide, the greater the radioactivity.
2. Radionuclides that have exposed cells through inhalation, and that have very short half-lives, such as krypton and carbon-11, are particularly pernicious because of their enhanced radioactivity, and because their short half-life defies proper monitoring. (They would have done their damage and decayed before a body count would be taken. Inhaled particles are, for the most part, not recorded on the film badges.)
3. The Baneberry venting would have emitted many short-lived radionuclides which, according to the Department of Energy, presents no threat of health damage to humans because there are no personnel present during the weapons tests. However, there were many personnel present during the Baneberry test, and body counts, even a few hours later, are too late to detect some of the short-lived but very toxic radionuclides.
4. In a short period of time, a short-lived radionuclide will discharge most of its radioactivity, whereas long-lived

radionuclides (plutonium, for example) would, in a short time, hardly begin to decay. (The Baneberry venting needs to be considered a short-period exposure.)

5. According to Gofman, it is as close as possible to medical certainty that Roberts's and Nunmaker's leukemias are directly attributable to the Baneberry venting. The chances are 3 out of 10,000 that these men contracted leukemia from anything *but* the Baneberry exposure. This judgment was echoed by Drs. Alice Stewart and Rosalie Bertell.

6. Gofman believes that the doses received by Roberts and Nunmaker were 100 times the external estimated doses recorded at the Nevada test site. He attributes this discrepancy to the alpha radiation, the inhaled radiation, and the short-lived radiation, which could not be recorded by either the film badges or the whole-body count.

7. Low-level radiation exposure below 25 rems can certainly cause leukemia and cancer. Gofman cited three well-known studies on low-level radiation:

   a. Sir Kenneth Potchin's study in Hiroshima/Nagasaki proved that 4.3 rems showed an excess of leukemia victims.

   b. According to Dr. Mondane's study, radiation exposure to the scalps of children induces six times the incidence of thyroid cancers at 6.3 rems (Israel, 1976 or 1977).

   c. Dr. Alice Stewart's study showed that .3-1.5 rems induced leukemia/cancer in children in a straight-line effect (Oxford study, 1956–58).

8. In 1974 Gofman estimated that 12,000 people per year would die from cancer/leukemia in the United States because of medical and dental X rays. Now, in 1979, he feels that number needs to be raised by two to three times as much—from 24,000 to 36,000 people per year.

9. In a study done in 1975 Gofman estimated that 116,000 persons had been consigned to plutonium-induced lung cancers from past atmospheric weapons tests. In the Northern Hemisphere the total number is close to 1,000,000 persons.

10. Based upon the data presented here for fatal lung cancers already due to weapons plutonium fallout in the United States, an estimate can be made for the future lung cancers to be produced by the developing nuclear industry. If that industry contains its plutonium to 99.99 percent, it will still be responsible for 500,000 *additional* fatal lung cancers annually.

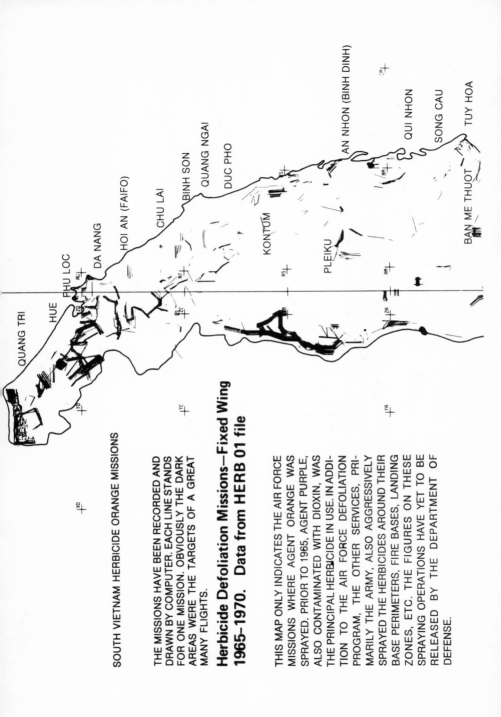

SOUTH VIETNAM HERBICIDE ORANGE MISSIONS

THE MISSIONS HAVE BEEN RECORDED AND DRAWN BY COMPUTER. EACH LINE STANDS FOR ONE MISSION. OBVIOUSLY THE DARK AREAS WERE THE TARGETS OF A GREAT MANY FLIGHTS.

Herbicide Defoliation Missions—Fixed Wing 1965–1970. Data from HERB 01 file

THIS MAP ONLY INDICATES THE AIR FORCE MISSIONS WHERE AGENT ORANGE WAS SPRAYED. PRIOR TO 1965, AGENT PURPLE, ALSO CONTAMINATED WITH DIOXIN, WAS THE PRINCIPAL HERBICIDE IN USE. IN ADDITION TO THE AIR FORCE DEFOLIATION PROGRAM, THE OTHER SERVICES, PRIMARILY THE ARMY, ALSO AGGRESSIVELY SPRAYED THE HERBICIDES AROUND THEIR BASE PERIMETERS, FIRE BASES, LANDING ZONES, ETC. THE FIGURES ON THESE SPRAYING OPERATIONS HAVE YET TO BE RELEASED BY THE DEPARTMENT OF DEFENSE.

QUANG TRI

HUE

PHU LOC

DA NANG

HOI AN (FAIFO)

CHU LAI

BINH SON

QUANG NGAI

DUC PHO

KONTUM

PLEIKU

AN NHON (BINH DINH)

QUI NHON

SONG CAU

TUY HOA

BAN ME THUOT

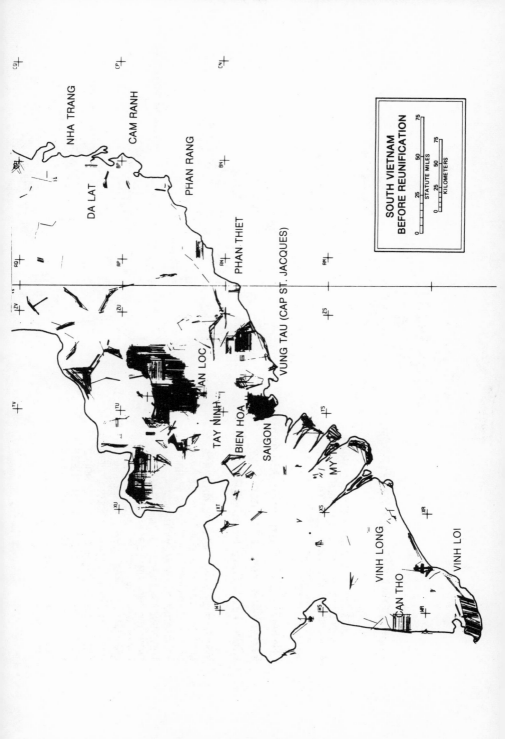

NHA TRANG

CAM RANH

DA LAT

PHAN RANG

PHAN THIET

TAY NINH

AN LOC

BIEN HOA

SAIGON

VUNG TAU (CAP ST. JACQUES)

MY

VINH LONG

CAN THO

VINH LOI

SOUTH VIETNAM
BEFORE REUNIFICATION

STATUTE MILES
0   25   50   75

KILOMETERS
0   25   50   75

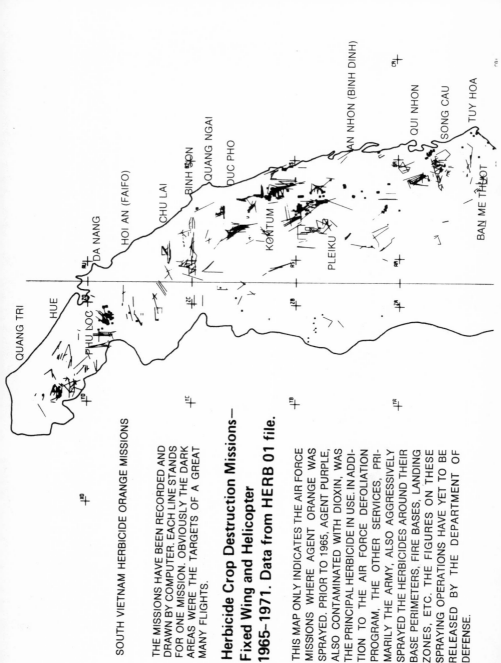

SOUTH VIETNAM HERBICIDE ORANGE MISSIONS

THE MISSIONS HAVE BEEN RECORDED AND DRAWN BY COMPUTER. EACH LINE STANDS FOR ONE MISSION. OBVIOUSLY THE DARK AREAS WERE THE TARGETS OF A GREAT MANY FLIGHTS.

Herbicide Crop Destruction Missions— Fixed Wing and Helicopter 1965–1971. Data from HERB 01 file.

THIS MAP ONLY INDICATES THE AIR FORCE MISSIONS WHERE AGENT ORANGE WAS SPRAYED. PRIOR TO 1965, AGENT PURPLE, ALSO CONTAMINATED WITH DIOXIN, WAS THE PRINCIPAL HERBICIDE IN USE. IN ADDITION TO THE AIR FORCE DEFOLIATION PROGRAM, THE OTHER SERVICES, PRIMARILY THE ARMY, ALSO AGGRESSIVELY SPRAYED THE HERBICIDES AROUND THEIR BASE PERIMETERS, FIRE BASES, LANDING ZONES, ETC. THE FIGURES ON THESE SPRAYING OPERATIONS HAVE YET TO BE RELEASED BY THE DEPARTMENT OF DEFENSE.

QUANG TRI

HUE

PHU LOC

DA NANG

HOI AN (FAIFO)

CHU LAI

BINH SON

QUANG NGAI

DUC PHO

KONTUM

PLEIKU

AN NHON (BINH DINH)

QUI NHON

SONG CAU

TUY HOA

BAN ME THUOT

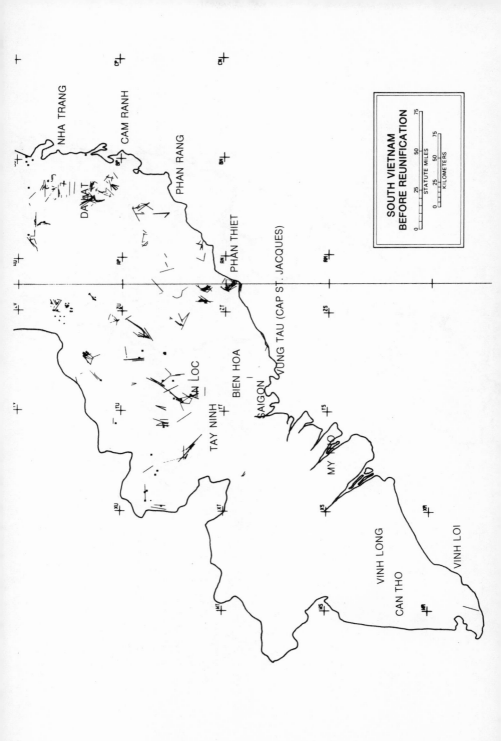

SOUTH VIETNAM
BEFORE REUNIFICATION

STATUTE MILES
0   25   50   75

KILOMETERS
0   25   50   75

NHA TRANG

CAM RANH

PHAN RANG

DALAT

PHAN THIET

VUNG TAU (CAP ST. JACQUES)

BIEN HOA

AN LOC

TAY NINH

SAIGON

MY

VINH LONG

CAN THO

VINH LOI

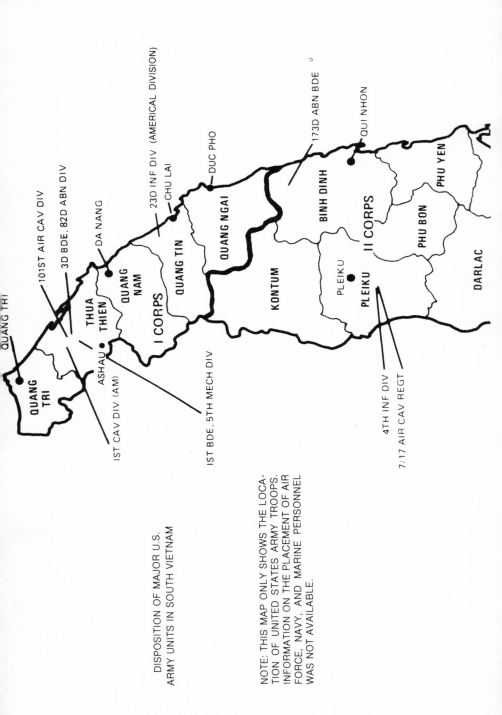

DISPOSITION OF MAJOR U.S.
ARMY UNITS IN SOUTH VIETNAM

NOTE: THIS MAP ONLY SHOWS THE LOCA-
TION OF UNITED STATES ARMY TROOPS.
INFORMATION ON THE PLACEMENT OF AIR
FORCE, NAVY, AND MARINE PERSONNEL
WAS NOT AVAILABLE.

QUANG TRI

101ST AIR CAV DIV

3D BDE, 82D ABN DIV

DA NANG

23D INF DIV (AMERICAL DIVISION)

CHU LAI

DUC PHO

173D ABN BDE

QUI NHON

1ST CAV DIV (AM)

1ST BDE, 5TH MECH DIV

4TH INF DIV

7/17 AIR CAV REGT

QUANG
TRI

THUA
THIEN

ASHAU

QUANG
NAM

I CORPS

QUANG TIN

QUANG NGAI

KONTUM

PLEIKU

PLEIKU

II CORPS

BINH DINH

PHU BON

PHU YEN

DARLAC

CITIZEN SOLDIER
175 Fifth Avenue, Suite 1010
New York, N.Y. 10010
(212) 777-3470

We have designed and distributed this questionnaire as part of our effort to identify and assist Vietnam veterans who may have suffered harmful effects by exposure to herbicides (Agent Orange) during military duty in Indochina. We urge you to answer each question as completely as you can. When you return the completed form to our office you'll be placed on our active mailing list and will receive informational mailings in the months ahead.

Your response to this questionnaire will assist our effort to develop a medical follow-up program for affected Vietnam vets.

I. Name _____

Address _____

_____ Zip Code

5. Home phone (___) _____
area code

Can we call you at work: If so,

(___) _____
area code

2. Sex: ☐ Male ☐ Female

3. Race ☐ White ☐ Black
☐ Hispanic ☐ Other (specify)_____

4. Date of Birth _____ _____ _____
mo. day year

6. Social Security No. ___ ___ ___ ___ ___ ___

7. Military Service # _____
(pre-1970) vets

8. What is your present occupation? _____

II. MILITARY SERVICE
This section deals with your service in the military and in Vietnam.

1. During what years were you in the military service? _____ _____
from to

2. During what period(s) were you in Vietnam? from _____ _____ to _____ _____
mo. year mo. year

3. What was your job (MOS)? _____

4. What unit were you assigned to in Vietnam? _____

5. What was your rank? _____

6. What type of discharge? _____

7. Were you ever injured or wounded in Vietnam? ☐ yes ☐ no → go to question 8.

Indicate the dates of each injury and whether you are receiving V.A. disability payment (show the percent disability):

Type of Injury (Describe)	Date of Injury		V. Disability		
	Mo.	Year	Yes	%	No.

8. Have you ever suffered mental illnesses or breakdown? ☐ yes ☐ no → go to question 9

Are you receiving V.A Disability for this? ☐ yes ☐ no If yes, _____ %

9. Were you ever given an anti-malaria pill called DAPSONE? (It's a small white pill that was given every morning)?
☐ yes ☐ no

10. Did you ever have malaria? ☐ yes ☐ no If yes, when? _____

III. HERBICIDE EXPOSURE

In this section we are interested in finding you what you remember about being exposed to defoliating herbicides such as Agent Orange which was used to kill jungle cover in Vietnam. If you believe you were exposed to such a chemical agent, either by directly loading it, spraying it or entering a freshly sprayed area, we would like you to describe **how** you were exposed and **when**. Fill in your answers below.

If you don't remember being directly exposed to herbicides check here: _____ Don't remember being exposed. and go on to Section IV.

How were you exposed to herbicides?	What year?	How long did it last?
EXAMPLE: Cargo loader for C-123 or spray helicopter OR Sleeping in sprayed fields	1969 1970	31 days (of duty) 13 weeks

IV. HEALTH HISTORY

The next series of questions is about your health history.

SKIN DISORDERS

1. Did you ever have acne as a teenager? ☐ yes ☐ no → Go to question #2

If yes, how old were you? _____

Did it ever come back again? ☐ yes ☐ no

How old were you when it came back? _____

2. Have you ever had a skin rash with blisters? ☐ yes ☐ no → question #3

If yes, when? _____ (year)

3. Have you ever experienced a change in your skin color? ☐ yes ☐ no → question #4

If yes, did it become ☐ lighter? ☐ darker? When did it begin? _____ (year)

---

4. Have you ever noticed an increased sensitivity to sunlight? ☐ yes ☐ no → question #5

   If yes, have any of the following developed (check box) ☐ blisters? ☐ sores ☐ worsening of rash?

   other (describe)_____ Year it began?_____

5. Did you, or do you have a fungus infection ("jungle rot")? ☐ yes ☐ no → question #6

   If yes, check correct box ☐ crotch ☐ feet ☐ legs other area_____ (specify)

   Year began_____

DIGESTIVE SYSTEM

	No	Yes	Has it happened more than once?	Year it first began
6. Have you lost 20 or more pounds without changing your diet?				
7. Do you regularly experience loss of appetite?				
8. Have you ever been repeatedly nauseous when you haven't had a flu or other sickness?				
9. Are you regularly troubled with constipation?				
10. Are you regularly troubled with diarrhea?				
11. Have you ever had jaundice (yellow eyes and skin)?				
12. Have you ever had hepatitis?				
14. Has a doctor ever told you that you had cirrhosis of the liver?				
15. Have you ever passed urine that is oak brown (coca-cola colored)?				

GENERAL HEALTH

16. How many hours do you normally sleep?_____

17. In addition, do you take regular naps? (at least 3 times per week) ☐ yes ☐ no

18. Do you usually wake up rested? ☐ yes ☐ no

19. Do you have episodes of severe dizziness or light headedness? ☐ yes ☐ no

20. Do you frequently feel as if you are about to faint (black-out)?(not related to drinking) ☐ yes ☐ no

21. Have you fainted/blacked-out more than twice? (not related to drinking) ☐ yes ☐ no

22. Is your vision ever blurred (other than needing new glasses)? ☐ yes ☐ no

23. Have you or your family ever noticed a personality change?

   Check box: ☐ depression ☐ fly off handle ☐ anxiety (uptight) ☐ irritable

   other _____

   When did this begin?_____ (year)

24. Do you often get into a violent rage? ☐ yes ☐ no

25. Is there any change in your desires for sex? Check box: ☐ increase ☐ decrease

    Year it first began?_____

26. Do you have any difficulty in maintaining an erection? ☐ yes ☐ no

27. Do you smoke cigarettes? ☐ yes ☐ no   If yes, how many cigarettes a day?_____

    How old were you when you began smoking regularly?_____

28. Do you drink alcoholic beverages regularly? ☐ yes ☐ no

    If yes, show how many glasses or shots each day.

    _____ beer

    _____ wine

    _____ liquor

MUSCLE AND BONE SYSTEM
We want to know if you've experienced unusual tightening, numbness, pain, swelling, or stiffness in any of the following joints (not associated with exercise or exertion). Please check any such experience below.

		Right side	Left side	SYMPTOMS IN JOINTS				
				Tingling	Numbness	Swelling	Stiffness	Pain
1	hands							
2	fingers							
3	wrists							
4	elbows							
5	arms							
6	shoulders							
7	hips							
8	knees							
9	ankles							
10	feet							
11	toes							
12	neck							

13. If you've checked any of the above, answer the following questions. Otherwise, go on to the next section.

	YES	NO
Do you need your hands to help you get out of a chair?	_____	_____
Do you have trouble climbing stairs without holding onto the railing?	_____	_____
Are you unable to do things which require holding your arms at shoulder level (as when you carry heavy grocery bags in front of you)?	_____	_____
Do you have difficulty holding hand tools or other items for prolonged periods (hammer, pencil, etc.)?	_____	_____

V. PAST MEDICAL HISTORY

In this section we are interested in any problems you may have seen a physician for or which a doctor diagnosed. Therefore, we want to know if you have ever been told by a **doctor** that you had any of the following conditions? If so, indicate the year that the condition first began.

	Yes	No	Condition	Year it began
1			Hay Fever	
2			Asthma	
3			Allergies of any type	
4			Tuberculosis	
5			High blood pressure	
6			Heart Disease	
7			Ulcer (stomach or intestine)	
8			Epilepsy	
9			Kidney disease	
10			Anemia	
11			Sickle cell anemia	

	Yes	No	Condition	Year it began
12			Venereal Disease	
13			Diabetes	
14			Goiter (thyroid swelling)	
15			Parasitic infection (dysentery)	
16			Tumors or cancer Type: _____	
17			Major injury or operation of any type (other than ones already described): Describe: _____	

VI. FAMILY HISTORY

Have you ever had children or tried to have children? (check)

☐ Yes   ☐ No ⟶   There are no further questions, thank you.

If possible, you should fill out this section with the natural mother(s) of the children. If this is not possible, you should complete this section as best you can.

a) Who is completing this section?   ☐ Mother   ☐ Father   ☐ Both

b) For each pregnancy, provide the information requested below. For multiple births (e.g. twins), list each child on a separate line. Include all live births, stillbirths, miscarriages, and therapeutic abortions.

Pregnancy Child No.	What happened with this pregnancy				Date		Sex (Check)		Birth Weight		For live births, is this child now living? (check)	
	Live Birth	Still-birth	Miscar-riage	Volun-tary Abortion	Mo.	Yr.	M	F	Lbs.	Oz.	Yes	No
1												
2												
3												
4												
5												
6												
7												

Did any of these children have birth defects? (check)   ☐ Yes   ☐ No
If yes, please check as many as apply to each child,
using the same child number as used in chart above.

Child No.	Mongoloidism	Clubfoot	Cleft lip/palate	Missing, deformed or extra fingers, toes	Heart defect	Defect of the digestive system	Spina bifida or other brain or spine defects	Condition requiring special education or care	Cerebral palsy	Hearing disorders	Other (specify)
1											
2											
3											
4											
5											
6											
7											

Resources

Veterans' Organizations working on behalf of herbicide or radiation victims.

Citizen Soldier
175 Fifth Avenue, Suite 1010
New York, New York 10010
(212) 777-3470

Veterans Task Force on Agent Orange
Attention: Ron De Young, Chairman
Columbia College
600 South Michigan Avenue
Chicago, Illinois
(312) 663-1600

National Veterans Law Center
American University
Washington College of Law
Washington, D.C. 20016
(202) 686-2741

National Association of Atomic Veterans
Attention: Orville Kelly
1109 Franklin
Burlington, Iowa 52601
(319) 754-7266

Citizens Hearings for Radiation Victims
317 Pennsylvania Avenue SE
Washington, D.C. 20003
(202) 543-0222

Committee for US Veterans of Hiroshima and Nagasaki
P.O. Box 14424
Portland, Oregon 97214
(503) 232-2641 and (503) 288-4405

Environmental Organizations active against domestic use of
2,4,5-T and 2,4-D (partial list).

Citizens Against Toxic Herbicides
Attention: Paul Merrill
2737 25A Street,
Clarkston, Washington 99403
(509) 758-5796

Friends of the Earth
Attention: Eric Jansson
620 C Street, SE
Washington, D.C. 20003
(202) 543-4312

Northwest Coalition for Alternatives to
Pesticides
P.O. Box 345
Eugene, Oregon 97440
(503) 344-5044

Citizens National Forest Coalition
John Stauber
Donna Waters
110506 Windmill Court
Chaska, Minnesota 55318
(612) 448-6700

Selected Bibliography

Books

Allen, James S. *Atomic Imperialism*. New York: International Publishers, 1952.

Alperovitz, Gar. *Atomic Diplomacy: Hiroshima and Potsdam*. New York: Simon & Schuster, 1965.

Amrine, Michael. *The Great Decision*. New York: G. P. Putnam's Sons, 1959.

Aronow, T., ed. *Fallen Sky*. New York: Hill & Wang, 1963.

Bernstein, Barton. *The Atomic Bomb: The Critical Issues*. Boston: Little, Brown, 1976.

Boffey, Philip. *Brain Bank of America*. New York: McGraw-Hill, 1975.

Bradley, Dr. David. *No Place to Hide*. Boston: Atlantic, Little, Brown, 1948.

Brown, A., and C. McDonald, eds. *Secret History of the Atomic Bomb*. New York: Dial Press, 1977.

Carson, Rachel. *Silent Spring*. Boston: Houghton Mifflin, 1962.

Chomsky, Noam. *At War with Asia*. New York: Vintage, 1970.

Committee of Concerned Asian Scholars. *The Indochina Story*. New York: Bantam, 1970.

Commoner, Barry. *The Closing Circle*. New York: Alfred A. Knopf, 1971.

———. *The Politics of Energy*. New York: Alfred A. Knopf, 1979.

———. *The Poverty of Power*. New York: Alfred A. Knopf, 1976.

———. *Science and Survival*. New York: Viking Press, 1967.

Devine, Robert A. *Blowing on the Wind: The Nuclear Test Ban Debate, 1954–1960*. New York: Oxford University Press, 1978.

Ensign, Tod, and Michael Uhl, eds. *Dellums Committee Hearings on War Crimes in Vietnam*. New York: Vintage, 1971.

Federal Civil Defense Administration. *Cue for Survival: Operation Cue.* Battle Creek, Mich.: 1955.

Fleming, D. F. *The Cold War and Its Origins.* New York: Doubleday, 1961, 2 vols.

Frank, Pat. *How to Survive the H-Bomb and Why.* Philadelphia: J. B. Lippincott, 1962.

Fowler, John M., ed. *Fallout.* New York: Basic Books, 1960.

Fuller, John G. *The Poison That Fell from the Sky.* New York: Random House, 1977.

General Accounting Office of the Comptroller General. *Health Effects of Exposure to Herbicide Orange in South Vietnam Should Be Resolved.* Washington, D.C., 1979.

————. *U.S. Ground Troops in South Vietnam Were in Areas Sprayed with Herbicide Orange.* Washington, D.C., 1979.

Gerstell, Richard. *How to Survive an Atomic Bomb.* New York: 1950.

Glasser, Ronald J., M.D. *365 Days.* New York: George Braziller, 1971.

Gofman, J., and A. Tamplin. *Poisoned Power.* Emmaus, Pa.: Rodale Press, 1971.

Gray, D., and J. Martens. *Radiation Monitoring in Atomic Defense.* New York: Van Nostrand Reinhold, 1951.

Greene, Graham. *The Quiet American.* New York: Viking Press, 1956.

Groueff, Stéphane. *Manhattan Project.* Boston: Little, Brown, 1967.

Hachiya, Michihiko. *Hiroshima Diary: Journal of a Japanese Physician.* Chapel Hill: University of North Carolina Press, 1955.

Hersey, John. *Hiroshima.* New York: Alfred A. Knopf, 1946.

Hersh, Seymour. *Chemical and Biological Warfare: America's Hidden Arsenal.* Indianapolis: Bobbs-Merrill, 1968.

Human Resources Research Office. *Desert Rock I, A Psychological Study of Troop Reaction to an Atomic Explosion.* George Washington University, 1951.

International Agency for Research on Cancer, Joint NIEHS/IARC Report. *Long-Term Hazards of Polychlorinated Dibenzodioxins and Polychlorinated Dibenzoflorans.* Lyons, France: United Nations, June 1978.

Jablon, Seymour. *The Origin and Findings of Atomic Bomb Casualty Commission.* Rockville, Md.: U.S. Bureau of Radiological Health, 1973.

Kindall, Sylvian. *Total Atomic Defense.* New York: Richard R. Smith, 1952.

Lang, Daniel. *Early Tales of the Atomic Age.* New York: Doubleday, 1948.

Lapp, Ralph. *Must We Hide?* Cambridge: Addison-Wesley Press, 1949.

————. *Voyage of the Lucky Dragon.* New York: Harper & Row, 1958.

Lawrence, William L. *We Are Not Helpless.* New York: New York Times Publications, 1950.

Lewallen, John. *Ecology of Devastation: Indochina.* Baltimore: Penguin, 1971.

Lewy, Guenter. *America in Vietnam.* New York: Oxford University Press, 1978.

Lieberman, Joseph. *The Scorpion and the Tarantula.* Boston: Houghton Mifflin, 1970.

Lifton, Robert Jay. *Home from the War: Vietnam Veterans, Neither Victims nor Executioners.* New York: Simon & Schuster, 1973.

McCarthy, Richard. *Ultimate Folly: War by Pestilence, Asphyxiation, and Defoliation.* New York: Alfred A. Knopf, 1969.

Metzger, H. Peter. *The Atomic Establishment.* New York: Simon & Schuster, 1972.

Mumford, Lewis. *The Human Prospect.* Boston: Beacon Press, 1955.

National Academy of Science. *The Effects of Herbicides in South Vietnam, Part A, Summary and Conclusions.* Washington, D.C., 1974.

————. *The Effects on Populations of Exposure to Low Levels of Ionizing Radiation.* Washington, D.C., 1972.

Nielands, J. B., et al. *Harvest of Death: Chemical Warfare in Vietnam and Cambodia.* New York: Free Press, 1972.

O'Brien, Tim. *Going After Cacciato.* New York: Delacorte, 1977.

Olson, McKinley C. *Unacceptable Risk: The Nuclear Power Controversy.* New York: Bantam, 1976.

Palmer, Gregory. *The McNamara Strategy and the Vietnam War.* Westport, Conn.: Greenwood Press, 1978.

Pike, Douglas. *Viet Cong: The Organization and Techniques of the National Liberation Front of South Vietnam.* Cambridge: Massachusetts Institute of Technology Press, 1966.

Primack, Joel, and Frank von Hippel. *Advice and Dissent: Scientists in the Political Arena.* New York: Basic Books, 1976.

Reinhardt, G. C., and W. R. Kintner. *Atomic Weapons in Land Combat.* Harrisburg, Pa.: Military Service Publishing Company, 1953.

Rose, Steven, ed. *CBW: Chemical and Biological Warfare*. Boston: Beacon Press, 1969.

Schlesinger, Arthur M. *A Thousand Days: John F. Kennedy in the White House*. Boston: Houghton Mifflin, 1965.

Schubert, Jack, and Ralph E. Lapp. *Radiation: What It Is and How It Affects You*. New York: Viking Press, 1960.

Shepley, J., and C. Blair. *Hydrogen Bomb: The Men, the Menace, the Mechanism*. New York: David McKay, 1954.

Shurcliff, W. A. *Bombs at Bikini: The Official Report of Operation Crossroads*. New York: Wm. H. Wise, 1947.

Smith, Alice Kimball. *A Peril and a Hope: the Scientists' Movement in America 1945–47*. Cambridge: Massachusetts Institute of Technology Press, 1965.

South Okanagan Environmental Coalition. *The Other Face of 2, 4-D*. Vancouver, B.C.: 1978.

Stavins, Ralph, Richard Barnett, and Marcus Raskin. *Washington Plans an Aggressive War*. New York: Vintage, 1971.

Stone, I. F. *The Hidden History of the Korean War*, rev. ed. New York: Monthly Review Press, 1969.

Thursfield, H. G., ed. *Brassey's Naval Annual*. New York: Macmillan, 1947.

Toynbee, Philip. *The Fateful Choice*. Detroit: Wayne State University Press, 1959.

U.S. Army. *Exercise Desert Rock*, Vols. I, II, III, IV, V, VII, VIII. Washington, D.C., dated variously 1952–1957.

U.S. Department of Defense. *United States–Vietnam Relations, 1945–67* (also known as *The Pentagon Papers*). Washington, D.C., 1971.

U.S. Departments of Defense and Energy. *The Effects of Nuclear Weapons*. Washington, D.C., 1977.

U.S. Navy. *Operation Crossroads: 4th Cruise of the Mighty Mac*. Washington, D.C., 1946.

U.S. Navy. *Operation Crossroads: The Official Pictorial Record of Joint Task Force*. Washington, D.C., 1946.

U.S. Navy. *Operation Sandstone: The Pictorial History*. Washington, D.C., 1948.

U.S. Navy. White, Clarence, ed. *Operation Sandstone: The Story of Joint Task Force 7*. Washington, D.C., 1949.

Veterans Administration. *The Vietnam Veteran in Contemporary Society*. Washington, D.C., May 1972.

Vo Nguyen Giap. *The Military Art of People's War: Selected Writings.* New York: Monthly Review Press, 1970.

Walton, Richard. *Cold War and Counterrevolution: The Foreign Policy of John F. Kennedy.* New York: Viking Press, 1972.

Weisberg, Barry. *Ecocide in Indochina: The Ecology of War.* San Francisco: Canfield Press, 1970.

Whiteside, Thomas. *The Pendulum and the Toxic Cloud: The Course of Dioxin Contamination.* New Haven: Yale Press, 1979.

————. *The Withering Rain: America's Herbicidal Folly.* New York: Dutton, 1971.

Young, Capt. Alvin, Lt. Col. John A. Calcagny, Lt. Col. Charles E. Thalken, and Maj. James W. Tremblay. *The Toxicology, Environmental Fate, and Human Risk of Herbicide Orange and its Associated Dioxin,* prepared for the Surgeon General, United States Air Force. Washington, D.C.: Oct. 1978.

Pamphlets, magazines, journals

Baldwin, Robert D. *Experience at Desert Rock VII.* Human Resources Research Office, Staff Memorandum. Washington, D.C.: George Washington University, 1958.

Brightman, Carol. "Weed Killers in Vietnam." *Viet Report,* June/ July 1966.

"Civilian Defense Against Atomic Attack." *Bulletin of Atomic Scientists,* Aug./Sept. 1950.

Commoner, Barry, and Robert E. Scott. "U.S. Air Force Studies on the Stability and Ecological Effects of TCDD (Dioxin): An Evaluation Relative to the Accidental Dissemination of TCDD at Seveso, Italy." Menlo Park: Linus Pauling Institute of Science and Medicine, Nov. 1976.

Democratic Republic of Vietnam. "Chemical Warfare." *Vietnamese Studies,* 29 (1971).

Human Resources Research Office (HumRRO). *Desert Rock I, A Psychological Study of Troop Reaction to an Atomic Explosion.* Washington, D.C.: George Washington University, 1951.

Langer, Elinor. "Chemical and Biological Warfare. I: The Research Program; II: The Weapons and the Policies." *Science,* Jan. 13, 20, 1967.

Library of Congress, transcript prepared by "Radiation Standards and Public Health Proceedings of a Second Congressional Seminar in Low-level Ionizing Radiation, Feb. 10, 1978."

Meselson, Matthew. "Chemical and Biological Warfare." *Scientific American*, May 1970.

Office of Defense Mobilization and Federal Civil Defense Administration. *Standards for Operation Alert; Attack Phase*. Washington, D.C., 1958.

Orians, G. H., and E. W. Pfeiffer. "Ecological Effects of the War in Vietnam." *Science*, May 1, 1970.

United States Department of Defense. *Medical Aspects of Atomic Weapons*. Washington, D.C.: United States Government Printing Office, 1950.

Westing, Arthur H. "Ecological Effects of Military Defoliation on the Forest of South Vietnam." *Bioscience*, Vol. 21, No. 17, Sept. 1, 1971.

————. "Poisoning Plants for Peace." *Friends Journal*, 16 (1970).

Wisconsin AgriBusiness Council. *The Phenoxy Herbicides*. Madison, Wisc.